Codes and Ciphers

Codes
and
Ciphers

Fred B. Wrixon

PRENTICE HALL GENERAL REFERENCE

New York   London   Toronto   Sydney   Tokyo   Singapore

PRENTICE HALL GENERAL REFERENCE
15 Columbus Circle
New York, New York, 10023

PRENTICE HALL and colophon are registered trademarks of Simon & Schuster Inc.

Library of Congress Cataloging-in-Publication Data

Wrixon, Fred B.
    Codes and ciphers / Fred B. Wrixon.
        p.   cm.
    Includes bibliographical references and index.
    Summary: An alphabetical exploration of the world of codes and ciphers and significant individuals involved in that field.
    ISBN 0-13-277047-4
    1. Cryptography.   2. Ciphers. [1. Cryptography—Dictionaries.
2. Ciphers—Dictionaries.] I. Title.
Z103.3.W75   1992
652'.8—dc20   91-42848

Designed by Richard Oriolo
Manufactured in the United States of America

10 9 8 7 6 5 4 3 2 1

First Edition

To My Family

Acknowledgments

My agent, Meg Ruley, and my editors Traci Cothran, Gerry Helferich, and Kate Kelly, deserve praise for their guidance and patience throughout the development of this text.

I would also like to express my special appreciation to Mr. David Kahn for his help. His classic, *The Codebreakers,* is the basis of all modern research in cryptology.

The following persons have provided much needed inspiration and information: Earl Coates, John Costello, Paul Dane, David Gaddy, Miss C. M. Hall, Louis Kruh, Robert Lamphere, Graydon Lewis, Edward Pleuler, Jr., Eric Schulzinger, Gustavus J. Simmons, and Miss Angela Wootton.

Prompt and efficient services were provided by the staffs and members of The American Cryptogram Association; The American Philosophical Society; The British Broadcasting Corporation; The British Museum; The Central Intelligence Agency; The Crown Publishing Group; The Federal Bureau of Investigation; The Imperial War Museum; The International Telecommunication Union; The Library of Congress; The Lockheed Aeronautical Systems Company; The Martins Ferry Public Library; The National Air and Space Museum; The National Archives; The National Security Agency; The Naval Cryptologic Veterans Association; The Naval Historical Center; The New York Public Library; The Ohio County Public Library; The Society of Wireless Pioneers; *The Encyclopaedia Britannica; The Encyclopedia Americana*; The U.S. Air Force Historical Research Center; The U.S. Army Communications Museum (Fort Monmouth, N.J.); The U.S. Army Military History Institute; The U.S. Army Signal Corps Museum (Fort Gordon, Georgia); The Veteran Wireless Operators' Association.

Contents

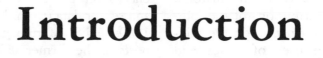

Introduction

By opening the cover of this book, you have entered the secret world of codes and ciphers. It is the realm of mysterious symbols, royal emissaries, microdots, diplomatic couriers, electronic interceptions, and space-age spies. From the years of yore to today's satellite age, ciphers and codes have protected private communications from prying eyes. This effort, however, has been challenged by equally energetic third-party observers and eavesdroppers, who have attempted to record visible or audible messages. The competition between the code and cipher makers (cryptographers) and code and cipher breakers (cryptanalysts) encompasses the science of cryptology (from the Latin *crypta* and Greek *kryptē<kryptós*, both meaning "secret" or "hidden," and *lógos* "word").

The beginnings of secret writing have been traced to Egyptian scribes of the pharaohs, while Arab civilizations of the 7th century A.D. were the first to develop formal solving processes. Later, Renaissance postal exchanges involved anterooms called "black chambers," where missives were surreptitiously opened and their con-

tents revealed. Royal cryptographers countered with expanded collections of codewords called *nomenclators*. Centuries afterward, these gave way to specialized telegraph codes for military or commercial use. Today, secret data is often shielded by computer-generated numbers before transmission.

The alphabetical entries in this reference cover the full scope of the art and science of cryptology, including:

1. The historic development of such methods throughout the world
2. Their application by various professions, including soldiers, entrepreneurs, musicians, scientists, and novelists
3. Biographies of major figures in the history of cryptology
4. Notable successes and failures on the part of code and cipher makers and breakers
5. The operation of the concealments themselves, ranging from simple letter or numeral substitutions to complex electronic mechanisms

Early in the planning stages for this

book, a decision was made not to present detailed descriptions of the advanced mathematics of cryptology. An entry or two would neither do justice to the material itself nor to the contributions of the individuals involved. Information on the military and espionage uses of codes and ciphers is also necessarily vague in some cases, owing to the security-conscious nature of those enterprises and the resulting restrictions upon information.

A word on terminology. *Cipher* and *code* are not synonymous within the framework of cryptology. Strictly speaking, in a code, entire words are replaced with other words or groups of letters and/or numbers. In the more complex cipher, on the other hand, the word to be concealed is broken down into its component letters, which are then replaced by other letters and/or numbers.

The general word *encryption* refers to either a code or a cipher. To *encrypt* a message is to either encode or encipher it; to *decrypt* it is to recover the original words.

Although cryptology is an ancient science, codes, ciphers, and the secrets they are intended to conceal are still very much in the news, as witness the John Walker family spy ring, which divulged U.S. Navy encryption processes along with weapons and sensor data (from the 1960s to the mid-1980s); U.S. Marine guards at diplomatic posts in the former USSR, who permitted Soviet access to top-secret encryption materials (1987); and U.S. Army warrant officer James Hall III, who turned over satellite eavesdropping intelligence (about presumably encrypted interceptions) to an agent of the Soviets (1989).

Even as this text was being prepared for publication, news reports revealed yet another U.S. embassy scandal. In April 1991, during a fire at the U.S. embassy in Moscow, KGB agents working among Soviet firemen absconded with materials from open safes that reportedly included computer disks and encryption data. Even in the age of Eastern European political reform and Third World resurgence, the age-old competition of spy versus spy and concealment versus revelation is still very much with us.

—FRED B. WRIXON

A-1, a designation given to a U.S. Navy CODE developed during World War I and to a rarely used State Department enciphered code (see ENCICODE).

Created by Lt. (j.g.) William "Poco" Smith, the Navy version of A-1 was intended to replace some increasingly impractical codes, such as the five-letter SIGCODE and a four-letter radio code. The A-1's five-letter code groups were equated with text words and phrases. Lt. Smith accomplished this with typed columns of mixed letter groups that he cut in segments and placed in a container. Then he withdrew the letter strips, typed them in other columns, and aligned them with the terms on the particular encoding list. The awkward construction was typical of many U.S. code-making efforts of the period. In fact, it took Smith so long to complete the A-1 that it was not distrib-

uted by the U.S. Government Printing Office until after the United States had entered the war, in 1917.

The U.S. State Department's version of A-1 was created in the early 1920s by government employees who were alarmed by breaches in diplomatic communications. This version was a superenciphered code (see SUPERENCIPHERMENT); that is, the original CODENUMBERS and CODEWORDS were further masked by transposing or substituting the letters and/or numbers in a process that combined codes with aspects of CIPHERS. Though the superenciphered messages were an improvement, the code was rarely used, and U.S. diplomats were shackled with antiquated codes throughout the 1920s and the early 1930s.

A-3, a device made to ensure radiotelephone security. The A-3 figured prominently in World War II message transmissions. This Bell Telephone creation was a band-splitter first put into operation in December 1937 on the circuit between the Mutual Telephone Company in Honolulu and Radio Corporation of America in San Francisco.

Band-splitting generally involved splitting a signal, such as the human voice, into smaller frequency bands and interchanging them. Thus, it affected the signal similarly to the way in which CIPHERS rearrange and segment written material. When a voice signal entered a band-splitter the signal was divided into bands by filters. These were then altered by modulators and sent through other band filters, an encoding device, and other modulators. Finally, at a concluding filtering point, a scrambled signal emerged.

On September 1, 1939, the A-3 carried the momentous news from Paris to Washington, D.C., that World War II had begun. Throughout the war, President Roosevelt used phones equipped with scramblers to communicate with Allied leaders such as WINSTON CHURCHILL (see CIPHONY; PULSE CODE MODULATION).

ABC Code,

ABC Code, a book of the commercial CODE that reduced the cost of words in telegrams and overseas cables.

As entrepreneurs learned the value of better, more rapid communications, they quickly realized that the fewer the words and figures needed, the less costly the message. Thus businesses began to devise their own lists of terms to replace money amounts, phrases, and even entire sentences. Eventually, simple words such as *hat* and *coat* became code words that might have meant, for example, "Send me the contract immediately at this address."

With the completion of the Atlantic cable in 1866 and the corresponding boost in transoceanic communications, the need for a money-saving commercial code was greater than ever. By 1874, Englishman William Clausen-Thue, a shipping manager, had developed the *ABC Code*, which was capably arranged and had a huge vocabulary. It soon became the first public CODEBOOK to achieve broad sales and longevity.

Additive,

Additive, a number or numbers added to a CODE to make it more difficult to DECODE.

Additives were introduced in the 1800s, when increased secrecy was needed for cables and telegrams. This secrecy effort was a type of SUPERENCIPHERMENT that used SUBSTITUTION involving numbers.

For example, suppose that one of the CODENUMBERS, also called the plain code or "placode," was 1162 7824 5286. To this number a single number, the "additive" (such as 2040), was added:

$$
\begin{array}{ccc}
1162 & 7824 & 5286 \\
+\,2040 & 2040 & 2040 \\
\hline
3202 & 9864 & 7326
\end{array}
$$

The other codenumbers in the message were also given this additive. The resulting cryptogram (also called an enciphered code or "ENCICODE") was then ready for transmission. While the additive was not special in itself, as long as its secrecy was maintained, it was easy for the communicators to use and did increase the difficulty for potential interceptors.

ADFGVX, one of the best-known field-ciphers in the history of CRYPTOLOGY. It was created and applied by Germany during a crucial stage of World War I, when the Kaiser was planning a major offensive in the spring of 1918.

The ADFGVX was set up with a design variously described as a 6×6 bipartite square, grid, or matrix. Twenty-six letters and 10 digits were placed in this design, with the coordinates being ADFGVX.

	A	D	F	G	V	X
A	F	L	1	A	O	2
D	J	D	W	3	G	U
F	C	I	Y	B	4	P
G	R	5	Q	8	V	E
V	6	K	7	Z	M	X
X	S	N	H	Ø	T	9

This configuration was used to substitute letter pairs for each letter of a message, such as ALL QUIET ON THIS FRONT TODAY.

The PLAINTEXT letter is found in the matrix, and the letters that are at its coordinates become the pair that replace it (e.g., *L* is replaced by *A* and *D*). The pairs always begin with the one in the vertical column at the left, followed by the one in the horizontal row at the top:

```
A   L   L     Q   U   I   E   T
AG  AD  AD    GF  DX  FD  GX  XV

O   N   T   H   I   S
AV  XD  XV  XF  FD  XA

F   R   O   N   T   T   O   D   A   Y
AA  GA  AV  XD  XV  XV  AV  DD  AG  FF
```

A biliteral cipher is the result. This is then placed in a second rectangle, or TRANSPOSITION matrix, with the encrypted letters written left to right in successive rows. A KEYWORD, in this case GERMAN, and the position of its letters in the alphabet indicate the numerical order in which the letters are to be read down each column. These columns are then taken from the rectangle and written in groups of five letters each until their total number is used to make the CIPHERTEXT.

Transposition matrix:

G	E	R	M	A	N
3	2	6	4	1	5
A	G	A	D	A	D
G	F	D	X	F	D
G	X	X	V	A	V
X	D	X	V	X	F
F	D	X	A	A	A
G	A	A	V	X	D
X	V	X	V	A	V
D	D	A	G	F	F

Ciphertext:

AFAXA XAFGF XDDAV
DAGGX FGXDD XVVAV
VGDDV FADVF ADXXX
AXA

Decipherment is accomplished with knowledge of the KEY and possession of the original matrix. The recipient knows the keyword and places the ciphertext letters in a rectangle according to the same numbered order. Then the letters are taken back through the sequences to the original 6×6 grid, also in the receiver's possession. This time, the letter pairs are used to find the original letters (and numbers, if used) at their coordinates.

CRYPTANALYSIS of such a method is a much different and more difficult matter. Yet, during World War I, a reserve artillery lieutenant, named GEORGES PAINVIN broke the ADFGVX and helped to save his native France.

Aeneas the Tactician (4th century B.C.),

Greek writer who in his text about military science (entitled *On the Defense of Fortified Places*) gave the world its earliest record of communications security. Aeneas tells of ancient peoples who were aware of the need to protect their messages from prying eyes.

In a form of STEGANOGRAPHY, the Greek alphabet was represented by holes cut through disks. Then the sender passed yarn through the appropriate openings, and the recipient unraveled the yarn to determine the proper order of the letters. Aeneas also told of making tiny holes in printed material to indicate a secret communication within a PLAINTEXT.

It is interesting to note that some systems very similar to these remained in use during both world wars.

Aerial Telegraph, a NONSECRET CODE

apparatus invented by Frenchman Claude Chappe. In 1794, when he and his employees installed it between Paris and Lille, 140 miles to the north, real speed was given to long-distance dispatches for the first time.

An advanced version of other systems that had developed over a number of years and were generally called semaphore (Greek: *seema*, "sign," + *phero*, "to carry"), the Chappe device was nonsecret in that the communications sent with it were visible to anyone with good eyesight or a telescope. It was a CODE in the sense that only the initiated knew the meaning of the signals.

The telegraph consisted of a post, a crosspiece (regulator), and wooden pieces (indicators) that were attached to each end of the crosspiece. The entire assemblage was often placed on its own tower, and sometimes it was mounted on a hilltop or a barn roof to maintain a clear line of sight. The center post supported the crosspiece and attachments. The indicators and regulator were moved into different positions by pulleys to create various configurations. The different arrangements indicated the words of the message. A watcher at the next tower studied the shapes with a telescope and recorded the signal, then in turn repeated the pattern to the next tower, and so on, until the message had traveled the entire distance.

Agony Columns,

personal advertisements especially popular in newspapers in the mid- to late 1800s. They acquired their nickname from the number of supposedly private lovers' communications contained in them. To avoid being caught in adulterous affairs or to circumvent parental restrictions, the smitten but often separated pairs corresponded in this disguised way. Because intermediaries could be disloyal and notes were susceptible to interception, the paramours sought the relative convenience and accessibility of the daily news.

Correspondents used systems ranging from simple SUBSTITUTIONS of alphabet letters (such as *A* for *B* and *M* for *O*) to more involved styles where numbers were equated with one or more letters. For example, standard alphabet letters and their corresponding positions indicated by numerals might be reversed: A = 1 through Z = 26 could become A = 26 through Z = 1. A column might have contained these numbers: 18 14 6 8 7 14 22 22 7 2 12 6 7 12 13 18 20 19 7.

Reasonably intelligent correspondents knew not to use commas or periods, which could give away the length of words or sentences. However, the above plea, I MUST MEET YOU TONIGHT, was not at all secure when read by cryptogram fanciers. As can be seen by even this one example, the repeating numbers virtually gave away duplicated letters. Those with even rudimentary skills in CRYPTANALYSIS were able to DECODE familiar phrases, salutations, and even rendezvous points, if mentioned often enough. Clearly, a number of readers found vicarious thrills and humor in the columns, which revealed others' secret trysts or heartbreaks.

Alberti, Leon Battista (1404–1472),

Florentine cryptologist known as the Father of Western Cryptology. Alberti was a model Renaissance man, adept in art, music, architecture, and writing. Among his architectural achievements were the designs of the original Trevi Fountain and the Pitti Palace. He also wrote architectural treatises, poetry, and fables.

It seems only natural that a man of so many interests would be fascinated by the means to conceal missives, but unlike other knowledgeable men who saw secret writing as an amusement, Alberti applied himself to its mastery.

He earned his reputation by solving CODES of increasing degrees of difficulty. Then his curiosity directed him toward the developing field of CIPHERS. As this means of transposing and substituting began to be used more frequently in the letters of other creative people, Alberti studied them and originated important concepts of his own. He wrote about letter frequencies in Latin and Italian sentences, and his study of how these aspects affect cipher solving is considered the first such presentation of CRYPTANALYSIS in the West. Applying his skills to cipher and code creation, he took CRYPTOLOGY a significant stride forward.

He made a CIPHER DISK with two copper plates, one small and one larger outside ring. On the smaller, movable ring, he placed letters at random. On the outer one, he placed 20 alphabet letters (minus *H*, *J*, *K*, *U*, W, and *Y*) and the numerals 1 to 4. These 20 letters were the PLAINTEXT. The lower-case letters on the inner ring then became the CIPHERTEXT.

Each correspondent had a matching disk and could change the alignment of the letters, informing the recipient of the new position. Each position shift initiated a new cipher alphabet. Because so many alphabet possibilities resulted, Alberti is credited with making the first polyalphabetic cipher (see POLYALPHABETIC SUBSTITUTION).

The outer circle's numerals were an additional important contribution. Alberti used groups of numbers such as 22, 333, and 4444 to form a code. When the encoded numbers were then applied to the letters of the disk, they were further enciphered. In other words, he had originated enciphered code.

Alberti was a visionary whose work was not fully appreciated in his day. It was not until the late 1800s that nations began to encipher their codes regularly over the broad range of diplomatic and military communications.

Alphabetical Typewriter 97, known as the 97-*shiki O-bun Injiki* to Japanese cryptographers in the late 1930s, an advance in Japan's cipher-making efforts. The device was numbered 97 for the year it was invented, 1937, which on Japan's ancient calendar was the 97th year of the 25th century.

In cryptological history, the "97" is important in two respects. First, it was a clearly different device from the American SIGABA and the Nazis' ENIGMA, both of which depended on the ROTOR to create their CIPHER variety. And second, the core of the Alphabetical Typewriter was a battery of six-level, 25-point telephone exchange switches. When combined with a plugboard, an intricate wiring pattern resulted. The many plug-in variations of the board helped with KEY changes and allowed for millions of encipherment combinations.

To operate the "97," the chosen key was set (a three-letter code was used to indicate numerals); a message was entered on the keyboard of the first electrical typewriter; the communication was sent through the maze of stepping switches enhanced by the keyed plugboard; and the enciphered message was printed on a second electrical typewriter.

The "97" was believed to be unbreakable. In fact, so confident was the Japanese foreign ministry that they installed it for transmissions between Tokyo and their embassies in Washington, London, and Berlin. However, some secondary diplomatic stations continued to use a less secure machine called the RED, which, unbeknownst to the Japanese, U.S. CRYPTANALYSIS experts had already broken. From these decryptions, the Americans learned that a new machine, dubbed PURPLE, was about to be activated.

Because some of the Red and Purple transmissions contained very similar subject matter, the Americans were able to decrypt certain parts of the Purple. Finally, a brilliant cryptanalyst named WILLIAM FRIEDMAN and the U.S. Army's Signal Intelligence Service succeeded in designing a near copy of the "97's" functions. The blueprint was built by an SIS technician, Leo Rosen, and this Purple analog was soon applied to deciphering more of Tokyo's diplomatic transactions, exerting a profound effect on the course of World War II.

American Black Chamber, nickname of American's post-World War I Cipher Bureau, under the direction of HERBERT YARDLEY. Named for the secret mail interception rooms of the late 1600s and the 1700s, this organization was financed by the U.S. State and War departments, largely due to Yardley's prescience and persistence.

After a year on New York's East 38th Street, the bureau's score of part-time staff members were given a more permanent workplace in a brownstone on East

37th Street near Lexington Avenue. In this four-story structure, Yardley and the others were eventually able to achieve surprising successes, despite their often makeshift materials and limited salaries.

One of their primary achievements was solving several of Japan's most important diplomatic CODETEXTS, a task made all the more difficult by the Japanese system of ideographic writing. Nevertheless, Yardley and his staff discerned that Tokyo was using a type of communication concealment called KATA KANA, which used some 70 syllables that had been given roman letter equivalents. The Chamber crew had obtained telegrams with common syllables and words that included *ari*, *aritashi*, *daijin*, and *gyoo*.

By using FREQUENCY counts and manipulating combinations of letter groups, the staff found links between a series of two-letter CODEWORDS (see CODENAME/ CODEWORD) and their hidden equivalents. Repetitions of the letters *RE*, *BO*, *UB*, and *OK* led to revelations like these:

RE UB BO   AS FY OK   RE OS OK BO
do i tsu   o wa ri   do ku ri tsu
(Germany)   (stop)   (independence)

The codebreakers reaped substantial rewards for their strenuous efforts. By the time of the important naval disarmament conference in Washington, D.C., in November 1921, the Black Chamber members were regularly reading Tokyo's as well as others' coded telegrams, thus helping the State Department to win acceptance of the Five-Power Treaty on terms very favorable to the United States.

However, appropriations limitations, the displeasure of telegraph companies, and an anti-spy, pro-diplomacy mood in Washington caused the Chamber to close permanently in 1929. Unemployed, then ruined by the Depression, Herbert Yardley published a highly controversial account of his experiences, *The American Black Chamber*.

American Black Chamber, The, a book written by HERBERT YARDLEY about the U.S. CRYPTOLOGY organization. "Scandalous" and "irresponsible" were two words livid critics used when it was published in 1931.

Introduced to a wide audience in articles in *The Saturday Evening Post*, the book was a financial and critical success. However, while literary reviewers were pleased with its narrative energy and cloak-and-dagger dramatics, other American cryptologists, including WILLIAM FRIEDMAN, believed that its candid revelations about American code breaking and CIPHER solving harmed U.S. intelligence in both the present and the long term.

Friedman's contention was seemingly proven when reports began to come in that other nations were changing their encoding methods. This was certainly true in Japan, where the book caused a particular sensation. Yardley's account of the decoding of Japan's diplomatic code during the important Washington Disarmament Conference was seen as a serious breach of honor in that country. Several historians have since argued that these disclosures were responsible for the Imperial Army and Navy's increased caution with their communications, demonstrated when they later initiated war plans in Asia.

For his part, Herbert Yardley claimed that his book was meant to alert free people to the dangers of weak CODES and narrow-minded cryptographic policies.

American Trench Code, a CODEBOOK that is an example of field CRYPTOGRA- PHY. The *American Trench Code* was created during actual warfare "in the field" when the United States entered World War I. The man put in charge of the important project was Howard Barnes, who had a captain's commission and a decade of CODE work with the State Department. Barnes and his associates may have been new to this task, but they caught on rapidly. By reviewing an available British code, asking questions, overcoming setbacks, and studying battlefield conditions, they were able to compile the *American Trench Code*, a ONE-PART CODE of 1,600 elements masked by a SUPERENCIPHER- MENT. One thousand copies were produced.

Barnes and his staff also developed a code of 500 elements called the *Front-Line Code*. Three thousand copies were made and distributed to the army, at the company level, for security maintenance. Both codes served to protect communications during the crucial early weeks of American Expeditionary Force action on the Western Front.

Anagrams, in CRYPTANALYSIS, a method involving the recovery of PLAINTEXT from CIPHERTEXT.

Unlike the hobbyist who deciphers standard anagrams from known letters (such as "now"–"won," "dear"–"read"), the *cryptanalyst* begins with the unknown, consider- ing such factors as the language in which the message is written, its length, the patterns and numbers of the groups of letters and/or digits used and any clues about the subject matter.

Once the analyst makes a break- through, such as with an opening phrase, a date, or an apparent letter pair, the work of substituting the known for the unknown begins.

When trying to recover the plaintext, a form of anagramming occurs with a process known as parallel reconstruction. This rebuilding of the KEY alphabet can be accomplished by placing ciphertext letters beneath those of a standard alphabet, the plaintext. After sometimes lengthy efforts involving experience and luck, the analyst discerns some of the plaintext/ciphertext equivalents and begins comparing the possibilities.

Plaintext: a b c d e f g h i j k l m n o p q r s t u v w x y z

Ciphertext: l n   v w z   x   c

Sometimes an analyst has the good fortune of finding clues in such primary arrangements. Here the apparent matchups of *b/l* and *d/n* would seem to indicate that ciphertext *m* would be plaintext *c*. A similar revelation seems likely with *v*, *w*, and *z*. Since *x* has been linked with *q*, the letter *y* becomes the more likely matchup with *j* of the plaintext.

Similarities of position may also lead to solutions. Suppose that another alphabet arrangement apparently indicates that *o* = *h*. If the solver finds a *p* in the encrypted message, he or she could try *i* as its plaintext with the assumption that if *p* follows *o*, then *i* follows *h*.

Pairs of identical letters, frequently used characters, common pairs such as *th*, and often-used vowels that combine with or adjoin particular consonants all can be useful in the anagram-solving process. Of course, the final proof is in the discovery of words that make sense. A good cryptanalyst includes anagramming and parallel reconstruction as a part of a broad repertoire of solving procedures.

Anglo-French Codebook, a pre-World War I English-French CODEBOOK. There are times when war plans are both timely and thorough. Such was the case when the French and English met at a London conference in 1911 and began the three-year development of War Plan W. The plan included a shared codebook with mutually accepted French/English word and phrase equivalencies, complete with instructions for their application.

Unfortunately for the English and French, the rival Central Powers emerged in World War I with similarly detailed, mutual planning.

Argot, particular language of thieves or the specialized vocabulary of people in the same workplace (see JARGON CODES).

Armed Forces Security Agency, an organization, created in 1949 to coordinate the armed forces intelligence and communications tasks. Although the AFSA was given control of strategic intelligence and communications tasks, the individual services still maintained tactical control of COMINT responsibilities in potential combat areas. Additionally, the U.S. Communications Intelligence Board

was created to coordinate data transfers among the AFSA, the FBI, and the State Department. However, what at first seemed an effective streamlining process soon encountered its own series of complications. For example, some historians blame the AFSA arrangement and its continued interservice and civilian security service rivalries for contributing to U.S. intelligence failure to recognize the danger signs of the Korean War.

This possibility, plus the admitted intelligence problems during the war, prompted President Truman in 1952 to establish the NATIONAL SECURITY AGENCY, which achieved much better coordination of intelligence gathering and security in the ensuing years.

Arnold—André Codes, CODES used by traitor Benedict Arnold and his co-conspirator, British Major John André, during the American Revolution. The account of their conspiracy has been documented in general history books and espionage texts alike. Yet what is rarely mentioned about the entire affair in 1780 is that the pair's use of codes contributed to the near success of their scheme.

As Arnold was planning to sell out the strategic West Point fortress and surrounding sites, including Stony Point and North Castle, he corresponded with André using a series of book codes. At first they used a code coordinated with Volume I of the fifth Oxford edition of Blackstone's *Commentaries*. Using a book method standard, three numbers made up a word: The first was the page, the second the line, and the third the word. Thus 35.12.8 elicited the word *general*. But many terms were difficult to find, and a number of proper names had to be spelled in their entirety. Much time was also lost counting the lines and letters, so Arnold discarded the system.

Next, the plotters tried Nathan Bailey's *Universal Etymological English Dictionary*. Its alphabetically listed terms were easier to locate than those in the *Commentaries*, and the Bailey book enabled Arnold and André to formulate a large portion of their conspiracy.

The patriots had their codebreakers (see COLONIAL CRYPTOLOGY), but the strength of the plotters' code was never tested. André was captured by three rebel militiamen whom he mistook for British soldiers. After appeals to spare his life were rejected and a deal to exchange him for Arnold failed, André was hanged as a spy at Tappan, New York. Arnold, escaping to the British lines, lived to see his name carved in the corridors of infamy.

ASCII, the American Standard Code for Information Interchange (pronounced "ask-key") was prepared by computer experts in 1964 as a means of conveying data in a standardized form.

This code is a list of the same binary digits (one and zero) that are used in the on–off electronic pulses of computer language. Such digits may represent numerous facts depending on how the computer is programmed. For standardization purposes, the ASCII has binary representations of decimal system numbers, punctuation marks, roman alphabet letters, and other keyboard characters. Here is a partial example of the code:

"	0	1	0	0	0	1	0
#	0	1	0	0	0	1	1
$	0	1	0	0	1	0	0
%	0	1	0	0	1	0	1
&	0	1	0	0	1	1	0
+	0	1	0	1	0	1	1
'	0	1	0	1	1	0	0
-	0	1	0	1	1	0	1
.	0	1	0	1	1	1	0
/	0	1	0	1	1	1	1
0	0	1	1	0	0	0	0
1	0	1	1	0	0	0	1
2	0	1	1	0	0	1	0
3	0	1	1	0	0	1	1
4	0	1	1	0	1	0	0
5	0	1	1	0	1	0	1

ASCII assigns a seven-bit string for encoding purposes. To this string an extra bit space is added as a mechanism for checking transmissions; this additional one or zero is called a parity bit.

ASCII has become one of the most frequently applied codes in the United States. International variations are used worldwide.

Atlantic, Battle of the (1939–1945), a World War II struggle to control the sea, as Nazi U-boat squadrons, known as wolf packs, wreaked havoc on merchant shipping.

CRYPTOLOGY played an important role in this battle. In addition to their skill and cunning, the U-boat commanders were aided immensely by German CRYPTANALYSIS, especially from the OKM (*Oberkommando der Kriegsmarine*), whose message solvers were able to peer into top-secret Royal Navy cryptomethods. For some time, this enabled the German naval high command to locate convoys, thus saving U-boats' fuel and time; keep the small German surface fleet away from a battle against potentially superior forces; sink British submarines; help surface raiders; and avoid entrapment of the wolf packs.

After much loss of life and naval tonnage, the Allies developed a multilevel plan to combat the wolf packs. In addition to better organized convoys, increased destroyer escorts, aerial surveillance defense, and sonar, improved CRYPTOGRAPHY for communications security was applied. Cryptanalysis, especially the British decryptions of German ciphers (see ENIGMA and ULTRA), gave the Allies access to vital facts such as the U-boats' refueling points. All these factors played a role in turning the tide of the Battle of the Atlantic.

Atomic Bomb Codes (1942–1945),
CODES and CIPHERS used to help protect the United States' top-secret atomic bomb development during World War II.

The massive project's CODENAME was the Manhattan Engineering District. Code names were also given to individuals, such as General Leslie Groves (*Relief*), Niels Bohr (*Nicholas Baker*), and Enrico Fermi (*Henry Farmer*); and to research centers, including Los Alamos (*Site Y*) and Oak Ridge (*K-25*). The bomb itself was referred to as *S-1*, the *Gadget*, and the *Thing*.

The Signal Corps used its cryptosystems to protect telegraphic communications. Telephone calls were also protected, but often by more personalized codes. Paper-borne codes were kept in places that ranged from safes to wallets (see QUADRATIC CODE). Conversations were also covered by prearranged JARGON CODES and self-styled double-talk.

However, in spite of these and other precautions, the atomic secret was being stolen even as it was being created. An extremely clever Soviet spy network had spread through the United States, Canada, and England to reach all levels of research and development (see IGOR GOUZENKO), and within four years of the first atom bomb detonations, the Soviet Union had its own nuclear weapon.

Autokey,
a type of KEY that changes with each communication, thereby giving more protection than one that is repeated with several messages. An even better form of this security is a message that is its own key. The key is kept running, or continuous, rather than being reused.

An application of the running key may be seen in an example whereby the letters of the PLAINTEXT communication provide the letters for the key (A is a priming key, explained below).

Key: (A) F I N   D H E   R N A M
Plaintext: F i n d   h e r   n a m e

This type of key had its letters generated by the message. Assuming the message continued, the key also continued.

Key: (R N A M)   E O   R A
Plaintext: (n a m e)   o r   a n

Key: N A D D R E S
Plaintext: a d d r e s s

Even though CRYPTOGRAPHY included keys and multiple alphabets by the 1500s, the autokey was a real advance in form and substance. The man who originated it was GIROLAMO CARDANO, a physician from Milan. However, his example was flawed by a *repeating* key that began again with each new message word.

Key:	F I N D	F I N	F I N D
Plaintext:	F i n d	h e r	n a m e

Key:	F I	F I	F I N D F I N
Plaintext:	o r	a n	a d d r e s s

Cardano's efforts were improved by a French nobleman named BLAISE DE VIGE-NÈRE, who provided a means for the CIPHER maker to set up a letter (called a priming key) that enabled the intended solver to make quicker progress with his own tables of alphabet equivalents.

In the example of the autokey with a running key above, the letter *A* represents the priming key. When the addressee knew this, he would be able to decrypt the first CIPHERTEXT letter. This known plaintext letter would then serve to decipher the second encrypted letter, and so forth.

Key:	(A) F I N	D H E	R N A M
Plaintext:	F i n d	h e r	n a m e
Ciphertext:	c q v l	p m z	x j u o

With priming key *A*, the recipient knew that ciphertext *c* was plaintext *F*. Using *F* as the key on the alphabet table, *q* became *i*. Each revealed character thus became the key for the next concealment.

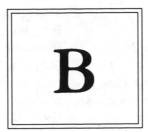

B

B-1, a CODE used by the U.S. State Department that had its own tables for encipherment. This factor gave it a modest element of security when it came into general use by State in the early 1920s.

B-1 is worth remembering if only because some experts considered it much more secure than a long-applied foreign service code called the GRAY CODE, which was so well known that its continued application seemed to be more the result of comfortable habit than an attempt to maintain security.

Controversial cryptologist HERBERT YARDLEY, still employed by the State Department during these years, said these porous codes belonged in the 1500s. He was right, but no one in charge heeded his advice. In the 1930s the B-1 was finally replaced by strip CIPHERS and CIPHER MACHINES.

Bacon, Sir Francis (1561–1626), English philosopher and statesman, the Baron Verulam, Viscount of St. Albans, and Lord Chancellor to Queen Elizabeth I. Some believed he was the true author of Shakespeare's major works (see SHAKESPEARE CIPHERS).

Regarding CRYPTOGRAPHY, Bacon developed a very clever form of STEGANOGRAPHY. With 24 letters (*u* and *v* were interchangeable, as were *i* and *j*), Bacon created this alphabet using the first two letters of his name.

a	AAAAA	e	AABAA	i	ABAAA
b	AAAAB	f	AABAB	k	ABAAB
c	AAABA	g	AABBA	l	ABABA
d	AAABB	h	AABBB	m	ABABB
n	ABBAA	r	BAAAA	w	BABAA
o	ABBAB	s	BAAAB	x	BABAB

p	ABBBA	t	BAABA	y	BABBA
q	ABBBB	v	BAABB	z	BABBB

With this method, *THE* became *BAABA AABBB AABAA*. Bacon called this process "bi-literal," and he proposed that it could be used to convey secret writing as well as audible signals with bells, horns, and muskets (for example, one bell ring for *A* and two for *B*.)

The steganographic aspect was built upon the alphabet by using different print typefaces and a cover text. In modern typeface we can illustrate this by having the *A*'s of the concealment in roman in the cover-text and the *B*'s of the masked words in italics. In order to hide the actual message *GO* (*AABBA ABBAB*), the typeface would be:

Be here soon

The letters *b* and e are roman for the first two *A*'s of *GO*. Then the *h* and *e* are italicized, the r and e are roman, and so on, according to the typeface variation designated for *A* or *B*.

G	O	(Hidden Message)

AA BBAA BBAB
Be *here soon* (Cover-Text)

Bacon's method combines aspects of steganography with concealment in apparently innocuous words and SEMAGRAMS with the slightly altered shapes of the letters themselves.

Bacon, Roger (1220–1292),
English friar renowned for having foreseen the telescope, advanced transportation methods, and human flight.

Bacon was ahead of his time in defining

aspects of CRYPTOGRAPHY as well. Though he did not personally make important advances in this field, his *Epistle on the Secret Works of Art and the Nullity of Magic* described masking secrets using arcane figures, SHORTHAND, and unusual alphabets. Some historians consider this book Bacon's most notable contribution to cryptography and science and believe that it influenced the works of SIR FRANCIS BACON three hundred years later.

BAMS Code,
the English Admiralty's Broadcasting for Allied Merchant Ships communications system which included the *Merchant Ships' Code*, a TWO-PART CODE with added SUPERENCIPHERMENT.

The code-broadcasting network was crucial to the coordination of supply ships that maintained the fragile lifeline of the British Isles during World War II. When the Royal Navy's transmission stations sent out an encoded message to a convoy captain, his radio operator would turn to the decoding section of the *Merchant Ships' Code*. An example of how such decoding pages were arranged is shown here:

50

36979	L	P	C	R	Island
980			D	Q	Locate
985			E	P	Port
990			F	N	Signal
996			G	M	Escort
37002	L	Q	H	L	Bay
010			I	K	Dock
015			K	J	Coast
021			L	H	Wind
027			M	G	Supply

38361	L R	B P	Convoy
376		C O	Tons
383		D N	Oil
392		E M	Direct
39420	L S	F L	Current
422		G K	Officer(s)
431		H J	Surface
440		I G	Fleet
447		J E	Buoy
453		K D	Channel
456		L C	100°

CODES like these look complicated, but when the numbers that superenciphered them were stripped away by an expert in CRYPTANALYSIS, compromised by the carelessness of radio operators, or divulged by treachery, such codes were quite vulnerable.

Bank Card Codes, CODES that increase the security of banking transactions at unattended terminals. This is accomplished with (1) a bank card containing a magnetically recorded primary KEY or account number (*ACCT*) and (2) a secondary key or personal identification number (*PIN*). A typical transaction follows these steps:

1. When the bank's card is placed in the terminal's card reader, the account number is read.
2. The cardholder then enters a personal identification number at the terminal's keyboard.
3. The card owner next makes a transaction request such as: Dispense $100 and debit checking account ACCT.

The security system checks to see that the ACCT is a legitimate one and that the cardholder's PIN correctly corresponds with the ACCT.

The personal identification number serves as a secondary key because it is intended to deny a segment of the private information to a potential thief. It usually consists of from four to six alphanumeric characters. Cardholders are advised not to write their PIN numbers in an accessible place, since, as with the CODEBOOKS of yore, the discovery of the personal identification code would subvert the protection system.

Baudot Code, named for its French inventor, J.M.E. Baudot, a CODE that was to the teletypewriter what MORSE CODE was to telegraphy.

The teletypewriter was an advanced form of telegraph with a receiver that printed messages at the receiving end. The striking of the transmitter's keyboard produced impulses that caused the receiver's corresponding keys to register.

Baudot arranged his code so that each character had five units (pulses), each of which was made up of either the presence of electrical current or its absence. He developed 32 combinations, 26 for letters and six for "stunts" (such as number and letter shifts and carriage returns).

The transmission was accomplished by commutators that rotated and produced the sequence of electrical pulses denoting which key had been pressed. The letter *A* was *mark mark space space space*, *N* was *space space mark mark space*, and *IDLE* was indicated by *space space mark space space*.

The letters were printed on paper tape,

with marks indicated by holes that perforated the tape. A pause in this pattern left a space. The tape was "read" by metal fingers that poked through the openings, made contact, and thus sent pulses. A space (intact tape) prevented the fingers from touching and interrupted the circuit until the next opening permitted another contact.

Here is a table of the Baudot Code with alphabet letters and teletype process symbols. 1 represents a mark and 0 a space.

Baudot Code

A 11000	B 10011	C 01110	D 10010
E 10000	F 10110	G 01011	H 00101
I 01100	J 11010	K 11110	L 01001
M 00111	N 00110	O 00011	P 01101
Q 11101	R 01010	S 10100	T 00001
U 11100	V 01111	W 11001	X 10111
Y 10101	Z 10001	α 01000	β 00010
Υ 11111	δ 11011	ϵ 00100	η 00000

α: *paragraph break* δ: *shift from letters to numbers*

β: *carriage return* ϵ: *idle*

Υ: *shift from numbers to letters* η: *blank space*

Bazeries, Étienne (1846–1931),

French army officer and cryptanalyst. Bazeries earned a reputation as a CIPHER solver while serving in the Franco-Prussian War of 1870–1971. He broke the official French military cipher and solved other supposedly "unbreakable" systems. High-ranking officers began to take notice; promotions and a position in the Ministry of Foreign Affairs followed his successes with CRYPTANALYSIS.

After a government assignment to reveal some concealed dispatches from the days of Louis XIV, Bazeries became interested in other old methods, including NOMENCLATORS that once protected the writings of French kings. He also solved messages in cases involving an anarchy trial and a pretender to the French throne.

Despite his reputation, the French high command did not heed Bazeries's warnings about the weaknesses of their own CODES. Finally, frustrated with the inertia of the military, Bazeries made a device of his own.

He called it a "cylindrical cryptograph." It was a system of simultaneous encipherment with multiple alphabets. There were a total of 20 rotatable disks, each of which bore 25 letters on its periphery. The device's KEY was the arrangement of the disks on its spindle; the particular order used for a given message was agreed upon by the intended communicators.

The sender turned the disks so that the first 20 letters of the message's PLAINTEXT appeared in a row:

SHEWILLTRAVELATSEVEN

The CIPHERTEXT letters were made from the numerous jumbled alignments of 20 letters in any other row, such as these:

ZLMANPQXVEYIOCUWGBKR

If the message contained more than 20 letters, the process was repeated by rotating the disks. The ciphertext was made from any other row of letters equal to the number needed.

It was assumed that the recipient had an exact replica of the device and the prearranged order of the disk alignment. The letters of the ciphertext were aligned across one row. Then the recipient simply checked the other rows to see the one and only row that contained the plaintext.

The French military rejected Bazeries's cylinder after the Marquis de Viaris, a vengeful rival, broke Bazeries's ciphers and his hopes for its acceptance.

Nevertheless, CRYPTOLOGY benefited from Bazeries's disappointment. In 1901, he avenged himself with a scathing book that attacked his critics and the military hierarchy. *Les Chiffres Secrets Dévoilés* (or "Secret Ciphers Unveiled") is considered one of the most informative and competent books written on the subject.

Beaufort Cipher, developed by Royal Navy admiral Sir Francis Beaufort (1774–1857), who was known for a numerical indicator of wind speeds, from less than one mile per hour (0 = calm) to a velocity of 72 or more miles per hour (12 = hurricane force).

His CIPHER, presented to the English public in 1857, took the form of a 4 × 5-inch card with a red-and-black-printed alphabet square and was advertised as a new method for veiling messages dispatched on postcards and telegrams. (The Beaufort cipher was actually very similar to an alphabet tableau [or table] of Frenchman BLAISE DE VIGENÈRE.)

Beaufort created the cipher by arranging the English alphabet on four sides of the square, with 27 letters down, 27 across, and A at each corner. Its KEY was derived from a name, place, or poetic phrase familiar to the user, who applied these directions:

1. Find the first letter of the message text in the side column (*C*).
2. From this letter, trace horizontally across the table until finding the first letter of the key (*P*).
3. At the top of the column containing *P* will be located the letter *N*, which will become the CIPHERTEXT letter.

ABCDEFGHIJKLMNOPQRSTUVWXYZA

BCDEFGHIJKLMNOPQRSTUVWXYZAB

CDEFGHIJKLMNOPQRSTUVWXYZABC

DEFGHIJKL...(ETC.)...WXYZABCDEF

To recover the PLAINTEXT, the receiver follows the same process, from ciphertext to keyletter and back. This form is also called True Beaufort to distinguish it from a slightly different technique called Variant Beaufort. In the variant form the cipher maker begins with the keyletter, uses it to locate the plaintext, and then, in its column, finds the ciphertext.

With the Beaufort name attached to them, both types of cipher gained respected places in the history of CRYPTOGRAPHY, although they did not really advance its progress significantly.

Belaso, Giovan (16th century), Italian nobleman who contributed to CRYPTOGRAPHY. In 1553 Belaso's little book *La cifra del. Sig. Giovan Batista Belaso* conveyed his idea for an easy-to-change KEY for polyalphabetic SUBSTITUTION CIPHERS. He called the key a "countersign" and proposed that it could be written with different languages as well as with differing numbers of words. Here is an example of Belaso's method. The PLAINTEXT words *THE PROUD CITY* are given the countersign *ROMAN GLORY*.

Countersign: R O M A N   G L O R Y   R O
Plaintext: t h e p r   o u d c i   t y

When pairing the keyletters and plaintext letters, the capital letters are changed to lower case. The keyletter thus paired signifies the letter from a chosen alphabet table that will encipher the plaintext letter. In the above example, *t* is enciphered by the table's *R* alphabet, *h* by its *O* alphabet, *e* by its *M* alphabet, and so on.

Belaso's small booklet was a significant improvement in written security. It provided surprising variety, since the number of alphabet sequences was expanded considerably. Different messages could be given different keys, and broken, forgotten, or pilfered keys could be exchanged quickly for others. Keys were made more important by such alterations, and those who wanted improved concealment took notice. Belaso had taken a step toward the modern use of keys, in which several are alternated during a communication.

Beobachtungs-Dienst (B-Dienst), translated as "Observation Service," the name given by the Commander of the German navy Adm. Karl Dönitz, to its small but very capable CRYPTANALYSIS group. The organization helped U-boats to destroy British ships in the battle of the Atlantic and contributed to major German successes on land.

In March and April 1940, as Hitler was formulating plans for the invasion of Nor-

way and the seizure of its rich ore supplies, the *B-Dienst* broke British CODES and revealed a Royal Navy plan to mine the harbor of Narvik, Norway. This knowledge helped the Nazis to arrange a decoy attack, fool the British, and successfully land invasion troops.

The *B-Dienst* broke many of the British merchant vessels' codes that were broadcast over the BAMS CODE network. In the second full year of the war, the *B-Dienst* was deciphering communiqués exposing the positions of entire convoys. Thus orders that were meant to direct supply-ship captains away from dangerous areas were instead used by the Germans to direct wolf packs to their prey. Throughout the spring of 1941, Allied losses increased to an alarming level, with an average of one ship being destroyed every 16 hours. By the winter of 1943, the *B-Dienst* was even reading an English broadcast called the "U-Boat Situation Report," and these warnings to the vessels actually helped the U-boats counteract the convoys' defenses.

By March 1943, the wolf packs were at the peak of their success. *B-Dienst* analysts were able to single out convoys at different ports and determine their courses, travel times, and speeds. From March 16 to March 19, with the loss of only one submarine, Dönitz's squadrons sank 21 vessels totaling 141,000 tons. These numbers indicate how desperate was the need for better communications security and new technology, such as long-range air patrols and sonar, that eventually helped to end the undersea menace.

Bible Cryptography, elements of word transformation in biblical scriptures. Noted

CRYPTOLOGY historian David Kahn suggests in his landmark book, *The Codebreakers*, that the instances of Bible cryptography are better considered proto-cryptography, since they do not have the same aspects of secrecy that fully developed CRYPTOGRAPHY provides. Nevertheless, the examples are fascinating from a historical point of view.

The word transformations are found in the Old Testament. Two of them are associated with a traditional Hebrew alphabet substitution of letters called *Atbash*, in which the first letter is replaced by the last, the second by the next-to-last, and so forth through the alphabet. *Atbash* also makes this process reciprocal, beginning with the last letter being replaced by the first.

Jeremiah 25:26 and 51:4 contain transformations in which *Sheshach* replaces *Babel* (a name for Babylon). The second of these exemplifies the apparent lack of a secrecy motive when Sheshach is followed by a phrase with Babylon in it:

How is Sheshach taken!
And the praise of the whole earth seized!
How is Babylon become an astonishment
Among the nations!

The name Babylon also appears in a cryptic form in Revelation. Among the beasts and monsters is a symbolic evil woman who bears the name Babylon. Babylon is interpreted as Rome and its empire in Rev. 17:15 as follows:

and on her forehead was
written a name of mystery:
Babylon the great, mother of

harlots and of earth's abominations.

Because passwords are often associated with CODEWORDS, though they are not necessarily synonymous, it is interesting in this context to note that the Bible mentions a password. In Judges 12:5,6 the men of Gilead tried to stop the defeated Ephraimites from escaping across the Jordan River by requiring that all passersby say the word *Shibboleth*. They knew that the Ephraimites could not pronounce the initial *sh* in the word, and all those who could not pass the test were slain.

Bifid Cipher, a concealment process created, along with the trifid, by Frenchman Felix Delastelle (1840–1902). Delastelle was a bachelor who worked for 40 years as a government tobacco inspector. When he retired, he began writing *Traité Élémentaire de Cryptographie (Elementary Treatise on Cryptography)*, in which he categorized and explained the principles of important crytographic methods, most of which were types of CIPHERS.

Delastelle's study led him to develop a type of FRACTIONATING CIPHER called the *Bifid*, using a 5 × 5 checkerboard. The letters *i* and *j* are considered interchangeable.

	1	2	3	4	5
1	d	v	m	q	a
2	l	h	y	r	u
3	o	f	p	n	c
4	z	k	w	b	s
5	x	e	t	i	g

To send the PLAINTEXT message *order three boxes*, write its letters in groups of a set length. Since five is a convenient arrangement number here, use it and replace each message letter by its coordinates (*e.g.*, o = 31). Place these numbers below each letter.

```
o r d e r    t h r e e    b o x e s
3 2 1 5 2    5 2 2 5 5    4 3 5 5 4
1 4 1 2 4    3 2 4 2 2    4 1 1 2 5
```

Encipherment is accomplished by combining the coordinated numbers horizontally and in pairs within each group representing a plaintext word. The word *order* would be 32, 15, 21, 41, 24, moving across the top row and then the bottom row.

These number pairs are then reconverted into the letter that is at their coordinates in the checkerboard (32 = *f*, 15 = *a*, and so forth) The CIPHERTEXT for the original message becomes

```
f a l z r    e u t r h    w g b d u
```

The intended receiver uses the same grid to reverse these steps and reveal the message.

Bigram, in CRYPTOLOGY, a letter pair (from *bi-*, "having two," + *gram*, "what is written"). Bigrams are often associated with CIPHERS because the primary units of ciphers are alphabet letters. Bigrams are combined in various configurations when making or solving cryptosystems. Another word for bigram is *digraph* (from the Greek: *di-*, "twice," + *graphos*, "to write").

Black Chambers, sites of surreptitious letter opening and reading. Their exact origin has remained shrouded in time. Some

historians believe they began in anterooms of palaces, where royal residents instructed servants to read intercepted missives. Other scholars think that these sites were purposely set up in buildings through which correspondence moved in the early years of mail service.

By the 1700s, the chambers' occupants were well-organized and well-paid employees of their respective nations. England had its Decyphering Branch, France its *Cabinet Noir* ("black chamber"), and Vienna the *Geheime Kabinets-Kanzlei*. Each of these groups had its nimble-fingered specialists who took impressions of wax seals, made molds, and forged amazing copies. Others then softened the seals and opened the letters with heated wires or knives. Once the contents were copied, the letters were carefully resealed and sent on to their destinations.

These efforts directly influenced CRYPTOGRAPHY because over time the letter openers steadily increased their CRYPTANALYSIS methods. Aware of these practices, the senders worked to improve their cryptomethods, and the see-saw battle was vigorously contended.

Black Code, named for the color of its binding, a U.S. military attaché's code. Given extra security by CIPHER tables, it was considered invulnerable in the early 1940s. In reality, it had been broken by German radio interception CRYPTANALYSIS.

Especially damaging to the Allied cause were the compromised messages sent by Col. Frank Fellers, the U.S. military attaché in Cairo, Egypt. Col. Fellers's detailed reports about British Middle East operations were sent to Washington in the

Black Code. In the latter part of 1941, German radio listening stations began snarling the transmissions. Their valuable contents were DECODED and sent to the "Desert Fox," Field Marshall Irwin Rommel.

Fortunately for the Allies, a surprise attack on a German wireless outpost in the dessert at Tel-el-Eisa revealed the compromising of the Black Code. The Allies then began to outfox Rommel with deceptive information sent in the same Black Code.

Bletchley Park, the idyllic Victorian-era estate near Bletchley, some 45 miles northwest of London, where the small British CRYPTANALYSIS group, the Government Code and Cypher School, moved as World War II was beginning. A number of brilliant individuals from diverse backgrounds with linguistic and mathematical skills gathered there. Support staff members were brought in and a mini-village arose. In often makeshift conditions, the enormous project of breaking German CIPHERS was begun.

The overall effort was given the name ULTRA. Among the vital successes was the solving of the major cipher device called the ENIGMA.

Members of the ULTRA group developed their own electronic cipher-solving machines, which were improved over time and evolved into COLOSSUS, a precursor of the modern computer. Such inventions, used with multilevel teamwork, allowed the Allies to win the often underestimated but crucial "brain battle" of World War II.

Blocking, the encrypting of a communication by segmenting it into blocks of letters or digits. By this process, a message is vertically blocked into groups of eight

characters and symbols, including * and . to indicate spacing and punctuation as in the following example.

Plaintext:

SELL•500•SHARES•OF•ACMO•
INDUSTRIES.•JAKE•SMITH.•

Vertical Alignment:

S	•	O	I	E	•	Block 1
E	S	F	N	S	S	Block 2
L	H	•	D	.	M	Block 3
L	A	A	U	•	I	Block 4
•	R	C	S	J	T	Block 5
5	E	M	T	A	H	Block 6
0	S	O	R	K	•	Block 7
0	•	•	I	E	•	Block 8

The enciphered text is made by arranging the new stack in horizontal blocks to generate eight groups of six letters that are sent sequentially.

Ciphertext:

Block 1	Block 2	Block 3	Block 4
S•OIE•	ESFNSS	LH•D.M	LAAU•I

Block 5	Block 6	Block 7	Block 8
•RCSJT	5EMTAH	OSORK•	O••IE•

Recovery of the PLAINTEXT is accomplished by regrouping the CIPHERTEXT into six-letter blocks, stacking them, and reading the characters and numbers vertically.

Blue, before World War I, the name of an elementary diplomatic CODE that was typical of the very poor security measures of the time.

During World War II, *Blue* was the name of the blue-bound book in which U.S. Navy cryptanalysts recorded their findings about a Japanese navy TWO-PART CODE of 85,000 groups.

The Blue book came into existence at the end of 1930, when U.S. analysts were assigned the very difficult task of uncovering a multilayered cryptosystem masked by KATA KANA, a complicated form of Japanese ideographic writing. OP-20-G, the Navy team in Washington, D.C., including Thomas Dyer, Lt. Joseph Wenger, and its shrewdly insightful leader, AGNES DRISCOLL, achieved an important first in CRYPTANALYSIS. It was the trainee Dyer who discovered a means of using IBM tabulating machines to sort the multiple potential solutions. This advancement not only helped to break the Japanese code but also had far-reaching consequences for the future of CRYPTOLOGY.

Burr, Aaron (1756–1836), a U.S. vice president and political conspirator.

Disaffected with his party, the Jeffersonian Republicans, and suffering setbacks in his political career, Burr renewed his association with a long-standing acquaintance, Gen. James Wilkinson, who was in command of the newly purchased Louisiana Territory. Using private financing and Wilkinson's connections, Burr acquired a huge tract of land in the region and retained a small army around 1806, leading to speculation that he was planning to seize more territory and establish an independent country in the Southwest.

Adding to the mystery was Burr's use of CIPHERS. In 1800, he had concealed a private letter, using a CIPHER DISK with numbers for POLYALPHABETIC SUBSTITUTION. For his correspondence with Gen. Wilkinson, Burr used symbols, combining them with a CODE made from John Entick's *New Spelling Dictionary*.

All of Burr's planning was nullified, however, when Wilkinson turned himself in and submitted a deciphered version of a Burr letter to President Jefferson. It was soon revealed that Wilkinson was a paid agent of Spain, a nation very interested in the Louisiana lands bordering on Mexico and its other southwest possessions.

Burr was tried for treason, and although finally acquitted, he met with financial and social ruin.

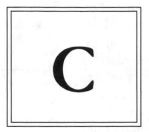

C

Cablegram, a communication method associated with national and international cables, linked most closely with CRYPTOLOGY when used with commercial CODES For business transactions. Companies learned that they could shorten messages and save money on cables by putting frequently used terms and even whole phrases into code. When this became popular and was used by companies around the world, various codes and their meanings were published in books, such as the *ABC Code*.

Caesar Substitution, a simple CIPHER bearing the name of Gaius Julius Caesar (100?–44 B.C.), who sent encrypted messages during his successful military campaigns in regions such as Gaul (now modern France, Belgium, and parts of the Netherlands, Germany, Switzerland, and Italy).

In his *Gallic Wars*, Caesar wrote about using Greek letters to mask his Latin communiqués. He also used rearrangements of the PLAINTEXT alphabet, essentially cyclical shift SUBSTITUTIONS. Using the modern 26-letter English alphabet, the method looks like this:

Plain:	a b c d e f g h i j k l m
Cipher:	D E F G H I J K L M N O P
Plain:	n o p q r s t u v w x y z
Cipher:	Q R S T U V W X Y Z A B C

The message *Gaul is ours* would become *JDXO LV RXUV*.

The intended recipient would know the alphabet shift and compare the CIPHERTEXT with the plaintext alphabet accordingly.

Card Cryptography, secret CODES, such as verbal and physical signals, by which cardplayers communicate with their confederates and cheat their opponents. For example, a shill might be positioned to look over a player's shoulder and convey the contents of the hand to the dealer.

Similarity, in Victorian whist parlors, partners often had a code to indicate the chosen suit of cards. "Did you know about young McElvoy?" might signal diamonds, and "Have you tried any of that cake?" could be the sign for hearts. Bridge partners have had a whole host of such tricks, ranging from hand and finger movements to the position of certain cards on the table. While opponents have suspected some or all of these methods, most players have accepted the schemes with good-natured resignation. However, in high-stakes international poker and bridge competitions, accusations of cheating have been made. Still, such schemes have been difficult to uncover even in the era of videotaped closeups.

Cardano, Girolamo (1501–1576), Milanese physician and mathematician. A native of Milan in an age of blossoming intellectual curiosity, Cardano strove mightily to establish himself as a great thinker. He wrote some 240 books, and among his personal papers was the first recorded writing on probability theory. As might be expected, CRYPTOGRAPHY was among Cardano's many interests. In two of his books about science, he included many of the known facts about secret writing, concealing with inks, and letter-opening techniques.

It was Cardano who originated the idea of the AUTOKEY, a KEY that changed with each message to provide greater security than would a key that was repeated. Cardano used the message's own words to make a CIPHER.

Key:	THE	THE	THENE
Plaintext:	t h e	n e w	t r a d e

Key:	THEN	TH	THENEWTR
Plaintext:	p o r t	i s	b e s i e g e d

His idea was ingenious but flawed, since his reuse of the key with every new PLAINTEXT word led eventually to multiple decryptions. Repeating the first key letters each time meant that ciphertext A might conceal plaintext g that had the key G. But ciphertext A could also represent plaintext r keyed by R. This same weakness left the entire mask open to removal should a cipher solver happen to discover the pattern. Therefore, except for the autokey idea, Cardano's system was forgotten (see BLAISE DE VIGENÈRE).

He made a second contribution to cryptography in a form of STEGANOGRAPHY called a GRILLE. His version was made of a rigid material such as heavy parchment or metal, into which rectangles were cut at different intervals.

The cipher creator placed the grille over new parchment and wrote the message in the openings, using complete words, letters, or syllables. After removing the grille, he wrote sentences incorporating the secret terms to complete the concealment. The receiver was in possession of a matching grille and, after aligning it, read the hidden words through the apertures.

One real flaw in the technique was the frequently awkward, contrived phrases used to "fill out" sentences and letters, which were a giveaway to the trained eye. Nevertheless, the grille survived and was used by rulers and ambassadors throughout the 16th century and into the 17th.

Chase, Pliny Earle (1820–1886), a Harvard graduate and professor of philosophy at Haverford College near Philadelphia, author of more than 250 magazine articles on a variety of scholarly subjects. In one of them, appearing in a periodical called *Mathematical Monthly* (March 1859) he presented the first known explanation of FRACTIONATING CIPHERS (see ADFGVX and BIFID CIPHER).

Other alphanumeric methods have equated alphabet letters with single numbers, triplets, or combinations of 0 and 1 (see BAUDOT CODE). Some of these systems were merely letter–number lists. Others had rows and columns of numbers to create coordinates in a form often called *checkerboard*. But these versions treated the digits as whole entities. Chase was the first to alter the top-and-side coordinates approach by separating, or "fractionating," the numbers. Then he applied different CRYPTOGRAPHY styles to them. His checkerboard arrangement had 10 columns of the letters *a* through *z* and three numbered rows, and included an ampersand and Greek letters.

	1	2	3	4	5	6	7	8	9	10
1	z	g	u	j	d	a	f	r	&	δ
2	o	c	s	m	q	v	x	b	p	θ
3	h	y	i	t	l	w	k	n	e	λ

He wrote his number coordinates vertically, beginning with the row number, then the column. Using this pattern, the PLAINTEXT word *divide* would have these numerical representations:

D	I	V	I	D	E
1	3	2	3	1	3
5	3	6	3	5	9

The next step was to multiply the lower line by 9 and replace it with the product:

$$
\begin{array}{r}
5\ 3\ 6\ 3\ 5\ 9 \\
\times\ 9 \\
\hline
4\ 8\ 2\ 7\ 2\ 3\ 1
\end{array}
$$

This created a new number variation:

1	3	2	3	1	3
4	8	2	7	2	3	1

Then Chase returned to his checkerboard's coordinates to change these numbers into letters again, reading them vertically as 4, then 18, 32, and so forth. 4 = j, m, or t, 18 = r, 32 = y, 27 = x, 32 = y, 13 = u, and 31 = h. This process made the final encryption j r y x y u h.

Chinese Cryptosystems, cryptographic methods devised by the Chinese from ancient through modern times.

The ancient Chinese, very early masters of writing and paper making, apparently did not develop complex techniques of CRYPTOGRAPHY in the centuries before western influence, probably because their ideographic characters did not lend themselves to the SUBSTITUTION or TRANSPOSITION methods of CIPHERS.

In the early 1800s, secret societies such as the Triads had a small CODEWORD system based upon multiple meanings of selected terms. This same group also developed a series of hand and finger configurations similar to a sign language. During the Opium War (1839–1842) when European powers forced Chinese ports to open, soldiers of fortune and drug peddlers alike had informal concealment names for themselves and their illicit trade.

By the time of World War II, the Chinese were still using insecure systems based on 19th-century commercial CODEBOOKS that equated ideographs with four-digit numerals used for telegrams. The adventurous HERBERT YARDLEY helped to solve Japanese encryptions for Chiang Kai-shek in the late 1930s, and the World War II Allies introduced to China their much better cryptomethods. During the Cold War, it is presumed that Soviet cryptologists shared some of their techniques with the Chinese before the Sino-Soviet split. Although Chinese has no alphabet and its characters are difficult to organize in ways that might be useful for cryptographic purposes, there are aspects of the language that lend themselves to encryption and CODES in existence that utilize them, both of which are surveyed below:

- The Chinese Telegraphic Code involves the assignment of four-digit CODE NUMBERS to approximately 8,500 common characters. Militarily speaking, this code is more practical for strategic than tactical applications.
- The 227 radicals, or ideographic characters, in the Chinese language make it possible to encode their various shapes. Each radical is numbered, as are any additional strokes needed to make it. The character 人 (*ren*, person) is encoded as 023,00 and the character 今 (*jin*, modern) is 023,03.

Digit	Shape	Digit	Shape
0	ㅗ	5	才
1	-/しし	6	口
2	リ	7	冖
3	丷	8	八 人 卜 丷
4	十乂	9	小 川 业 忄

The Chinese four-corner method.

- The Four Corner method, illustrated below, encodes with a series of generic shapes, each of which is equated with the numerals 0 through 9.

A character is then separated into four quadrants, beginning counterclockwise from the top left. Each quadrant is concealed by the number of the generic shape that most closely corresponds with its actual shape. Thus 人 is encoded as 8 and — is 1. With just 9,999 possible codes, a fifth digit is frequently added to represent the middle section of the character. Thus 主 becomes 80101.

Pinyin, or Romanization, is a system of using roman letters to represent the phonetic content of characters. This system is the one most used by U.S. news organizations. It is also well suited for machine cryptosystems.

Gwoyeu Romatzyh, a second form of romanization. It is a tonal spelling process that can encode both phonetic and tonal aspects.

The Chinese National Phonetic Alphabet, a primarily *Pinyin* method, using 37 phonetic symbols instead of roman letters. It is easily applicable to manual ciphers

Initials				Medials			Finals		
b	p	m	f	i	u	ü	a	o	e
ㄅ	ㄆ	ㄇ	ㄈ	ㄧ	ㄨ	ㄩ	ㄚ	ㄛ	ㄜ
d	t	n	l				ie	ai	ei
ㄉ	ㄊ	ㄋ	ㄌ				ㄝ	ㄞ	ㄟ
g	k	h					ao	ou	
ㄍ	ㄎ	ㄏ					ㄠ	ㄡ	
j	q	x					an	en	
ㄐ	ㄑ	ㄒ					ㄢ	ㄣ	
zh	ch	sh	r				ang	eng	el
ㄓ	ㄔ	ㄕ	ㄖ				ㄤ	ㄥ	ㄦ
z	c	s							
ㄗ	ㄘ	ㄙ							

The Chinese National Phonetic Alphabet.

because its arrangement closely resembles a true alphabet.

Church, Benjamin (1734–1778), a double agent who used CIPHERS to exchange information with other Tories and British military commanders.

American history texts mention Benjamin Church as a traitor to the patriots' cause, yet in comparison to Benedict Arnold, Church is an obscure figure indeed. However, espionage-related books, especially those dealing with the American Revolution, do offer detailed accounts of his life and misdeeds. A trained physician and member of Paul Revere's Boston spy ring, Church used his position to gain information that he then passed to Thomas Hutchinson, royal governor of Massachusetts. He later reported to Hutchinson's successor, British Gen. Thomas Gage. Some historians believe that it was Church who told Gen. Gage of the Colonials' cache of military supplies in Concord during the fateful spring of 1775. The double agent used a type of symbol cipher in his communications. This secret, along with his trysting partner, was to prove his undoing. In fact, it was Church's mistress who began his downfall by entrusting one of his ciphered letters to a former lover named Wenwood in Newport, Rhode Island. Instead of giving the missive to British officers as requested, Wenwood became suspicious and gave the letter to Gen. George Washington. The mistress was summoned, questioned, and divulged the physician's name. Washington sought help from amateur cryptanalysts Rev. Samuel west and Elbridge Gerry and Massachusetts militia Col. Elisha Porter, who removed the doctor's cipher mask to reveal facts about colonial privateers, rations, ammunition, and currency, among other damning revelations. Church was imprisoned, then expelled from Massachusetts. Aboard a schooner bound for a West Indies exile, he was lost at sea.

Churchill, Winston (1874–1965),

British prime minister and statesman. It was during Churchill's tenure as First Lord of the Admiralty that a very important CODE came to his attention. In September 1914, not long after World War I began, a German light cruiser was wrecked in the Baltic Sea (see MAGDEBURG). An important CODEBOOK was lost, but not to the depths of the sea, where the book's lead lining should have sunk it. Instead it and another were found by the Russians, who turned them over to Churchill and the British Admiralty. After some difficulty the codes were decoded and put to use (see ROOM 40).

By the time of World War II, Churchill had risen to prime minister. Once more he was in a crucial position to see the importance of the newest advances in communications intelligence and security. He is credited with understanding the real importance of the early effort to solve German CIPHERS. In those dark months when England faced Hitler alone, it was Churchill who used the powers of his office to support the various intelligence staffs. One of these was the fledgling group at BLETCHLEY PARK, whose efforts were eventually called ULTRA and whose achievements included solving the German's ENIGMA cipher. Churchill later called the conflict a "Wizard War," and the wizardry of the British cryptanalysts contributed much to England's ultimate victory.

Cifax,

the encipherment of an electronically transmitted image. This type of communications concealment is technically considered a branch of CRYPTOEIDOGRAPHY, that, according to author David Kahn, is masking the content of pictures. Because the process is similar to the one whereby a word's letters are transposed or substituted by CIPHERS, the word *cifax* was derived from *cipher* + *fax* (for facsimile).

The wirephoto process was invented by Frenchman Edouard Belin. According to this method, a photograph was placed on a rotating drum and its surface was viewed by a photoelectric cell. The cell then converted the image into an electric current, emitting more current to correspond to the dark and light areas of the photo. These variations in current were then transmitted to the receiving point.

At the recipient's location, a similar drum turned at the same speed. It had light-sensitive paper that revolved under a light source, with the degree of illuminating released in proportion to the fluctuating current of the transmission until the paper was fully exposed.

Belin discovered a means to provide concealment for this process. He knew that if the drums were accidentally turned at different intervals, the electronic pattern was disturbed and image distortion resulted. But if the sender and recipient had a predetermined KEY that indicated the pattern of intervals, this became an encryption. The recipient operated his machine by the same arrangement to achieve decryption. Without the key, a third party received only blurred lights and shadows.

Other creative people altered the wirephoto's current by splitting it into frequency bands in levels of brightness or altering time transmissions. But none of these processes ever really gained acceptance, largely because there was no profit to be made from intercepting wirephotos. This situation changed in the 1950s with the expansion of television. Then cifax methods became an issue once more as sponsored television confronted subscription viewing for the first time. Devices to scramble TV signals to nonsubscribers rapidly advanced with the expanding technology.

Cipher, a method of concealment in which the primary unit is the letter.

One of the major terms in CRYPTOLOGY, the word *cipher* is from the Arabic *sifr*, meaning "nothing." However, the name notwithstanding, ciphers meant a lot to the advanced Arab civilization that flourished in the 7th century. After a period of disuse, ciphers were again applied in some limited forms by Catholic church officials in the Middle Ages. Thereafter, they gained significance as an alternative to CODES for making messages unintelligible to all but those intended to have them.

Sometimes the cipher's letter unit is a pair (BIGRAM or digraph) and, rather infrequently, larger letter groups called polygrams. Ciphers commonly split letters within words and syllables; for example, the word *and* might be divided as *a-nd*.

Ciphers are applied to communications in a variety of ways. Two of their main functions are SUBSTITUTION and TRANSPOSITION. Both involve types of letter transformations. Substitution replaces the message letters with numbers, symbols, or other letters. Transposition shifts the original text, causing the normal order of the letters to be disarranged. With substitution the word *freedom* could become *iuhhgrp* and 6 18 5 5 4 15 13, or follow an even more complex pattern. Transposition keeps the original letters but moves them, to become, perhaps, *romefed or demofer.*

Throughout much of their history, ciphers have had a KEY, or function that determines the operations of a given cipher. A KEYWORD might signify the pattern of letters in a cipher alphabet, while a KEYNUMBER would specify the order of the letters in a transposition. In the first example, the alphabet is the series of letters that is equated with the original message letters, or PLAINTEXT, in order to begin a concealment process with a keyword such as *here*. In this case the intended communicators have arranged to make the first and third letters set the pattern of the alphabet.

Plaintext: h i j k l m . . . z
Cipher alphabet: r s t u v w . . . j

Here *h* and *r* are ten letters apart in the alphabet. This is the key or function that directs the resulting arrangements through the standard 26 letters, including $z = j$. Using this particular alphabet, the word *message* becomes *wocckqo.*

In the case of a keynumber and a transposition, the prearranged digits could be

34512. This means that the third letter of the original word is transposed to be first, the fourth letter is second, and so on. Applying this keynumber to *leave* makes it *avele*.

In the 20th century, ciphers began to supersede codes as a concealment method. This was largely because ciphers' ability to operate on letters and syllables made them easily adaptable to modern electronics, digital equations, and tabulating machines. Codes, in contrast, lost favor because of their dependence on replacing whole words and often bulky word lists.

New advances in mathematics and COMPUTER science have expanded cipher applications to the point where the term *key* now includes TWO-KEY CRYPTOGRAPHY and PUBLIC KEYS. Still, the basic relationships among cipher, key, transposition, and substitution maintain their place at the foundation of the multimillions of computer-generated concealment possibilities.

Cipher Disk, used to arrange alphabets, numerals, or symbols for encrypting and decrypting purposes. The terms *cipher disk* and *cipher device* have often been used interchangeably. For the purposes of this text, the word *disk* is defined in two ways. When it appears in lowercase letters, it is intended to describe a circular object that forms a small part of a larger mechanism, as in the case of ETIENNE BAZERIES's "cylindrical cryptograph" and THOMAS JEFFERSON's "cypher wheel," both of which have spindles on which a series of circular pieces are placed in varied arrangements to alter the alphabet letters on the circles' outer edges.

The disks described in this entry (referred to elsewhere in capital letters) are

A Mexican cipher disk. (From *The American Black Chamber* by Herbert Yardley, Bobbs-Merrill, 1931.)

more elaborate dials or rings. They are frequently in pairs that contain numbers, letters, or symbols to conceal words with CIPHERS or CODES.

Beginning with LEON ALBERTI's two copper plates and continuing through the symbols and numbers of GIOVANNI PORTA's invention, disks generally have a similar circular design. They permit the turning of one or more of their rings in order to achieve different alignments of the figures or characters on their facing surfaces, thus providing polyalphabetic encipherment (see POLYALPHABETIC SUBSTITUTION).

Cipher Machine, a mechanism used to encrypt and decrypt messages. Although the term has been used synonymously with CIPHER device, it is more properly reserved for more mechanical, and later electrical, encryption machines.

The hand-operated versions include the disklike PLETTS DEVICE and the WHEATSTONE CRYPTOGRAPH. Both allowed the "dialing" of letters to alter the cipher.

However, these alignments were still accomplished manually.

By the early 1900s, a number of often impractical gear-and-sprocket inventions had been introduced, which were operated by moving a dial or pushing a button to activate gears that turned themselves. One of the better methods is exemplified by the contribution of mathematician LESTER HILL, who is credited with inventing algebraic CRYPTOGRAPHY. But his machine for POLYGRAPHIC substitution never became popular.

With the advancements first of telegraphy and then of the fledgling radio doing so much to speed communications, CRYPTOLOGY seemed to be falling behind. Then a large leap forward occurred when American EDWARD HEBERN blended technology with cryptographic needs in 1917 and invented the wired codewheel called the ROTOR. This applied the speed of electrical responses to the alphabet and number variations needed to encrypt words for ever more rapid messages. Hebern's rotor, along with its rivals such as those of BORIS HAGELIN and Arvid Damm, signaled the arrival of cryptology's machine age.

Ciphertext, the result of applying a CIPHER method to a given text (the PLAINTEXT). The new, enciphered communication is the ciphertext.

Ciphony, a primary form of oral secrecy involving speech modification with scrambler devices. Because these techniques affect parts of a communication, they have an effect similar to the one CIPHERS have on segments of words. Thus the word *ci-*

phony derives from *cipher* plus *telephony* (the science of telephonic transmission).

Not long after Alexander Graham Bell patented the telephone, people were trying to find ways to make speech more secretive. This has been accomplished with frequency and time variations.

The various frequencies in the human voice (measured in cycles per second) enable changes to be made. In a version of SUBSTITUTION, frequencies are altered. One method is a band-shift whereby the frequencies are moved down or up. Another type of ciphony is band-splitting, which divides the frequency into smaller bands, then mixes them. Once the bands are segmented into subbands, a scrambling mechanism rearranges and alternates them in fractions of seconds.

Other scrambling methods include inversion, covering messages with "noise," and amplitude modification. Inversion involves turning human speech "upside down." Vocal tones of low frequency pass through the inverter and come out much higher, while the opposite happens to those of high frequency. "Noise" is achieved by a phonograph record of music or other sounds being electrically placed over the intended message, thus acting like a NULL in a cipher that mixes false letters or symbols with the real ones. The recipient has to have a descrambler identically synchronized with the originating scrambler in order to separate out the unwanted noise.

The third type of scrambling method, amplitude change, is also called wave-form modification. This technique has a changeable electric current that creates alterations in the volume level of the voice. The person receiving the message unscrambles it with a current arranged to reverse the fluctuations.

Time variation ciphony is accomplished with magnetized tape. In time-division scramble, or T.D.S., a recording mechanism takes segments from speech in intervals of seconds, and mixes their order. The recipient's descrambler is equipped with an equal number of recording heads that return the sound segments to another magnetic tape in their proper order.

Scrambling devices began to achieve popularity in the late 1920s and 1930s and saw widespread use during World War II (see A-3). Expanded by Cold War and private industry concerns, ciphony now encompasses such transmissions security factors as: Citizen's Band sets secured by pseudorandom changes in the frequency spectrum between caller and receiver; the NATIONAL SECURITY AGENCY's Electronic Secure Voice Network of phone scramblers; and encrypted, digitalized voice signals (see PULSE CODE MODULATION).

Civil War (United States, 1861–1865),

a war in which concealment systems played an important role, although they did not affect the outcome.

Union Gen. George McClellan, for example, used a type of word TRANSPOSITION in 1861 during his victorious campaign along the Ohio River Valley and in western Virginia. The CIPHER was created by Anson Stager, first superintendent of Western Union. Mr. Stager's cipher grew in importance as Union commander John C. Freemont and detective Allan Pinkerton applied it in the West and East, respectively. In 1862, the Stager transposition came into use throughout the Union Army, thanks to the first large-scale wartime use of the telegraph. In fact, President Lincoln frequently visited the telegraph room in the War Department to keep informed of unfolding events.

The Stager cipher was readily adaptable to telegraphy because of its easy arrangement. The message was written in lines and transcribed using the columns that the lines formed. Secrecy was provided by the order in which the columns were read, namely down one column and up another. As time passed, further security was added by NULLS, CODENAMES for special terms, and multiple directions that formed a larger maze of ROUTES necessary to trace the message.

The various branches of the Union Army did not all use the Stager cipher. Some forces, for example, continued to use elementary word transpositions and members of the new Signal Corps, such as Sgt. Edwin Hawley and Maj. ALBERT MYER, devised other methods. Hawley's polyalphabetic creation (see POLYALPHABETIC SUBSTITUTION), was a set of 26 wooden pieces bearing different CIPHERTEXT alphabets used with a KEYWORD, became the first American cipher method to be patented. Myer, the Signal Corps' commander, also developed a CIPHER DISK as well as a signaling system for flags, torches, and other hand-held objects.

Both sides were often able to intercept such visual signals, though a number of them were purposely falsified. But the South's efforts in CRYPTOGRAPHY and CRYPTANALYSIS did not compare favorably with those of the North. Gen. Albert Sidney Johnston used a CAESAR SUBSTITUTION to communicate with Gen. Pierre Beauregard during the devastating Battle

A Confederate cipher disk. (Courtesy of The Museum of the Confederacy, Richmond, Virginia. Photograph by Katherine Wetzel.)

of Shiloh, and Johnston and Confederate President Jefferson Davis used a dictionary for a book CODE. Southern naval officers sent messages in dictionary-based codes as they planned attacks on Northern shipping.

The South's cryptographers also put their faith in BLAISE DE VIGENÈRE's method, with its table of 26 alphabets, row shifts, and KEY alphabet for encipherment. Yet because of transmission errors by their own cipher clerks using MORSE CODE, the Confederate officers often had a more difficult time deciphering their own communiqués than did the Union cryptanalysts (see THE SACRED THREE).

Cleartext, a communication that has not been concealed. Such messages are also called *in clear* or, sometimes, *in plain lan-*

guage. Cleartext is differentiated from PLAINTEXT, with the latter being the original text that is recovered after decryption, or CRYPTANALYSIS. Sometimes cleartext messages are sent in error, causing diplomatic embarrassment or loss of life in battle.

Clock Code, a means whereby pilots communicated during World War I. Clocks and watches have been used for CODES and CIPHERS because their numerals equated with letters, words, symbols, other numbers, and so on. However, this particular clock was not mounted on a wall or strapped on anyone's wrist. In order to direct artillery fire, both the aerial observer and the artillerymen receiving the reports worked with a "clock" that had imagined inner circles and clockface numerals.

The target for the artillery barrage was considered to be at the center of the clock. Its axis, represented by the 12 o'clock-to-6 o'clock line, was thought of

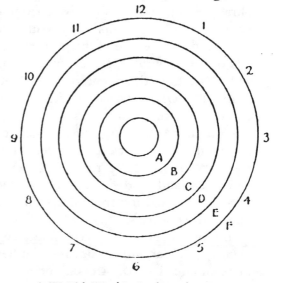

A World War I clock code.

as true north and south. The digits 1 through 12 on the periphery formed coordinates for better locating the position of artillery hits and misses.

The coordinates were completed with roman letters in the concentric rings. The circles represented radial distances of 50, 100, 200, up to 500 yards in estimated distance from the target. If greater accuracy was sought, rings of 25 and 10 yards in radius and identified with the letters *Y* and *Z* were used.

When a round was fired, the aerial observer noted its impact point with reference to the number–letter coordinates, such as *A*12 or *E*3. In the case of *A*12 the gunners would have been very close indeed, near the target and just above it on the north–south axis. But the *E*3 coordinates, at the outer ring and well to the right, meant much readjustment was needed.

Code, a word, number, letter, or symbol used to replace words, letters, and phrases. The name is derived from the Latin *codex* ("tree trunk" or "writing tablet"). Codes were one of the primary methods of secret writing for centuries. Codes and CIPHERS both appeared as brief letter SUBSTITUTIONS in early Vatican archives dating from the 1300s and were used by the Mediterranean city-states. Both concealment methods were included in NOMENCLATORS, collections of cipher alphabets and coded names that influenced secret writing from the 15th to the mid-19th centuries.

In more recent times, codes became especially popular with businesses. Gathered in commercial CODEBOOKS, codes short-ened messages and made sending telegraph or cable transmissions less expensive. Two other important applications were in World War I field CRYPTOGRAPHY, by which messages were exchanged with the trenches, and World War II CODENAMES/CODEWORDS that concealed the facts about a number of important plans and missions.

Throughout their varied history, codes have been generally consistent in form. Codewords or CODENUMBERS may replace a word or phrase of varied length. They deal with whole words and specific entities.

Code				Plaintext
A	C	F	H	component
D	G	J	N	compose
G	I	M	O	composed
J	M	O	Q	composer
N	P	R	U	composing
P	S	U	Y	composite
S	V	X	Z	composition
V	Y	A	D	compositor

ACFH stands in for *component*. But if another tense or a slightly different meaning is sought, the other code letters would be used (for example, *DGJN* for "compose" but *GIMO* for "composed"). Codes differ from ciphers in this respect because the latter divide the PLAINTEXT word into its various parts (*e.g.*, separating pairs of letters like *th*).

Codes can be further concealed as codenumbers and through an enciphering process whereby numerical codegroups are added to a numerical KEY. The sum constitutes a numerical encipherment (see ENCICODE).

Codebook, either a collection of code terms or a book used to encode and DE-CODE messages.

Small groups of CODES were once kept on large folded pieces of parchment called NOMENCLATORS. To protect these codes, and sometimes to hide them from prying eyes, covers were added, creating codebooks.

Another type of codebook was a text chosen as a basis for encoding and decoding communications. In this system, three numbers were often used to signify a particular word—the first for the page number, the second for the line, and the third for the word. Terms not found in the text could be given a separate alphabet, or equated with other words or CODENUMBERS. Variations on this method involved counting paragraphs, using *L* or *R* to indicate the right or left column, and making an enciphered code by adding preset numbers to the three standards, page, line, and word (see ENCICODE).

Dictionaries, with their alphabetized word lists, were often used in this manner. In fact, Benedict Arnold and John André used Nathan Bailey's *Universal Etymological English Dictionary* as an encoding book while plotting against West Point (see AR-NOLD–ANDRÉ CODES).

Codebooks with substantial collections of nonsecret code terms were prepared and sold to companies to help them save telegraph and cable charges by condensing their messages. Briefer codebooks were prepared by the military during World War I. These included *The American*

Trench Code and the *Front-Line Code*, both of which were ONE-PART CODES used with SUPERENCIPHERMENTS. Not as complicated as the commercial codes, they were meant for quick use in life-and-death situations.

Codenames/Codewords, terms that are often applied interchangeably in fiction, but in fact differ in the field of CRYPTOLOGY.

A *codename* refers to an operation such as wartime concealments for a person (a spy's cover) or for an object such as a secret weapon.

A *codeword* is used more as a signal, exemplified by the JARGON CODES of D-DAY. In general, a word that masks another.

Codenumbers, numbers that function like CODEWORDS when they replace the words of an original message. At one time when large CODEBOOKS were still used by consulates and military commanders alike, both CODENAMES and codenumbers were applied as concealments.

Codewords were more reliable, since codenumbers were susceptible to error when MORSE CODE was the primary means of transmission. An added or deleted dot would have altered a digit in such a way as to completely change the original intent.

Codenumbers could be changed into letters by the application of a KEY. Long words with no repeating letters, such as *countryside*, could be exchanged for numbers (1 = *C*, 2 = *O*, 3 = *U*, and so on). Using this system, the number 34957 could stand for *unity*, or a number of combinations within a given word could occur by altering the equations.

Codetalkers, members of U.S. Indian Nations who concealed messages in both world wars, using linguistic cryptosystems.

In World War I, members of the Choctaw Nation, Muskhogean Indians originally from the region of Louisiana and Georgia, practiced linguistic concealments for the American Expeditionary Force. In October 1918, Choctaws with the 142nd Infantry saw combat in the area of Chufilly and Chardeny during the Meuse-Argonne campaign, using a telephone exchange to convey messages that completely fooled the Kaiser's most skilled eavesdroppers, with concealments such as:

Military Term	Choctaw
allies	apepoa
artillery	tanamp chito, tanamp hochito
talk	anumpa
tank	oka aialhto chito

The original Choctaw language did not have direct equivalents for all military phrases, and between the wars, few efforts were made to develop formal CODES equating Indian and armed forces' terms. But World War II caused a widespread reassessment of all communications security (COMSEC), and many methods were expanded and applied.

During the anti-Axis conflict, Indians from the Choctaw, Comanche, Kiowa, Navajo, and Pawnee Nations proudly served as codetalkers. Their varied languages combined with CIPHER lists and CODEBOOKS protected many dispatches and saved Allied lives.

Comanche	Pronunciation	Military Term
enemy	tu-wa-ho-na	enemy
sewing machine	techa-keena	machine gun
red belly	ex-sha-bah-nah	soldier
tank	wah-ke-ray	tank

Navajo		
ahead	nas-sey	advance
hid	di-nes-ih	camouflage
defense	ah-kin-cil-toh	defense
potatoes	ni-ma-si	grenade
short big gun	be-el-don-tso-quodi	howitzer

Codetext, a coded message. Very similar to CIPHERTEXT, codetext differs mainly in that a CODE, rather than a CIPHER, conceals the text.

Colonial Cryptology, cryposystems used in the colonies of North America. The American patriots did not have the type of organized CRYPTOGRAPHY or CRYPTANALYSIS that was prevalent in Europe. Still, they were responsible for both outstanding personal achievements and unusual methods worthy of inclusion in the history of CRYPTOLOGY.

Gen. George Washington was well served by the amateur cryptanalysts Rev. Samuel West, Col. Elisha Porter, and Elbridge Gerry, who broke a CIPHER-concealed letter of double-agent BENJAMIN CHURCH, ending his treachery.

The colonists used CODES to conceal the activities of the spy group known as the Culper Ring. Robert Townsend of New York (Culper Jr.) and Samuel Woodhull of Long Island (Culper Sr.) corresponded with Gen. Washington using a NOMENCLATOR and a dictionary-based code provided by spymaster Maj. BENJAMIN TALLMADGE of the Connecticut Dragoons. Their messages were given an extra level of concealment with *stains*, or INVISIBLE INKS. Through the efforts of the Culper group, important information was successfully conveyed to Washington, allowing him to protect his outnumbered troops and to maneuver successfully against the British.

Benedict Arnold's plot, with John André, to deliver West Point to the British nearly succeeded, with the help of a dictionary-based code (see ARNOLD—ANDRÉ CODES). Their conspiracy was not revealed by letter interception or cryptanalysis. Rather, André was captured by an alert rebel patrol, and the well-woven scheme unraveled.

The British and their Loyalist allies used several cryptography and STEGANOGRAPHY systems, with varying levels of success. Early in the war, Benjamin Thompson sent an invisible-ink missive to British headquarters in Boston, describing some of the plans of the rebellious New England troops. Later, Sir Henry Clinton, British commander of New York, rendered his correspondence more secure with an alphabet table, a nomenclator, a number SUBSTITUTION, and a type of GRILLE. Clinton used the latter in a letter sent to Gen. John Burgoyne in 1777.

During the final campaign of the war, cryptanalysis again benefited the colonial forces at a crucial time. JAMES LOVELL, a Boston school teacher, solved intercepted British dispatches revealing Sir Henry Clinton's plans to rescue Charles Cornwallis, commander of the British forces at Yorktown. This knowledge enabled Washington's ally, French Adm. de Grasse, to block the relief attempt, and Cornwallis was left to face Washington's well-orchestrated siege alone. He was soon forced to surrender, marking the patriots' final victory.

Colossus, an early form of COMPUTER used to break the German ENIGMA ciphers during World War II. Huge by today's standards, Colossus was a marvel of its time. It was the brain child of Alan Turing, a noted mathematician, who also developed the Turing machine, another landmark in the development of the computer. Working in 1940 with England's BLETCHLEY PARK staff, including A. Dillwyn Knox; Max Newman, a Cambridge mathematician; and Thomas Flowers, a British post office engineer, Turing was instrumental in solving Enigma.

ULTRA, the struggle to decipher Enigma, began after Polish agents managed to smuggle a replica of the German cipher machine and a description of its functions out of Poland before that country's fall. Later in the war, after the British had broken early ciphers, the Germans improved their security efforts with cryptographic teletypewriters using a mechanism called the *Geheimschreiber* (a.k.a. T52 CIPHER MACHINE). In conjunction with a teleprinter, this device automatically encrypted and sent a message that had been typed on a keyboard in CLEARTEXT.

The Bletchley staff countered by using electromechanical machines called "bombes" to continue to reveal Enigma secrets. Then Turing and his team created electronic devices to match the speed of the *Geheimschreiber*/T52; a series of these resulted in the protocomputer named Colossus.

Described as being the size of three large wardrobes, Colossus had recently developed vacuum tubes that made the telephone exchange-type switches of previous decrypting devices seem plodding by comparison. Its eventual total of 2,400 tubes could solve intercepted German messages at the then astounding rate of thousands of characters per second. The machine's high development cost was quickly justified by the information it provided Allied commanders.

COMINT, an acronym for communications intelligence, one of the primary categories of SIGINT (signals intelligence). COMINT is defined by the National Security Council Intelligence Directive No. 6 as "the interception and processing of foreign communications passed by radio, wire, or other electromagnetic means, and by the processing of foreign encrypted communications, however transmitted." The directive continues, "Interception comprises search, intercept, operator identification, signal analysis, traffic analysis, cryptanalysis, decryption, study of plain text, the fusion of these processes and the reporting of results. Excluded from this definition are the interception and processing of unencrypted written communications, press and propaganda broadcasts."

Compaction, the process of reducing the length of an enciphered message in order to reduce its chance of being solved. Compaction is based on the principle that "less is more." In a basic example of the method, every third character, space, or punctuation mark is removed. The deleted components are then sent by a different means to the intended recipient, who collates the CIPHERS in order to restore the message. Thus the decryption KEY consists of the deleted letters and the rule for their removal.

Plaintext: SELL•700•SHARES•OF•ACMO•
INDUSTRIES.•NATE•SMITH.

Compaction: SEL•00SHRE•O•
AMOINUSRIS•NAE•MIH•

Removed Characters: L7•ASFC•DTE•TST

Compartmentation, CODES that are a part of the U.S. government's security classification system, restricting access to information that pertains to national security.

Established and revised by a series of presidential executive orders, the three primary security classifications in descending order are Top Secret, Secret, and Confidential. Compartmentation codes provide subclassifications for these primary categories.

Computers, electronic devices for mass information storage, retrieval, and distribution.

Computers are crucial to any modern nation's security. The use of machines for collecting and analyzing intelligence was first initiated by military personnel in the mid-1930s, when U.S. Navy and Army signals intelligence (SIGINT) groups began using tabulating machines with rapid digital circuitry. These devices used a punch-card format and were considered high-tech in their day. However, the costly inventions were limited because each was built to at-

The Mark I. (Courtesy of the Cruft Photo Lab, Havard University. Photograph by Paul Donaldson.)

tack a specific cryptosystem. If that CODE or CIPHER was changed or canceled, the device was relatively useless.

With the outbreak of World War II, the SIGINT team worked with Kodak, IBM, and Bell Laboratories among others to develop machines with greater speed and increased flexibility. Allied nations such as Great Britain were involved in similar pursuits (see COLOSSUS). But after the defeat of the Axis powers, academia continued the research in this area. The University of Pennsylvania and its Moore School of Electrical Engineering were responsible for a crucial advance in 1946 with their ENIAC, an electronic numerical integrator computer with 18,000 electron tubes housed in a 30-by-50-foot room and with a total storage capacity of just 20 numbers. The seminal ENIAC was followed by the Naval Security Group's Atlas (1950), the Army Security Agency's

Abner (1952), and then the NATIONAL SECURITY AGENCY's Harvest (1962) and Stretch (1962).

Today's smaller and smarter progeny of these behemoths are the primary means by which all the diverse intelligence data, from spies' whispers to satellite surveillance, is compiled. Nations also protect their communications with computer-generated encryptions to achieve the highest level of communications security (see COMSEC).

On the other side of the coin, the computer is vital to modern decryption techniques. Its speed and capacity to process volumes of material enable would-be solvers to consider the millions of letter, syllable, and number combinations and other FREQUENCY possibilities necessary to uncover clues in an encryption shield.

COMSEC, communications security, defined as "the protection resulting from any measure taken to deny unauthorized persons information derived from the national security-related telecommunications of the United States, or from any measure taken to ensure the authenticity of such telecommunications."

In the United States, a large measure of this vital work is conducted by the NATIONAL SECURITY AGENCY at its Fort Meade, Maryland, headquarters. Known as COMSEC, the NSA's Office of Communications Security has technicians, mathematicians, and engineers who develop theories, test devices, and evaluate systems to protect communications. They use COMPUTERS to study the potential strength of CIPHER models, to make cryptographic equipment for military communications, and to provide security processes ranging from phone scramblers to encryptions for missile telemetry.

Construction Tables, tables of letters used to form encryptions. Each table consists of a square of single letters and two squares of letter pairs, one at the side and the other at the top. The pairs are set up so that all of those in either a row or column in the square differed by two letters.

In order to avoid transposing adjacent letters, the squares are arranged to have an odd number of places on each side. To alter a 26-letter alphabet, one letter is either discarded or an extra character (*i.e.*, &, *, %) is added. (Later, all the words made with this character are removed from the supply of terms.) A brief example of such a table made with a six-letter alphabet *B, C, D, E, F, G,* and # as the extra character, is shown at right.

To make a five-letter CODEWORD, the word compiler then takes two elements from the same column and two from the same row. The fifth or single letter is at the pivot of the chosen row and column. A codeword sequence could then follow a pattern such as this:

BB (column) + *B* (single letter) + *BB* (row) = *BBBBB*

BB (column) + *B* (single letter) + *CC* (next row pair) = *BBBCC*

The letters would continue from *BBBBB, BBBCC . . . BBB##* for just one group of numerous choices to replace the given PLAINTEXT words. Thus the encryption maker had a two-letter differential, which helped him or her to avoid TRANSPOSITIONS of alternate letters and resulting transmission errors.

BB	BC	BD	BE	BF	BG	B#
CC	CD	CE	CF	CG	C#	CB
DD	DE	DF	DG	D#	DB	DC
EE	EF	EG	E#	EB	EC	ED
FF	FG	F#	FB	FC	FD	FE
GG	G#	GB	GC	GD	GE	GF
##	#B	#C	#D	#E	#F	#G

B	C	D	E	F	G	#		BB	CC	DD	EE	FF	GG	##
C	D	E	F	G	#	B		CB	DC	ED	FE	GF	#G	B#
D	E	F	G	#	B	C		DB	EC	FD	GE	#F	BG	C#
E	F	G	#	B	C	D		EB	FC	GD	#E	BF	CG	D#
F	G	#	B	C	D	E		FB	GC	#D	BE	CF	DG	E#
G	#	B	C	D	E	F		GB	#C	BD	CE	DF	EG	F#
#	B	C	D	E	F	G		#B	BC	CD	DE	EF	FG	G#

Contact Chart, a tool, used by a CODE breaker or CIPHER solver, to analyze the FREQUENCY of certain letters or letter combinations in encrypted text.

A frequency count is often written with each letter of the alphabet paired with the total number of times that letter appears in the message being analyzed:

A B C D E F G H I J . . . Z
8 16 13 15 7 10 12 9 11 18 . . . 19

However, a cryptanalyst cannot solve the code or cipher by simply comparing frequencies to standard lists of most-used or least-used letters in a given language. Nor can letter SUBSTITUTION be checked until the shield is broken. If the crypto-method is sophisticated, the original message may be very difficult indeed to reveal. Still, once letters have been found to show some frequency tendencies, these are studied. Because every language has characteristic frequencies, some pattern generally emerges.

Contact charts assist in this analysis by taking advantage of the fact that certain letters are often found in pairs or groups. As a chart begins to take shape and reflect some of the potential combinations, it begins to have a personality of its own.

27	V	V	X	L	Z	J	B
23	X	V	X	L	Z	J	B
20	L	V	X	L	Z	J	B
19	Z	V	X	L	Z	J	B
18	J	V	X	L	Z	J	B
16	B	V	X	L	Z	J	B

In this chart of high-frequency letters, the letter being counted appears at the left. The same letters are placed in rows to the right, and their contact points are noted. The marks below each show the number of times that it follows the subject letter. Tallies above indicate how many times the letter in that row precedes the subject letter.

In the above example, X has preceded V three times and followed it twice. Thus the letter pair (digraph) has occurred five times—$XV(3)$ and $VX(2)$.

A properly constructed contact chart gives clues about the real letters of the message, because the letters follow the characteristics of the language being used. For example, in English, the letter e is the most common vowel. Therefore, its discovery might cause the entire fabric of the encryption to unravel. The next three high-frequency vowels are a, i, and o; of special interest to potential solvers is the fact that they are not frequently found together. So when a digraph in the chart appears to have a very infrequent association, it may prove to be a rare pair in the PLAINTEXT. In English, ai, oi, and ao are rather infrequent, for example, while io is used more often.

Consonants also have certain tendencies. The letter n is often preceded by a vowel. So a CIPHERTEXT letter in the chart often preceded by the same enciphered letter might signify a plaintext n preceded by a vowel. Pairs of consonants such as t and h also may be hidden by a frequent digraph pair revealed by the chart. Some consonants are located side by side in a standard alphabet, yet tend to pair with many other letters rather than with each other. This also provides important clues for the cryptanalyst.

After finding such contact possibilities with the chart, the analyst then begins the next level of the puzzle, trying these findings in the cryptic message to see whether coherent patterns emerge.

Copek, CODENAME for a highly secure cryptosystem linking U.S. Pacific bases with Washington, D.C., before and during World War II. Its messages were sent by the U.S. Navy's ECM (Army's SIGABA) machine, whose electric ROTORS assured an advanced level of encipherment for its day.

The Copek-associated organizations and their radio network exemplified some of the best and worst aspects of communications security of their time. Copek linked Washington's Negat Station with the U.S. Navy's intelligence centers Hypo (Hawaii) and Cast (at Cavite in the Philippines). These sites had different responsibilities for intercepting and breaking Japanese cryptomethods: The Hypo group tried to reveal the CODE of the Japanese admirals, while the Asiatic Fleet intelligence squad at Cavite used their PURPLE machine to try to solve the main Japanese navy operational cryptosystem (see JN25).

The Copek system was kept secure partly because it was not used as frequently as other methods. However, due to questionable, overcautious, security decisions, the Hypo center in Hawaii did not have decipherments of the "J" SERIES of TRANSPOSITION ciphers used by Japan's consulates, despite the fact that one such consulate was located near the important U.S. naval base at Pearl Harbor. Many critics of U.S. preparedness on the eve of the war believe that, had the base had access to these ciphers, several warning signs could have been recognized in time to counter the Japanese attack of December 7, 1941.

Coral Sea, Battle of the (May 7–8, 1942),

a World War II engagement in which U.S. radio interception and CRYPTANALYSIS of Japanese naval messages laid the groundwork for the thwarting of Japan's plan to attack Port Moresby, New Guinea, and thereby threaten Australia.

The COMINT center for the Pacific Fleet in Hawaii had applied its skills of signals interception, traffic analysis, and cryptanalysis to determine that the Japanese Imperial Fleet was preparing a campaign, codenamed "RZP", in the southwest Pacific, targeting Port Moresby, New Guinea, which was an important fortress in its own right and a vital part of the larger Australian defense plan.

U.S. naval forces were divided at the time, with two aircraft carriers participating in the DOOLITTLE RAID against Japan. But the Commander of the Pacific Fleet, Adm. Chester Nimitz, took a calculated risk and ordered the carriers *Yorktown* and *Lexington* to disrupt the invasion plan.

The two ships and their accompanying Task Force 17, commanded by Rear Adm. Frank Fletcher, met the Japanese navy on May 7, 1942, in a region northeast of Australia called the Coral Sea. American flyers sunk the light carrier *Shoho*, an escort for troop transports. Japan's naval cryptosystem JN25 (including the newer JN25b) transmissions were detected at more than one point during the battle, but in the midst of the conflict, Rear Adm. Fletcher was not always certain of the reliability of the decrypted CIPHERS.

On May 8, the U.S. and Japanese fleets continued to fight the historic encounter. It was the first naval engagement conducted solely with aircraft, and the opposing ships never even sighted each other. The Japanese carrier *Shokaku* was damaged, and some of their support vessels were sunk. The U.S. Pacific fleet was dealt a shock with the loss of the carrier *Lexington* and the damaging of the *Yorktown*.

Rear Adm. Fletcher was later criticized for not making better use of the tactical radio intelligence at his disposal, and some historians believe he let a decisive victory slip from his grasp. However, others focus on the positive outcome of the battle, which thwarted the planned Japanese assault on Port Moresby as well as delivering a blow to Japanese morale.

Crime Codes and Ciphers,

cryptosystems used by criminals with varying levels of success. The ARGOT of thieves' dens in 12th-century Europe and the JARGON CODES, or slang terms, used to gain entry to private gambling clubs or speakeasies in our own century had similarities that transcended time.

Criminal gangs have used various gestures for initiation and recognition. A number of signaling methods, including torches, flags, horns, and so on, have also been used as signs to begin an illegal activity.

These obvious audial or visual methods were rendered virtually obsolete with the rise of professional police forces and advances in investigative technology, however, and criminals began to employ CODES and CIPHERS. When bootleggers in the 1930s used offshore vessels to smuggle illegal liquor, the U.S. Coast Guard used radio direction-finding and the cryptanalytical skills of ELIZEBETH FRIEDMAN to disrupt their plans and win convictions. Soon, however, the rumrunners were improving their cryptomethods to the point where Friedman considered them superior to a number of systems used in World War I.

Illegal gambling has also made use of CRYPTOGRAPHY to keep secret records of bettors and transactions. Many "bookie codes" are elementary SUBSTITUTION codes using symbols and abbreviations. A bookmaker for horse races might have lists that remind him or her of just enough to keep the records straight while masking the truth from an inexperienced observer, as follows:

Horse Race Bets	Decryption
DD	Denise Doe (Bettor)
5 A 3 2	Fifth race at Aqueduct (Wager) Horse #3 $2 to win
JQP	John Q. Public
7 P 6 22	Seventh race at Pimlico Horse #6 $2 to win, $2 to place
SC	Stella Citizen
3 P 5 442	Third race at Pimlico, Horse #5 $4 to win, $4 to place, $2 to show
5 P 7 XX2	Fifth race at Pimlico, Horse #7 No win, no place, $2 to show
8 A 6 42	Eighth race at Aqueduct, Horse #6 $4 to win, $2 to place
18	$18 total wager of Stella Citizen

Drug dealers have also made use of cryptography. One such case in the 1970s involved a professional chemist who was convicted of manufacturing phencyclidine (PCP) based on CRYPTANALYSIS of some of his notebook ciphers.

The chemist had used a substitution method of one- and two-digit numbers. Here are the CIPHERTEXT and the PLAINTEXT letters that were uncovered:

1	3	11	19	37	55	87	4	12	20	38	56	88
A	B	C	D	E	F	G	H	I	J	K	L	M

21	39	57	89	22	40	72	23	41	73	24	42	74
N	O	P	Q	R	S	T	U	V	W	X	Y	Z

This decipherment enabled the analysts to read the particular CIPHER, but they also needed to recover the KEY to the system to make their case convincing. Further applications of FREQUENCY patterns, CONTACT CHART studies, and other solving methods yielded the following table:

1					
3	4				
11	12				
19	20	21	22	23	24
37	38	39	40	41	42
55	56	57	72	73	74
87	88	89			

Using their knowledge of the suspect's profession, the cipher breakers concluded that the system was based on the first six columns of the Periodic Table of Elements, which the chemist had posted on his wall. The numbers of the elements in the first column were identical to the first seven cipher equivalents.

Atomic Number   1   3   11   19   37   55   87
Letter   A   B   C   D   E   F   G

The atomic numbers for the first six columns of the Periodic Table were the key for the cipher. With the key, the analysts read all the chemist's notebooks and exposed the full range of his operation.

Cryptanalysis, the process of solving a CODE or CIPHER. Coined by the brilliant cryptologist William Friedman in 1920, this term is derived from the Latin *crypta*, the Greek *kryptē<kryptós*, "secret, hidden," and German *ana*, "up, throughout" and *lysys*, "a loosing." Cryptanalysts, who are outside the intended exchange of the communication, must first intercept the message, then acquire clues to its PLAINTEXT by a number of processes.

Terms such as DECODE, DECIPHER, and *decrypt* are sometimes used interchangeably, but they are not, strictly speaking, synonyms. As the names imply, *decode* means to break a code and *decipher* means to solve a cipher. *Decryption*, a more general term, can refer to either. The intended recipient of an encrypted message has the KEY that operates the concealment system. The third-party analyst seeks such a revelation.

Much more involved than mere guess-work, cryptanalysis requires skill and experience with letter FREQUENCY counts; CONTACT CHARTS; statistics; characteristics of different languages; slang and ARGOT; and various fields of activity (such as diplomacy, commerce, and the military).

In ancient times, cryptanalysts were thought of as practitioners of black arts, and it took centuries for them to gain acceptance. Eventually, however, with organized, government-supported efforts such as the BLACK CHAMBERS, the profession of cryptanalysis came into being. Today, in the microchip era, satellites, specialized sensing devices, COMPUTERS, and other high technology all play a crucial role in the cryptanalyst's art.

Cryptoeidography, coined by historian David Kahn, this word is derived from the Greek word *eidos*, meaning "form," two methods of rendering pictures secret. One version, CIFAX, modifies electrical patterns to distort an image. The second system involves optical alterations.

For most of history, distortion of pictures was useless to CRYPTOGRAPHY because there was no means by which the intended recipient could restore the original. As technology advanced, a level of secrecy was achieved with microphotography (see MICRODOT). Yet this reduced the size and was thus a type of STEGANOGRAPHY, or hiding the presence of the message rather than altering the content of the message itself.

According to author Herbert McKay's magazine articles (1946 and 1950), stereoscopic PHOTOGRAPHY influenced optical concealment. In the stereoscopic technique, two photos are taken by two cameras set up a short distance apart. When viewed through a device called a stereoscope, they appear to have one image. This inspired a similar process with written material.

The PLAINTEXT communication was incorporated into a covering text, which was not a mask or GRILLE that screened the message from view but was instead an innocuous text. The CIPHER builder then typed this material on a sheet of paper. Next a second sheet was typed that left out the plaintext; the paper was moved slightly, and the plaintext letters were put in again. The sheets were sent by different means to the intended recipient, who then placed them in a stereoscope. The 3-D effect caused the plaintext to appear in relief.

Beginning in the 1950s such clever but awkward methods gave way to fiber optics, which provide direct delivery of an image to the recipient. By electronically shuffling the thousands of tiny points of dark and light that compose a fiber-optics image, the sender can encode a visual message. Decryption is achieved by sending the jumbled image back through an identical cluster of fibers, thus reversing the mixing process. (See CIFAX for a discussion of the distorting of image through electronic means.)

Cryptography, from the Greek *kryptē< kryptós*, "secret, hidden," and *graphia*, "writing," the means of encoding or enciphering communications meant to be decoded or deciphered by the planned recipient (see DECODE and DECIPHER). The ways to accomplish this goal have been ex-

panded and made more complex by technological advances.

CODES and CIPHERS are means of transforming original messages (PLAINTEXT) into CODETEXT and CIPHERTEXT. Codes are a form of SUBSTITUTION whereby the main plaintext unit, the word, and sometimes a series of words, is replaced by the letters or words in the code, which may consist of words, letters, numbers, syllables, phrases, and symbols. The results can be further hidden by SUPERENCIPHERMENT (for example, CODENUMBERS can be altered by a substitution process).

The basic unit of ciphers is the letter or sometimes a group of letters. Ciphers have two main functions called *transposition* or *substitution*. Transposition shifts the location of characters in a text without changing their identity—as in *tineityd* or *ntidtiye* for *identity*. Substitution would replace the letters of this word with symbols, numbers, or other letters, such as 75684392 or hfmrzklc, either of which could mean identity. These cipher changes are accomplished with a KEY, which sets the rules under which the transposition or substitution is made (see CRYPTANALYSIS, TWO-KEY CRYPTOGRAPHY, CIPHER MACHINE, and COMPUTER).

Cryptology, derived from the Greek *kryptē<kryptós*, "secret, hidden," and either *lógos*, "word," or *ology*, "science," the science that includes message concealment (CRYPTOGRAPHY), the solving of such a communication by the intended recipient (see DECODE and DECIPHER), and the solution of a message by an unauthorized third party (CRYPTANALYSIS).

With technological advances, cryptology has come to include signals security and its competitor, signals intelligence (SIGINT). Each has several advanced technological subsets, including electronics security, electronics intelligence (ELINT), communications security (COMSEC), and communications intelligence (COMINT).

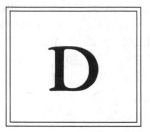

D-Day (June 6, 1944), codenamed Overlord, the Allied attack on Nazi-held Europe and the most massive invasion in history. CRYPTOLOGY played an important role in its success, as shown in the following examples.

- British ULTRA decryptions of the German ENIGMA and later cryptosystem machines revealed much important information from many levels of the German command.
- U.S. MAGIC's decipherments of Japanese diplomatic messages between Berlin and Tokyo (concealed by the PURPLE machine) were shared with England, enabling the Allies to learn about German plans and fortifications revealed to the Japanese.
- Resistance groups intercepted written messages, radio transmissions, and other communications by the Nazis. Because this work required proximity to the *Wehrmacht* camps, the Resistance used passwords, OPEN CODE signals, and other surreptitious means to convey messages, arrange rendezvous, and protect identities.
- Scores of CODENAMES and CODEWORDS were assigned as the leaders of the massing forces tried to maintain secrecy.
- The Allies practiced many types of COMSEC (communications security) measures, from the "Loose lips sink ships" campaign to enciphered ship-to-shore and air-to-ground transmissions.
- Innumerable real and false JARGON CODES—in single sentences, poems, personal messages, and even weather broadcasts—filled the airwaves over the English Channel as D-Day drew

nearer and resistance groups recognized signals or awaited further orders to initiate their own assignments, such as sabotage, seizures of strategic sites, and ambushes of *Wehrmacht* patrols or reinforcements.

Decipher,

to remove the CIPHER from the words, numbers, or other characters (the PLAINTEXT) that it has concealed (the Latin prefix *de* means "away from"). The intended recipient of the message can decipher it by use of a KEY or keys. The key provides the directions through the maze of a given cipher. A cryptanalyst, on the other hand, is one who tries to intercept the message and use CRYPTANALYSIS to break its cipher shield without benefit of the key.

Terms that are often used synonymously with *decipher* are *decrypt*, *recover*, and *locate*. Although *decode* is often used as a synonym for *decipher*, strictly speaking, the former refers to the solving of a CODE while the latter refers to the solving of a cipher.

Decode,

to discover a code's PLAINTEXT, ideally when done by its intended recipient. A cryptanalyst is someone other than the intended receiver who tries to obtain the message and remove its concealment (see CRYPTANALYSIS).

Words that are used synonymously with *decode* are *solve*, *locate*, *recover*, and even *decrypt* when it does not confuse a code with a CIPHER method. Although *decipher* is sometimes used as a synonym of *decode*, strictly speaking the latter refers to the solving of a CODE, not a cipher.

DES,

the Data Encryption Standard chosen in 1977 by the United States National Bureau of Standards as the officially sanctioned method of protecting unclassified COMPUTER files in federal departments. Developed by IBM, the DES is a single-KEY encryption system; in other words the same key encrypts and decrypts data. It is an algorithm (a set of procedures) designed to protect information that is in binary code form (two components, primarily 1 and 0 in varied sequences). Its increased application in large-scale integrated electronic computer chips has made the DES a primary part of commercial information security.

The Data Encryption Standard is a product block CIPHER. Its key begins as a sequence of eight decimal numbers chosen from zero to 127. For the computer language of bits (zeros and ones) the decimal numbers are turned into their seven-bit binary equivalents, including an extra eighth bit added at the end for verification purposes, not concealment. When activated, the key is eight decimal numerals multiplied by seven bits, or 56 bits in length.

The message also undergoes conversion to binary digits and is represented in ASCII form. This American Standard Code for Information Interchange is a collection of roman alphabet letters, decimal numbers, punctuation marks, and keyboard symbols with binary equivalents. The CODES in the ASCII style also have eight bits. With the message encrypted in blocks of eight characters times eight bits, each block begins as 64 bits.

At the time of its inception, the 56-bit key was itself a very substantial defense.

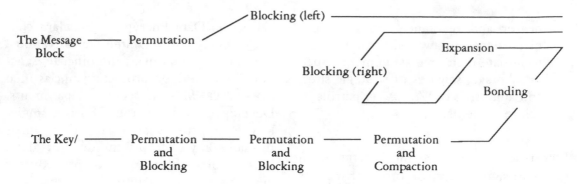

A third-party solution seeker using a computer to try all the combinations of 56 ones and zeros, even at a million tries a second, was facing 1,142 years of attempts. Though this time frame has been narrowed over the years by computer advances, a number of experts still consider the DES a strong transmission guardian.

The block cipher undergoes 16 rounds, or iterations, through the algorithm built into the microchip. The encryption processes include: BLOCKING, COMPACTION, EXPANSION, PERMUTATION, and SUBSTITUTION. An added process, known as *exclusive OR,* bonds parts of the encryption at points throughout the procedure. The OR operation is identified by a circled plus sign. It is a function of the logic gates in a computer's circuitry. The rules of this operation are: when combining unlike bits (one and zero), the result is a one; if like bits (two zeroes or two ones) are united, zero results:

$$
\begin{array}{cccc}
1 & 0 & 1 & 0 \\
\oplus & & & \\
1 & 1 & 0 & 1 \\
\hline
0 & 1 & 1 & 1
\end{array}
$$

This OR operation becomes involved with the rearranged keys, called subkeys, and pieces of the message bits. The OR procedure bonds the subkeys with the bits and causes the transmission to be fully affected by the special nature of the key, thus adding certain variety to the concealment.

Along with this special bonding, a series of procedures occur with the message block and the key. The former has its bits rearranged in a permutation stage similar to the term TRANSPOSITION in function. The new arrangement is divided into a right-side and a left-side block and the right-side block is changed by a formula before it joins the key. The key's bits (decimals changed to binary numerals) are transposed and split into two blocks; these blocks then undergo another permutation. Specific bits move from the blocks and are then realigned as a single sequence in a compaction stage. A segment of a flow chart is shown above.

This sequence of steps is a part of a single round. There are 15 additional iterations in the complete process for concealing a message block including nonlinear substitution.

The DES algorithm achieves 70 quadrillion encryption possibilities for a given communication. The planned receiver can DECIPHER it by using the chosen key and reversing the order of the stages beginning with the 16th round.

However, this process is dependent upon key secrecy and the protection of keys can be a security problem. Other processes developed in the late 1970s and early 1980s now rival the DES as security measures (see TWO-KEY CRYPTOGRAPHY).

Diaries, personal records, the privacy of which was often protected by concealment techniques. Throughout much of history it was fashionable for both men and women to enter in their diaries a record of their daily activities.

One of the early famous notebook keepers was the creative genius Leonardo da Vinci (1452–1519). In order to conceal some of his futuristic ideas (considered heretical at that time), he wrote in a backward script that was incomprehensible to the uninitated without viewing it in front of a mirror.

Perhaps the first diary in the American colonies to be kept in SHORTHAND was that of Virginian William Byrd (1674–1744). His style was later identified as "La Plume Volante" (the flying pen), developed by William Mason.

Perhaps the most notable diary using a concealment technique was that of SAMUEL PEPYS. The British civil servant wrote for almost 9½ years in a form of shorthand called *tachygraphy*, which he augmented with passages in different languages and NULLS of his own invention. However, Pepys's personal record did not gain its renown because of its masking method but because it contained a fascinating account of the world in which he lived.

Dogger Bank, Battle of (January 24, 1915) a World War I confrontation of dreadnoughts that was a prescient combination of intelligence gathering and CRYPTANALYSIS.

The foresight of WINSTON CHURCHILL and former First Sea Lord Adm. Sir Arthur Wilson had led to a successful use of radio direction-finding to intercept German naval call signs and communications, which were provided to the British cryptanalysts of ROOM 40. Additionally, the Admirality had had the good fortune to recover German naval CODEBOOKS from the wreck of the German light cruiser MAGDEBURG.

In January 1915, these factors coalesced into a chance to catch the elusive German fleet that had been shelling England's coastal villages. The decryption experts in Room 40 had learned that German vessels would have a rendezvous at Dogger Bank, a shallow part of the North Sea off the northern English coast. The British sent Vice Adm. Sir David Beatty to meet them, and in the fierce fighting, the German capital ships *Derfflinger* and *Seydlitz* were badly damaged and the *Blücher* was sent to the depths.

The Dogger Bank victory gave the Room 40 staff, the application of cryptanalysis, and radio intelligence a much needed boost.

Doll Code, a JARGON CODE used by a World War II Japanese spy, Velvalee Dickinson, a Madison Avenue doll-shop owner.

Beginning in January 1942, Dickinson sent letters in this type of OPEN CODE to addresses in South America. The contents apparently contained facts about dolls, their clothing, and repair needs. One letter had phrases about a wonderful doll hospital and broken English dolls. Another referred to a Siamese temple dancer while a third mentioned seven Chinese dolls. They bore postmarks from different locations in the United States and basically appeared to be news exchanged by hobbyists, yet they were actually intended for Japanese agents and contained facts about American warships.

Questions first arose when a letter was returned from Buenos Aires, Argentina. Marked "unknown at this address," the correspondence was taken back to the apparent sender, a resident of Portland, Oregon. The woman had no idea about the communication and took it to the Federal Bureau of Investigation. Four other letters were addressed to the same South American location and were returned to senders who had been Dickinson's customers. She had used their addresses and imitated their signatures.

The FBI's Technical Operations Division applied its CRYPTANALYSIS skills to discover that the condition of the dolls actually referred to repairs being made on U.S. ships in certain navy yards. The numbers of miniatures mentioned far too closely matched the actual totals of war vessels to be just a coincidence.

Bureau agents arrested the recently widowed Dickinson in January 1944. Threatened with the death penalty for espionage, she pleaded guilty to censorship violations by using illegal CODES. In August 1944, she received a sentence of 10 years in prison and a ten-thousand-dollar fine.

Doolittle Raid, the famous bombing raid on Japan that was planned with the crucial help of the United States' solving of the Imperial Navy's encryptions such as the JN25. In early 1942, Allied morale in the Pacific was sorely in need of a boost. U.S. forces at Pearl Harbor had been devastated. The Philippines was under heavy attack, and the combined U.S. and Philippine defense forces were being pushed down the Bataan Peninsula. The Japanese army and navy had made big gains in a wide area of Southeast Asia. Where could the United States strike back?

The answer became known as the Doolittle Raid, which was greatly helped by the CRYPTANALYSIS of Japanese radio messages by Joseph Rochefort's crew at Station Hypo in Hawaii.

The Joint Chiefs of Staff and Pacific Fleet Comdr. Chester Nimitz agreed on a bold plan. A two-carrier group, with the CODENAME *Task Force Mike*, led by Adm. William Halsey, sailed toward the Japanese home islands in April 1942 with a secret mission. Aboard the carrier *Hornet* were U.S. Army B-25 medium bombers. On the carrier *Enterprise* were fighter planes to protect the ships.

This mission directly benefited from reliable knowledge of the locations of Tokyo's many naval and air squadrons. The difficult and sometimes confused efforts to drive wedges into the Imperial Navy's cryptomethods now started to pay some much-needed dividends.

Because the Americans had broken the Japanese CIPHERS, admirals Nimitz and Halsey were fairly certain about the locations of Tokyo's naval and air squadrons. They also knew about some of Japan's immediate intentions, all of which gave them the freedom to risk the bold attack.

On April 18, against great odds, Col.

James H. Doolittle lifted his own bomber off the *Hornet*'s lurching deck and led 16 B-25s into history. Though relatively little damage was done in Japan, the supposedly impenetrable skies over its cities had been breeched. Allied confidence lifted as banner headlines declared, "DOOLITTLE DOOED IT."

Driscoll, Agnes (1889–1971), U.S. cryptanalyst.

Born in Illinois in 1889, Agnes Driscoll earned an undergraduate degree from Ohio State University. After employment as a music director and mathematics department head in Texas schools, she entered the Naval Reserve in 1918. By this time her varied skills in languages, mathematics, and statistics, among other fields, had given her a special foundation for a career in CRYPTANALYSIS, unusual for a woman in that era.

After working in the office of the Director of Naval Communications, she joined the ranks of the Department of Ciphers at the Riverbank, Illinois, estate of GEORGE FABYAN. Here she was directly influenced by the cryptologic research and writings of WILLIAM FRIEDMAN, another Riverbank employee.

Driscoll applied her training to solve an "unbreakable" message made on a machine of ill-fated inventor EDWARD HEBERN, for whom she also worked in a struggling California encryption machine business in 1923. After returning to Washington, D.C. she maintained a long and very productive career in cryptanalysis.

A woman in a "man's world," Driscoll was responsible for training officers such as LAURENCE SAFFORD and Joseph Roche-

Agnes Driscoll. (Courtesy of the National Security Agency.)

fort, who would become pivotal figures in U.S. Navy decryption during World War II. Driscoll herself contributed substantially to U.S. understanding of Imperial Japan's CODEBOOKS, CIPHERS, and encryption mechanisms at a time when such work was generally unheralded.

In 1926 she solved a KEY that opened the Japanese RED codebook for further U.S. study. Her accomplishment is exemplified by the fact that the codebook in question held about 100,000 code groups, with three groups often equated with each

Japanese term. Additionally, the words were concealed by SUPERENCIPHERMENT.

Throughout the 1930s, as Pacific Fleet listening posts and the ON THE ROOF GANG tracked the Imperial Navy in its own fleet exercises, people such as Agnes Driscoll were given the COMINT intercepts to solve. In 1935 she recognized cipher traffic that appeared to be created by a machine. It was labeled M1, and she developed a manual process to decipher the intercepts. Working with graph paper and sliding cipher sequences, she found the combination *to-mi-mu-ra*. Further effort revealed that this was the name *Thompson*, which was appearing in Japanese foreign office traffic.

Naval Intelligence used the decryptions to break an espionage cabal operating on both coasts in 1936. Pacific Fleet radio-man Harry Thompson and cashiered navy officer J.S. Farnsworth (Agent *K*) were passing gunnery and engineering data to Japanese agents. The U.S. traitors were convicted and imprisoned.

These experiences helped with the breaking of Japan's JN25 encryption series begun in 1939. Driscoll again led the attack on its three separate elements, including a codebook, an ADDITIVE book, and the beginning point of the additive flow (indicated at the beginning of messages). The knowledge gained from this painstaking work directly contributed to later decipherments before and during the BATTLE OF THE CORAL SEA and the BATTLE OF MIDWAY.

After the war, Driscoll worked with the top-secret NATIONAL SECURITY AGENCY, retiring in 1959.

E

Edgers, Dorothy (1908–1957), U.S. linguist. A specialist in the Japanese language, Edgers entered history because of something she noticed that went unheeded by her busy superiors.

As a former resident of Japan, Edgers had 30 years of direct experience with the subtleties of the language. This knowledge had helped her obtain employment as a translator with the *Z* section of OP-20-G in Washington, D.C.

On Saturday, December 6, 1941, a collection of decrypted, but not translated, Japanese diplomatic messages was placed on her desk. They were concealed in consular CIPHERS such as the low-grade cover called the *PA-K2*. However, while these were rather easy to break, the general intelligence emphasis had been directed toward other communications. Thus there was no special priority to decipher or translate these transmissions.

But Edgers noticed something of particular interest in one of the decryptions. She mentioned it to her brother and fellow linguistic expert, Fred Woodrough, who advised her to continue with it, which she did until well after normal working hours. While working on the decryption, she had a chance to mention the communication to her superior, Lt. Comdr. Alwin Kramer. But the overworked Kramer was concentrating on other, higher-level messages such as PURPLE and did not consider it important. Thus when Edgers completed her efforts, she left them on the desk of a chief clerk.

What she had found was the lights message, a cable from Japanese consul Nagao Kita in Hawaii to Tokyo concerning an agent near Oahu and signals such as lights from a beach house sent to a Japanese submarine. The information to be exchanged

Dorothy Edgars. (Courtesy of the British Broadcasting Corporation.)

by this system directly concerned the Pacific Fleet at Pearl Harbor, but the translation did not leave Comdr. Kramer's desk in time to be seen, understood, and appreciated.

Election of 1876, a race for the Oval Office in which secret communications about vote buying subverted the election. The presidential election of 1876 has often been cited as a prime example of a corrupt era in U.S. politics. The close victory of Republican Rutherford B. Hayes over Democrat Samuel J. Tilden was credited to fraudulent vote counts and bribery, tainting Hayes, a previously unsullied three-time governor of Ohio.

Tilden, governor of New York, had built a fine reputation and had gained nationwide fame as the man who had led the fight to stop William M. "Boss" Tweed and the corrupt Tammany Hall political machine in New York City. In fact, the Democratic Party had seemingly had success with their accusations of Republican misconduct in high places and in the condemnation of their opponents' controversial Reconstruction policies. When the ballots were tallied, it appeared that the Democrats had won the presidency for the first time in 20 years. Tilden's popular margin of "victory" was some 250,000 votes—giving him 184 electoral college votes, one short of complete election success.

However, there were disputed vote counts in part of Oregon and in three southern states, Florida, Louisiana, and South Carolina, and local election boards, favoring the Republicans, negated enough Democratic votes to declare Hayes the winner. Democrats claimed the election had been stolen, and the boiling controversy overflowed into Congress, where a Republican-controlled Senate and a Democrat-dominated House were in a standoff. An election commission of five members each from the Supreme Court, the Senate, and the House was chosen to settle the issue. But when one of the Supreme Court justices was replaced by a loyal Republican, this led to a straight party vote of eight to seven for Hayes, who went on to occupy the Oval Office after he was given all of the disputed electoral college votes.

Many believed that Samuel Tilden had been cheated. Then in 1878, the *New York Tribune* and CRYPTANALYSIS reversed this opinion with startling revelations. The *Tribune* was a Republican paper but overcame early skepticism about its credibility with facts uncovered in encrypted telegrams that had been obtained from Western Union by a Congressional investigative committee, Republican members of which provided the wires to the *Tribune*.

Some clues to the messages exchanged between Tilden men in Oregon and others back east were found in a CODE based on a dictionary's words and page numbers. Different wedges were driven into other codes by *Tribune* editors John Hassard and William Grosvenor. A third independent analyst was Edward Holden, who became interested in the *Tribune*'s articles about CIPHERS while working at the U.S. Naval Observatory in Washington, D.C.

Several of their most illuminating discoveries showed the communications to be encrypted in a method similar to the TRANSPOSITION used during the Civil War. But the method used by the politicians was much simpler and therefore more vulnerable. With telegrams of 15, 20, 25, and 30 words, one of four KEYS was used. Longer messages were concealed by two or more keys. A code list was applied to the names of some persons and to special words. One such list included word equivalents such as Bolivia/proposition, Glasgow/hundred, Edinburgh/thousand, and London/canvassing board. These terms were used to discuss proposals, money amounts, and deal with groups that controlled votes.

A key for encipherment of 20 words might have appeared like this:

17, 7, 1, 10, 3, 13, 11, 20, 4, 18, 16, 14, 9, 15, 5, 19, 6, 12, 2, 8.

A message about a vote-buying deal was first arranged with the PLAINTEXT as follows:

```
 1      2      3      4      5  6
Received the proposition to present at
 7      8      9  10   11        12
planned daylight hour a hundred thousand
13    14       15    16 17         18
for favorable decision of first canvassing
         19    20
board. Reply soonest.
```

Applying the key to establish the order of the words and the code list for the special terms, the concealed communication then became:

First planned received a Bolivia for Glasgow soonest to London of favorable hour decision present reply at Edinburgh the daylight.

The cryptanalysts solved such ciphers as well as MONOALPHABETIC SUBSTITUTION and checkerboard methods of SUBSTITUTION whereby pairs of numbers or letters at the checkerboard's coordinates replaced other letters. The *Tribune* created growing reader interest by teasingly presenting the ciphers and then eventually revealing their solutions.

The result was a backlash against the Democrats and big Congressional gains for the Grand Old Party, especially in the Northeast. Though his nephew William Pelton was a direct recipient of the telegrams, Tilden denied any direct involvement in the scheme. But the exposé brought down his rising star, and he descended into political oblivion.

ELINT, electronics intelligence, a major segment of signals intelligence. Within ELINT are the divisions of RADINT (radar intelligence) and TELINT (telemetry intelligence).

ELINT is defined by the National Security Council Intelligence Directive No. 6 as "the collection (observation and recording) and the processing for subsequent intelligence purposes of information derived from foreign, noncommunications, electromagnetic radiations emanating from other than atomic detonation or radioactive sources."

Electronics intelligence can include data acquired by spy planes eavesdropping on radar bases, satellites' interception of telemetry signals from missiles in flight, and the location of radio beacons (used for navigation). This information is combined with that gained from other sources, such as human intelligence (HUMINT), to assist CRYPTANALYSIS in various ways.

The CIPHER solvers are often able to pick up clues from the position of a radar station and the range of its equipment. For example, an encrypted message from another military site to the radar center might contain orders for the radar crews over a given time frame. If the activities at the radar station could be matched with portions of the encryption, a wedge could be driven into the particular concealment.

Radio beacons do not directly help the analysts decipher secret messages. However, their location can be compared with encrypted surface-to-air communications intercepted by communications intelligence (COMINT). Solved references to a known beacon site could help an analyst break into the cipher protecting the foreign air force.

Electronics Security, a primary branch of signals security, that tries to counteract the ELINT (electronics intelligence) efforts of other nations. Below are three examples of how the two functions oppose each other.

Electronics Security	Electronics Intelligence (ELINT)
missile telemetry (encrypt signals)	satellites (intercept signals)
radar (shift frequences)	aircraft (record emissions)
radio beacons (emit false signals and falsify sites, maintain periodic silence)	aircraft (locate sites, record data)
	radio stations (detect radio signals)

These counteracting efforts have been further enhanced by methods such as dropping metal strips from planes to fool radar, jamming, decoys, and electronically bending an enemy's navigational beams.

Such interwoven technological competitions have expanded CRYPTOLOGY far beyond the pencil-and-paper level and have come to be called E.C.M. (electronic countermeasures) and E.C.C.M. (electronic counter-countermeasures). Both are often referred to in a special category, ELECTRONICS WARFARE.

Electronics Warfare, combat of electronics security and electronics intelligence (ELINT) through electronic countermeasures (E.C.M.) and electronic counter-countermeasures (E.C.C.M.). Cryptologic techniques are related to these methods in general both as they are involved in the conflicting interests of maintaining secrecy versus gathering intelligence and because transmissions among the practitioners are encrypted.

Consider nations *A* and *B* as enemies. *A* has electronic security needs for its radar emissions that it protects by shifting their frequencies, whether they be early-warning systems or short-range tracking. The early-warning systems also direct attention to aircraft that don't answer the radar's electronic interrogation: A friendly plane transmits a prearranged electronic CODE that identifies it as belonging to a nonthreatening craft.

The shifting frequencies are intended to confound the electronic intelligence of *B*'s satellite, air, ground, and other intelligence stations, which try to find and interpret *A*'s radar location, antenna beam motions, frequency, and pulse repetition rates (radar's "fingerprints"). The military intelligence planners of *B* seek this information in order to develop ways to protect their own bombers and missiles from radar detection should they choose to attack. *B* seeks protection by developing electronic countermeasures such as jamming, ejecting chaff (metal strips), creating false radar echo techniques, and designing new weapons (such as stealth technology). *A* would counter with electronic counter-countermeasures, including devices to "see through" jamming systems and technology to find the true echo pattern and, thus, the *B* airplane or missile reflecting it.

At other levels of the intelligence conflict, *B* is trying to intercept and record everything from *A*'s missile telemetry to telephone calls between *A*'s bases con-

veyed by microwave methods. Because *A* wraps such data transmissions in code and more often in CIPHERS, *B* uses electronics intelligence to try to take signals from space or the earth's airwaves, then attempts to unwrap the encryption protections by using COMPUTERS and human analysis.

These measures, countermeasures, and encrypted signals are so intertwined that experts are now generally applying the designation of electronics warfare to encompass all of them.

Encicode, a combination of the words *enciphered* and CODE that refers to the PLAINTEXT message after it has been concealed by a code and then hidden by additional CIPHER methods. The process of providing such layers of protection is known as SUPERENCIPHERMENT.

The first known enciphered code was developed by Florentine LEON BATTISTA ALBERTI in the 15th century. His CIPHER DISK included two circular copper plates, one with a sequential 20-letter alphabet plus the numbers 1 through 4 and the other with letters in random order. When the random letters of the movable plate were aligned with the numbers, they were encoded by them. These numbers were next enciphered with the disk once more as if they were original plaintext. In this way, *140* could mean "Genoa," then would become *n q v z* with one plate position and *d 1 p r* at another.

Enciphered code did not become as popular as the NOMENCLATOR, a combination of a partial code and a cipher, whose code-like groups of names, words, and syllables and a separate cipher alphabet gained precedence. It was not until the widespread need for cost-effective business communications in the later 1800s that enciphered codes greatly increased in usage. They helped keep down telegram and cable costs and increased security, using, for example, the letter group *d h n u y* to say "Complete the deal Wednesday."

For even better security, these letters underwent further SUBSTITUTIONS by different letters. When these substitutions were themselves replaced by numbers, the original code became an enciphered code. Moreover, a business that covered its plaintext messages with CODENUMBERS could rearrange those numbers to encipher them, as below:

Plaintext	Codenumber	Encicode
Send	1429	9412

Also, codenumbers could be given even greater security by adding a KEYNUMBER called an ADDITIVE to the original codenumber (the plaincode, or *placode*). The total was the ENCICODE.

Placode	45271
Keynumber	+ 13425
Encicode	58696

The Enigma, the primary cipher machine of the Third Reich. (Courtesy of the National Security Agency.)

Enigma, often used to describe something puzzling and mysterious, the name given to a CIPHER MACHINE by its inventor, German engineer Arthur Scherbius.

In the early 1920s, Scherbius developed a series of such devices, which evolved from a machine the size of a cash register to a more manageable, portable model. The Enigma machine enciphered messages by applying the principle of the ROTOR (a wired wheel that provided several electrical contacts for message-sending variations). As Scherbius improved his machines, including their switch systems and type-writer keys, he added variations to the rotor, including different wire contact arrangements and gears to change the progression sequences of the rotors.

The Enigma had a number of appealing qualities, and a corporation was formed to manufacture and promote it. But a war-weary world and the financial instability of Germany's Weimar Republic limited the chances of financial success for a new firm based on a secrecy device. The invention failed to be profitable, and another group of business partners assumed control.

In a multifaceted twist of fate, both political and economic conditions favored such businesses after 1933. After the Nazi hierarchy and Germany's military leaders concluded that the Enigma provided satisfactory communications security (COMSEC), production of the machines increased, and the ink on the company's books turned from red to black.

Though sources vary, historians generally agree that it was a group of Poles who first introduced the secrets of the Scherbius machine to the Allies and enabled British intelligence centers such as BLETCHLEY PARK to develop and maintain a top-secret program called ULTRA, which provided crucial decryption material all through World War II.

The Enigma machine itself was an electromechanical device that was improved through successive versions designated A through D. Model A began with four rotors driven by four geared wheels. Different numbers of teeth in the gears allowed variations in the rotors' positions for producing polyalphabetic encipherments. The presence or absence of the teeth channeled the electrical pulses into different paths to the output stage of the machine.

Both the C and D versions were cryptographic advancements over A. They also had four rotors with 26 contact points each. However, the fourth rotor was a "half," also called a "reflecting," rotor that had contact points on only one of its faces. These points were interconnected and sent ("reflected") the incoming pulses back through the rotors whence they came.

This process meant that the cipher alphabets thus produced were reciprocal. If PLAINTEXT Q enciphered into N, then plaintext N would become CIPHERTEXT Q. Furthermore, none of the letters represented themselves because the reflected pulses didn't follow their original passage through the wires. Models C and D both had these aspects, with some minor variations. That is, C had a reflecting rotor that had only two positions in the machine; the keyboard was set in the regular alphabet's A-to-Z sequence. The D model had a reflecting rotor that could be changed but did not move during the encryption process.

Mechanisms such as an added plugboard, ratchets, notches, and pawls, along with variable turning speeds of the rotors, were all part of the Enigma. Decipherment was accomplished by knowledge of the rotors' order (fast, medium, or slow) and their starting positions during encipherment. Typing the ciphertext letters enabled recovery of the plaintext, which was indicated by glow lamps under the given letters.

With the information provided by the Poles, British analysts, using technological marvels of their own (COLOSSUS and *bombe*), were able to solve intercepted transmissions on a regular basis. Their top-secret operation, ULTRA, provided ongoing data from advanced Enigma models on land and beneath the sea. The Enigma was expected to protect the German armed forces. However, it was fallible, and revelations gained from it contributed immensely to the destruction of the Third Reich.

Expansion, simple form of concealment that expands, or stretches, the PLAINTEXT message in order to encipher it.

The process can be compared to the "secret language" called Pig Latin, in which the first consonant sound (or consonant blend) of each word is moved to the end of the word and the suffix *ay* is added, transforming the word *trade*, for example, into *adetray*. If a word starts with a vowel, the suffix *way* is added.

Expansion is a less complicated encryption process than the related methods BLOCKING, COMPACTION, PERMUTATION (TRANSPOSITION), and SUBSTITUTION, and it is often combined with one or more of these other methods. In the basic example of expansion below, a dot simply represents a space between the words and digits when placed above the line. When placed on the line, it indicates a period.

Plaintext:

SELL•900•SHARES•OF•ACMO•INDUSTRIES•NATE•SMITH.

Expansion:

ELLSAY•009AY•ARESSHAY•OFWAY•ACMOWAY•INDUSTRIESWAY•ATENAY• ITHSMAY.

Fabyan, George (1867–1936), U.S. businessman and philanthropist and early employer of cryptologist WILLIAM FRIEDMAN. A wealthy textile dealer, Fabyan had numerous hobbies and interests. He established an intellectual community on an idyllic five-hundred-acre estate, called Riverbank, near Geneva, Illinois, and invited talented people to gather and study different questions of their times.

Fabyan was intrigued by the debate over the authorship of William Shakespeare's works and tended to believe some enigmatologists who insisted that SIR FRANCIS BACON was the real Bard. Believing that the answer was hidden somewhere in the plays and sonnets, he hired scholars from various fields to find the proof.

Among his staff was a young Cornell geneticist named William Friedman. Neither Fabyan nor Friedman ever linked Bacon with Shakespeare's works (see SHAKESPEARE CIPHERS); however, Friedman was soon solving concealed messages belonging to other nations that had been obtained by the State and Justice departments. Thus Friedman and some of Fabyan's Riverbank staff comprised the first actual cryptanalytical organization in the United States. From this beginning, William Friedman later became the premier U.S. cryptanalyst, among *the* best the world has ever produced.

Fax Encryption, a method of ensuring the privacy of facsimile communications. As facsimile technology expanded rapidly during the 1980s, there was also an increase in the number of thefts of faxed material, since the technology that produced facsimiles was also being applied to steal them.

This pattern is part of the ongoing history of protecting messages from third parties who want to use such information for their own purposes. From the capturing of couriers by the ancients and the medieval mail readers working in BLACK CHAMBERS to the radio eavesdropping of World War II and the photo reconnaissance conducted by today's satellites, the defense and attack strategies continue to evolve.

A fax transmission is pilfered by thieves who tap phone lines, then use high-fidelity recording equipment and modified fax machines to convert clandestinely recorded signals into documents. The response to this has been encryption devices to protect document transfers.

In a standard fax transmission, the document is scanned and converted into binary data. These sequences of 1s and 0s are then sent over the phone lines to the receiving fax location. With an encryption device, the binary codes are rearranged and electronically generated in a nonlinear mathematical algorithm (a CIPHERTEXT, in cryptographic terms). The recipient equipment has a security device that recognizes the encrypted signal and recovers the original document (or PLAINTEXT) ensuring that it arrives only at its intended destination.

FBI, the Federal Bureau of Investigation.

The FBI has played a role in U.S. counterintelligence since its early years as the Bureau of Investigation (1909) within the Justice Department. Its involvement in this sphere generally increased during World War I with the growing threat of espionage and subversion. After the 1918 armistice, FBI departments expanded their repertory of standard investigative techniques to include broader surveillance, electronic intelligence such as hidden microphones and telephone wiretaps, and an organized nationwide data bank. Laboratory skills were also enhanced, including the ability to detect INVISIBLE INKS.

From concerns about the Kaiser's agents, the FBI turned its attention to the Prohibition-era problems of gangsterism and bootlegging. The criminals' small, personal CODE lists and CODENAMES (sometimes just nicknames) were not formal systems; much more elaborate concealment methods were used by seafaring rumrunners (see ELIZEBETH FRIEDMAN). Some gambling schemes and numbers-racket tabulations were recorded in codes to protect customers' names and to keep secret accounts. When confiscated by local police, these were sent to the FBI for decrypting (see CRIME CODES AND CIPHERS).

During World War II, the FBI was kept busy with a new wave of concerns about spies and saboteurs. Surveillance of embassies, consulates, and pro-Axis meeting sites was supported by black bag entries, wiretaps, and informers.

Following the events of December 7, 1941, counterespionage efforts were redoubled. In the famous case of the DOLL CODE, postal censors in the FBI's Technical Operations Division (T.O.D.) discovered that U.S. naval secrets were being conveyed to Japanese agents in the form of letters about children's toys written by the owner of a Madison Avenue shop.

The FBI's previous research with invisible inks brought additional dividends during the capture of eight Nazis in 1942. Having landed by U-boat on Long Island and in Florida, their plan to destroy strategic sites was foiled. Amid their cache of explosives and personal items was hidden writing discovered on the leader's handkerchief. When revealed by chemical processes, the writing was found to contain mailing addresses in Lisbon, Portugal, and the United States.

Third Reich scientists countered with a top-notch achievement of STEGANOGRAPHY, the *Mikropunkt* (or MICRODOT). To FBI director J. Edgar Hoover, this MICRODOT was "the enemy's masterpiece of espionage." It was a laboratory employee who first noticed a shiny spot masked as a typewriter's period on an envelope carried by a suspected German agent. While the technicians and censors rushed to find falsely dotted *i*s, FBI counterespionage agents were applying some camera and audio methods too. With the help of a radio operator pretending to a be a Nazi, the FBI foiled the Reich with a FUNKSPIEL of its own. While sending encrypted but false intelligence data through the airwaves, Bureau agents formed links to German operatives. When the latter came to a seemingly safe office, they were photographed through one-way glass, resulting in the breaking of a major espionage ring.

During the Cold War, the FBI counterespionage efforts continued. In 1947–1948, an FBI and Army Security Agency partnership opened the cipher lock of the KGB CABLES and uncovered an espionage cabal of scientists and engineers and their associates.

The FBI's own Cryptanalytical and Translation Section has continued to solve illegal betting, smuggling, and theft-ring codes, whether in letter, number, or SYMBOL CRYPTOGRAPHY. Occasionally they have also worked on coded messages of murderers sent in the mail to police officials and news organizations. Some of the cases are broken with the discovery of names, dates, or clues particular to a crime, but other codes are so bizarre and so limited in their letter FREQUENCY that they imitate virtually unbreakable one-time systems.

Since 1952, the majority of signals intelligence data has been directed to the NATIONAL SECURITY AGENCY (NSA). Encrypted electronic transmissions, interception of microwave signals, and other forms of signals intelligence are now handled by NSA antennas, COMPUTERS, and analysts, whose discoveries are conveyed to the FBI for investigation and possible criminal proceedings.

Fists, a term that describes the distinctive touch of radiotelegraph operators when they send messages, whether encrypted or not. The word was part of the vocabulary of radiotelegraphy by the time World War II began. To the experienced, the patterns of such radio signals are as unique to a given individual as handwriting. Fists are said to be heavy, light, rapid, methodical, and so forth. Both encryption makers and solvers must be alert to such characteristics as they seek to outmaneuver one another.

Fortitude, during World War II, the CODENAME for the tactical operations of cover and deception intended to hide the actual timing and location of the D-DAY assault stage on Western Europe (which was itself codenamed NEPTUNE). The operations consisted of Fortitude north (directed at Scandinavia), Fortitude south (Belgium and the Channel coastline of France), and Fortitude south II (the Channel areas after D-Day).

The overall fortitude arrangements had their birth at a conference called "Rattle" held in Largs, Scotland, beginning in June 1943. This conference determined that the site of the crucial Allied landing would be in Western Europe. It also formulated the broad strategy of aerial, electronic, espionage, camouflage, and other deceptions that would keep the German defenders off balance.

Fortitude north was intended to keep some 27 Nazi divisions in Norway, Denmark, and Finland under threat of imminent attack. An operation codenamed SKYE created a mythical British Fourth Army of 350,000 men supposedly assembled in Scotland, along with a nonexistent Fifteenth Corps from the United States and equally imaginary Russian troops.

Fortitude south involved the fictitious First United States Army Group (FUSAG), which was seemingly poised to strike at the Pas de Calais in France in order to pin down the powerful German Fifteenth Army and keep it away from a direct defense of Normandy. The deceptions that enhanced this trick were codenamed QUICKSILVER.

All these deceptions involved the concealment and analysis of CODES and CIPHERS. Several were accomplished by radio tricks wherein the Allies made intentional cryptographic errors designed to give misleading details about the imaginary armies and other forces.

Radio messages from southern England were conveyed to a mock headquarters in Dover, leading German eavesdroppers to conclude that a large force was poised in Dover, another site opposite the Pas de Calais. These misconceptions were further enhanced by squadrons of dummy vessels purposely gathered in the ports of southeastern England, as wireless deception and reports by double agents created a sense of real activity around the nonexistent naval forces. The same types of encrypted messages were sent to false air bases containing plywood bombers and fighters. The contrived radio reports and agents' "intelligence" was verified by the Luftwaffe when their aerial reconnaissance sighted these harmless air forces.

The success of these and many other operations with sabotage squads, airborne troops, naval commandos, and resistance units combined to make the invasion of June 6, 1944, a monumental achievement.

Fractionating Ciphers, a system that conceals PLAINTEXT with two or more letter or number equivalents that are then enciphered (often by TRANSPOSITION). The next stage is a recombination of new multiliterals, which are then replaced by a single encrypted letter. It is possible, using a matrix and a KEYWORD, to initiate an aperiodic fractionation process, so called because the keying process depends on the entire message. A keyword such as *profitable* can generate a mixed alphabet. For a 5 × 5 square, *v* and *w* are combined in one cell.

	1	2	3	4	5
1	p	r	o	f	i
2	t	a	b	l	e
3	c	d	g	h	j
4	k	m	n	q	s
5	u	vw	x	y	z

A combination is enciphered in vertical dinomes (two-number sets) beneath the plaintext. The dinomes are found at the horizontal and then the vertical coordinates of the message letters.

Message: b e g i n p r i v a t e a u d i t
Dinomes: 2 2 3 1 4 1 1 1 5 2 2 2 2 5 3 1 2
         3 5 3 5 3 1 2 5 2 2 1 5 2 1 2 5 1

The CIPHERTEXT is formed by grouping the digits in pairs beginning on the top left and continuing horizontally through the numbers to the lower right. This group of dinomes is then converted to CIPHER letters by using the matrix.

Second Dinome Sequence:

22 31 41 11 52 22 25 31 23

a c k p v a e c b

53 53 12 52 21 52 12 51

x x r v t v r u

The resulting ciphertext is *a c k p v a e c b x x r v t v r u.*

Fractionating can also be used for periodic encipherment. This time the plaintext is placed in five-letter sets with dinomes, generated with the previously mentioned key, placed below them. It is periodic because the method is applied to each letter group in turn.

Plaintext: s e c r e t a c c o u n t l o c a t e d
Sets of 5: s e c r e t a c c o u n t l o c a t e d
Dinomes: 42312 22331 54221 32223
         55125 12113 13143 12152

Periodic ciphertext is constructed by horizontally reading pairs of digits within each set of five letters, resulting, with the first set, in the series 42, 31, 25, 51, 25. The number sequence would continue with the pairs under each set: 22, 33, 11, 21, 13; 54, 22, 11, 31, 43; and 32, 22, 31, 21, 52.

The previously mentioned stage of converting these pairs into letters is used here.

42 31 25 51 25 . . . etc.

m c e u e

The resulting ciphertext is *m c e u e a g p t o y a p c n d a c t v.*

Fractionation can also be accomplished with a tripartite alphabet rather than a matrix.

a 111	g 131	m 221	s 311	y 331
b 112	h 132	n 222	t 312	za 332*
c 113	i 133	o 223	u 313	zb 333*
d 121	j 211	p 231	v 321	
e 122	k 212	q 232	w 322	
f 123	l 213	r 233	x 323	

Using the previous plaintext, an encryption is made with trinomes (three-number sets) in columns below the letters.

*This method adds a 27th character. The *a* and *b* are needed to differentiate this from a 26-letter alphabet.

Plaintext:

```
s e c r e    t a c c o    u n t l o    c a t e d
3 11 2 1    3 1 1 1 2    3 2 3 2 2    1 1 3 1 1
1 2 1 3 2    1 1 1 1 2    1 2 1 1 2    1 1 1 2 2
1 2 3 3 2    2 1 3 3 3    3 2 2 3 3    3 1 2 2 1
```

The ciphertext follows the previous format, whereby the trinomes are read horizontally within each five-letter group, as, in the case of the first group, 311, 211, 213, 212, and 332. Returning to the tripartite alphabet, these numbers are replaced by the cipher letters s j l k z a.

Ciphertext: s j l k z a   s d a m z b
x m j q r   c a b p m

The addressee will know the special arrangement for za/zb and deciphers accordingly (see ADFGVX, BIFID CIPHER, and PLINY EARLE CHASE).

Franklin, Benjamin (1706–1790), U.S.

statesman, inventor, and author. This creative, multifaceted Boston native also contributed to Colonial communications secrecy.

In the early months of conflict with England, Franklin recognized the talents of Charles William Dumas of the Netherlands, a German-born sympathizer of the Colonial cause who was a well-traveled classical scholar and translator. It was Dumas who suggested to Franklin that Britain's rivals Spain and France should be approached for assistance.

In 1776 Franklin advised the Colonial Secret Committee of Correspondence to make Dumas a secret agent. This was done, and the experienced European rewarded the Committee with a series of diplomatic accomplishments.

Dumas took advantage of Holland's neutral status and his friendship with ship captains to transmit to the patriots letters containing important facts from the Continent about the Colonial struggle. In his communications he used CODENAMES such as *Concordia* (for himself) and *le grand facteur* (for Duc de la Vaugoyon, the French ambassador at The Hague).

Historian Ralph E. Weber credits Dumas with "the best, most reliable and least confusing cipher used in correspondence between the Continental Congress and its foreign agents." This cryptosystem was based on the consecutive numbering of every letter and punctuation mark in a French passage, of which a portion is shown here, followed by its translation and a sample of the CIPHER.

Voulez-vous sentir la différence? Jettez les yeux sur le continent septentrional de l'Amérique. Dans les résolutions vigoureuses de ces braves colons vous reconnoitrez la voix de la vraie liberté aux prises avec l'oppression.

Do you want to feel the difference? Glance at the continent of North America. In the vigorous resolutions of those worthy colonists you will recognize the voice of true liberty at grips with oppression.

1	v
2	o
3	u
4	l

5	e
6	z
7	= (division or hyphen)
8	v
9	o
10	u
11	s

According to Weber, these lines and the others in the passage, with 682 symbols, probably originated in an essay provided, but not penned, by Dumas. For the purposes of CRYPTOGRAPHY, this cipher provided a moderate amount of concealment since it included different numbers for often-used letters; for example, *e* had 128 different numbers, *a* had 50, and *o* had 44.

Franklin and Dumas also used a one-part NOMENCLATOR in their correspondence. This method, with its SUBSTITUTION alphabet, was possibly designed by Dumas. It consisted of 928 elements and words with a rather small number of CODE symbols for often-used words. Here are some examples:

1 Aberdeen	183 Deceitful	418 Intercept
2 Above	184 Declare	419 Interest
3 Abroad	185 Defeat	420 Keep

Franklin used this system to write from the Colonial ministry at Passy near Paris when he was conducting high-level diplomatic efforts for the rebel cause. His sagacity and charm are justly credited with winning many friends for the colonies.

However, his wisdom was not absolute. His usually sharp mind apparently failed him when he could not understand several cipher variations sent to him by JAMES LOVELL, the master cryptologist of the Continental Congress. Lovell was forced to send several varied designs before his correspondent successfully deciphered them.

Franklin's judgments of others may not have been foolproof, either. His trusted friend and protégé Edward Bancroft was hired as the secretary of the Colonial legation in France, in which position he had access to official records and encrypted dispatches. He had served Franklin as a spy and knew the espionage craft well. In the 1880s, it was finally revealed that Bancroft was actually working as a double agent for the British and that he even managed to turn Franklin's colleague Silas Deane toward the royal side.

However, several historians believe that the wily Franklin knew of Bancroft and Deane's duplicity and may have been using their treason for his own purposes by allowing them to pass along false documents, rumors, and misdirections.

Whatever his skills in espionage, there is no doubt that Franklin's timely diplomacy was responsible for securing the pivotal alliance with France that turned the tide of victory in favor of the rebellion.

Fraternal Cryptography, cryptosystems used by many fraternal organizations throughout history to ensure the secrecy of their words, ceremonies, and correspondence.

CIPHER methods that have been revealed over time include the FREEMASONS' CIPHER and the ROSICRUCIANS' CIPHER, both of a type also referred to, for vague reasons, as the "pigpen." Though no longer a mystery, the Freemason and Rosicrucian versions of this type are still fascinating ciphers that make use of a "tic-tac-toe" design.

A B C	D E F	G H I
J K L	M N O	P Q R
S T U	V W X	Y Z

In some versions, as in example A below, the position of the letters in the original (left, middle, or right) was indicated by a dot in an angle of the design. Other variations had letters indicated by combinations of plain- and dot-containing designs, as in example B.

A.

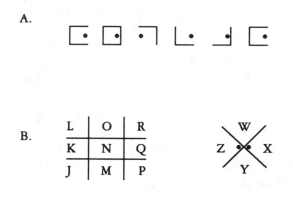

B.

In example A, both the angles of the matrix and the dot positions combine to conceal letters. Angles are open at the sides, top, or bottom and, in the case of the letters M, N, and O, a "box" is formed. The placement of the dots (left, middle, or right) in a given angle indicates the PLAINTEXT letter. In A, the dots and

angles form R, O, S, I, C, R, part of the word *Rosicrucians.*

In B, a combination of matrix angles as well as other designs with dots make similar types of SYMBOL CRYPTOGRAPHY. In this style, letters are represented by plain matrix angles while the dots are placed in some or all of the other designs (*e.g.,* Z and X).

Generally speaking, such methods used to conceal writing are basic MONOALPHABETIC SUBSTITUTIONS with passwords, CODEWORDS, or CODENUMBERS that designate special persons, documents, and so forth. They help to preserve secrecy, but fraternal organizations find their real security in the loyalty of their members.

Freemasons' Cipher, the method of secret writing used by Freemasons to protect their business from public scrutiny.

The first Freemasons were skilled intinterant stoneworkers who were not members of the medieval guilds. By the 1700s in England, the Freemasons and guild members alike gathered in formal meetings as members of lodges. In 1717, four such groups met in London and formed the Masonic Grand Lodge. These fraternal bodies quite naturally picked builders' tools as their symbols. They also incorporated the precepts of different religions in their practices and charitable efforts.

As divulged by disaffected former members, the Masons used a method of secret writing quite similar to the ROSICRUCIANS' CIPHER: Matrix and other design angles have dots that replace letters as shown in this example:

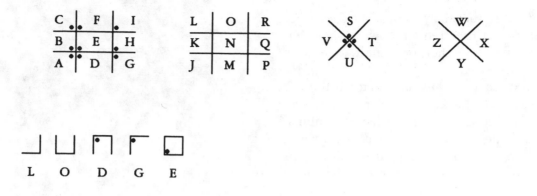

As a result of these security breaches, a number of U.S. Masonic Grand Lodges no longer created written ciphers, preferring to use vocal instructions in private ceremonies.

Frequency, with reference to CODE and CIPHER solutions, the number of times a letter or digit appears in the encryption. This is a primary clue for a cryptanalyst, because every legitimate language has discernible patterns for vowels, consonants, and syllable pairs.

An analyst generally begins an assault on a cryptomethod by counting the letters, numbers, and any other symbols used and by noting with which other letters or figures they appear.

Standard tables of letter usages are consulted for different alphabets in various languages. Some letters can be expected to appear often. In English, the most frequently used letters are *e, t, a, o, n, r, i, s,* and *h.* Infrequently used letters such as *q, x,* and *z* are also important since they may be covered by enciphered letters that occur only a few times. This does not

mean that frequent letters are easily recognizable in the ciphertext. Still, general patterns often begin to appear in the counts. When viewed in a horizontal alignment, they form recognizable peaks and valleys. Analysts sometimes use dashes to make their tallies, as below:

A B C D E F G H I J K L M

N O P Q R S T U V W X Y Z

A pattern often emerges when number totals are used:

X G L W C Q U B K I V A P
30 28 27 27 26 24 23 20 20 18 16 15 11

R D N Y E J T M S Z O F H
9 9 8 8 8 7 6 5 4 3 2 2 1

Does this mean that the group *XGLWCQUBK* is some combination of *etaonrish*? Perhaps one or more of the most common letters can be found there.

However, the analyst must next look for patterns in the frequency with which letters appear together, or contact. (See CONTACT CHART.)

Frequency studies have entered the age of COMPUTERS as these marvels help review millions of possible letter combinations. The tools of the pencil-and-paper analysts have been adapted to microchips and have achieved heretofore unimagined speed.

Friedman, Elizebeth (1892–1980),

U.S. cryptanalyst. Born in August 1892 as one of nine children of an Indiana dairyman, Elizebeth Smith came to the field of CRYPTOLOGY in an indirect way. After graduating from Michigan's Hillsdale College, she was working at a Chicago library when she met GEORGE FABYAN, an Illinois textile merchant who used a portion of his wealth to finance scientific experiments in such fields as chemistry, acoustics, and CRYPTOGRAPHY. The latter was of special interest to him since he was trying to find encrypted in Shakespeare's works the name of the real author, whom Fabyan believed to be SIR FRANCIS BACON.

While working at Fabyan's Riverbank estate in Geneva, Illinois, Smith met and eventually married a young geneticist named WILLIAM FRIEDMAN. First with the Shakespeare plays and then with current CIPHER materials generated by World War I, the Friedmans began careers that were to make them the world's premier encryption-solving pair.

In the 1930s, Elizebeth Friedman made important contributions to CRYPTANALYSIS while working for the U.S. Coast Guard in its efforts against waterborne

Elizebeth Friedman. (Courtesy of the Elizebeth Friedman Collection, George C. Marshall Foundation, Lexington, Virginia.)

rumrunners. Maintaining Prohibition at sea was difficult because the smugglers communicated with foreign liquor-bearing vessels, fast speed boats, and shore-based contacts using radio messages in CODE and cipher. To counteract this, the Coast Guard had to patrol the shoreline with far too few vessels and too little manpower to do a thorough job. Furthermore, they had

had no luck in breaking the encryptions—until Friedman applied her particular skills.

With the help of Coast Guard interception stations in California and Florida, a large number of encrypted messages were provided for her. But discovering the particular cipher clues in many of them proved to be a difficult task indeed, as the smugglers were very well organized and often used sophisticated message systems developed by professional cryptographers. The resulting cryptosystems were more complex than those used by the United States during World War I. For example, they combined the PLAINTEXT of a commercial code (such as the ABC CODE) with numbers, found these new sums in another business code, took the term by that number, and masked the term with a letter SUBSTITUTION process.

Plaintext	Meet	East Cove
ABC Code	34816	57161
+ 2000	54816	77161
Ajax Code (word)	CIMBU	GAZRO
Substitution result	DGVAZ	WHBQE

Plaintext	Await	Orders
ABC Code	25380	62097
+ 2000	45380	82097
Ajax Code (word)	JEPTY	NAMOK
Substitution result	SRIKM	JTFCL

The effort to break such an enciphered code (ENCICODE) involved the painstaking study of hundreds of commercial codes as well as trial-and-error attempts to unmask the other combinations of words, numbers, and substitutions used. However, Friedman's success led to the capture of

vessels, the seizure of contraband, and the convictions of bootleggers, including members of the large Consolidated Exporters Corporation in 1933. Friedman's skills were applied to other smuggling operations in the 1930s, including the Lim opium ring in Canada, which used the Chinese language in its concealments, and the Ezra brothers' drug ring in the San Francisco area.

On a less serious note, Friedman's final major contribution to cryptology was a collaborative work with her husband. In their early days at the Fabyan Riverbank estate, they had studied Shakespeare's plays for cipher clues to the real author. As a conclusion to their mutual careers, the Friedmans decisively debunked the enigmatologists' theory of Francis Bacon's authorship in their book *The Shakespearean Ciphers Examined* (see SHAKESPEARE CIPHERS).

Friedman, William (1891–1969), American cryptologist. Born Wolfe Friedman in Russia; his parents came to the United States, and in Pittsburgh, Pennsylvania, the boy, renamed William, grew up with a keen interest in science.

His abilities in genetics enabled Friedman to gain employment with GEORGE FABYAN, an Illinois businessman with varied interests. While Friedman began research with livestock and grains at Fabyan's Riverbank estate, he matured as a brilliant original thinker.

He became involved in CRYPTOGRAPHY through Fabyan's search for encrypted evidence that SIR FRANCIS BACON was the real author of Shakespeare's plays. While on this quest, William met Elizebeth Smith, who later became ELIZEBETH FRIEDMAN. The two became a famous husband-and-wife team in the field of CRYPTOLOGY (a term coined by William in 1921).

Before World War I, the Riverbank group was solving encryptions of other nations for Washington. When the United States entered the war in 1917, Friedman and the small but highly motivated staff began a training program for the government, and he began to create a series of cryptology monographs for its courses that became pillars of cryptology.

William Friedman. (Courtesy of the National Archives.)

Number 15 was published in 1917 and entitled *A Method of Reconstructing the Primary Alphabet from a Single One of the Series of Secondary Alphabets*. The primary alphabet was exemplified as a mixed alphabet such as that in a VIGENÈRE tableau to make a polyalphabetic encipherment method. The secondary alphabet was found in organized stages by CODE and CIPHER solving (CRYPTANALYSIS—coined by Friedman in 1920). A primary alphabet built upon a KEYWORD such as *absolute* could be arranged thusly:

Plaintext: a b s o l u t e c d f g h
Ciphertext: e c d f g h i j k m n p q

Plaintext: i j k m n p q r v w x y z
Ciphertext: r v w x y z a b s o l u t

The analyst would not know the order generated by the keyword unless he gained it by other intelligence. Therefore the recovery process is set up alphabetically, with the lower row of letters becoming the secondary alphabet and the keyword becoming somewhat hidden.

Plaintext: a b c d e f g h i j k l m
Ciphertext: e c k m j n p q r v w g x

Plaintext: n o p q r s t u v w x y z
Ciphertext: y f z a b d i h s o l u t

The original alphabet could be drawn out of the maze of letters by creating links of letters and spreading them out in arranged patterns. The solver makes the connections by starting with the letter beneath *a*, which is *e*. The analyst then locates this letter in the PLAINTEXT alphabet and uses the letter below it, *j*, as the second part of the linkage, and so forth.

After completing the first chain, the solution seeker writes letters out in trial intervals with increasingly wide spaces until plaintext parts of the keyword can be discerned.

	1	2	3	4	5	6	7	8	9	10	11	12	13
1	e	j	v	s	d	m	x	l	g	p	z	t	i
2	e		j		v		s		d		.	.	.
3	e			j			v			s			d

	14	15	16	17	18	19	20	21	22	23	24	25	26
1	r	b	c	k	w	o	f	n	y	u	h	q	a
2													
3	.	.	.										

Discovery of a primary alphabet is important to finding the solutions of other messages believed to be based upon it. Such knowledge can also help reveal other keywords of different lengths. Ideas about the choice of KEY systems can provide clues to the keying methods in different communications from the same source.

The publication numbered 16 dealt with solutions of running-key ciphers, polyalphabetic ciphers set up with lengthy texts in attempts to provide more concealment. Friedman demonstrated how to break them with a table of high-FREQUENCY keyletters and plaintext characters equated with known cipher letters and alphabets. Using only these letters, he applied an ANAGRAM process to find sensible text in both the key and the plaintext.

Among Friedman's other writings were cipher solutions, a description of cryptology-related literature, and methods of discerning CIPHER MACHINE encryptions. Within these important documents was the landmark Riverbank Publication No. 22. Written in 1920, it is described by cryptology historians as the single most influential document of its kind on the science.

No. 22 was entitled *The Index of Coincidence and Its Applications in Cryptography.* The fundamental techniques of the science are found within it. One method enabled an analyst to rebuild a primary cipher alphabet with no need to speculate about plaintext letters. The second technique, monumental in scope, linked cryptology and mathematics by presenting the distribution of letters as a curve with characteristics that could be quantified with statistics. This was a pivotal link between often arcane cryptology and accepted mathematical principles.

In 1925, while solving a message concealed by the cipher machine of EDWARD HEBERN, Friedman further developed his statistical approach with what was called the *kappa* test. (The Greek letter *kappa* [κ] designates a constant in mathematics.) The test deals with coincidences and percentages of letters appearing in plaintext and ciphertext. These factors are quantified as decimals and can be applied in probability studies of cryptomethods.

The existence of the *kappa* values permits a solver to arrange multi-alphabet ciphertexts to find the characters in each alignment (column) that have the same keyletter. These alignments permit a solution by superimposition, as developed by AUGUSTE KERCKHOFFS. Briefly stated, a superimposition process involves placement of letters from several messages to find those encrypted by the same keyletter. Anagramming, frequency, and position studies can lead to the discovery of the ciphertext equivalents for each character. This in turn makes easier analysis of the system as a monoalphabetic one. Completing the connection with Friedman's findings, the *kappa* test of probabilities and coincidence quantities shows whether a superimposition has indeed linked matching encryptions.

William Friedman's individual brilliance was combined with that of other talented members of the U.S. Army's Signal Intelligence Service in the late 1920s and 1930s. He and his team, including SOLOMON KULLBACK, FRANK ROWLETT, and ABRAHAM SINKOV, assisted the Allied victory in World War II by combining decrypted Japanese intercepts, Friedman's statistical/mathematical analysis, U.S. Navy cryptanalysts, and arduous effort to solve a top-level Japanese diplomatic code designated PURPLE. This revelation provided crucial data on the Axis powers throughout the war.

After the war, Friedman continued his work with the Defense Department and then the NATIONAL SECURITY AGENCY beginning in 1952. Though he retired in 1955, he continued to be a consultant for some years thereafter.

Friedman lived to see his discoveries and techniques used with COMPUTERS. By the 1960s, computers were applying his *kappa* test to find rates of coincidence in encryptions so quickly that it must have amazed even him, one of cryptology's true giants.

Funkspiel, German for "radio game," the use of an enemy's own radio set/network to transmit false information.

Once wireless exchanges became a primary part of military operations, means of protecting transmissions (COMSEC) or intercepting and solving them (COMINT) increased accordingly. A third element of radio use was found in the *funkspiel* (radio game) type of chicanery. At its fundamental level, a radio game involves capturing or compromising an enemy's wireless station. Because an outright capture must be swift to snare the operator, equipment, and cryptomethods (CODE lists, CIPHER numbers, and alphabets) intact, compromising an enemy radio agent (as with bribes, threats to family, and threats of torture or death) was easier than a full-scale raid.

It was also desirable to achieve acquiescence by the original transmitter in order to keep the same FIST, the operator's unique and personal way of sending a message, and avert suspicion. If the game was successful, the compromised station could be used to transmit all types of false information and to confound enemy operations.

In 1940, a highly successful U.S. radio game was accomplished by the FBI with the help of a double-agent named William Sebold.

A native of Germany and a World War I veteran, Sebold had returned from the United States to his homeland in 1939 to visit his mother. But his immigration card contained facts about his previous employment with a U.S. aircraft manufacturer, and this drew the attention of the *Gestapo*. They learned that Sebold had done some jail time as a young man and had not mentioned this when applying for citizenship in the United States. Blackmailed by this past sin, Sebold was persuaded to join the espionage training center at Hamburg. But he remained loyal to his adopted country and reported all to the U.S. consulate in Cologne.

Sebold returned to the United States in February 1940, a full-fledged operative with radio skills and postage-stamp-sized microphotos of documents, including the names of German agents and transmission instructions, hidden in his watchcase. Following orders to set up a front, he established the Diesel Research Company in the Knickerbocker Building in Manhattan. He also began broadcasts of the agents' information from his radio in a Centerport, Long Island, home. Sebold appeared so efficient that more and more *Abwehr* spies sent their messages through him.

This *funkspiel* was a major success for the FBI, whose agents actually operated the Centerport radio to transmit both screened and false data to Hamburg. Furthermore, the Manhattan Diesel Research office was equipped with cameras, one-way mirrors, and audio devices to record the spies who visited Sebold. Thus the FBI was able to conduct a series of raids in June 1941 and break a major espionage network.

Counterintelligence groups of the Third Reich also had good fortune with radio games. One of the most successful *funkspiels* is credited to an *Abwehr* branch in the Netherlands called *Section IIIF*. Beginning in January 1942, its NORDPOL radio game led to the compromise of the underground movement in Holland. Until concluded in April 1944, the operation accounted for a huge cache of captured money and matériel meant for Resistance groups and resulted in the demise of many Allied agents.

G

Geheime Kabinets-Kanzlei, the name for Austria's eighteenth-century BLACK CHAMBER, which was considered by many experts to be Europe's best. Located in Vienna, a crossroads city between western and eastern Europe, this chamber was situated near a number of important embassies. The mail intended for diplomats was instead surreptitiously brought at an early hour from the post office to the chamber, where a well-organized staff went to work with mechanical precision.

One group opened letters by melting the seals, after copying their wax insignia and forging the designs for future use. The letters were then copied and the envelopes resealed and returned to the postal system in time for regular delivery, after which cryptanalysts brought their knowledge to bear. Copies of solved letters were sent to Austrian military, diplomatic, or court officials.

The *Geheime Kabinets-Kanzlei* continued its work for years despite the suspicions of foreign diplomats.

Genetic Code, the CODE through which genetic information is transferred from the genes to the proteins that make up an organism.

The chromosomes in the cell nucleus contain genes, which in turn hold deoxyribonucleic acid (DNA), a substance that determines the genetic makeup of an organism.

Like all nucleic acids, DNA is a long molecular chain made up of three types of molecules that are linked.

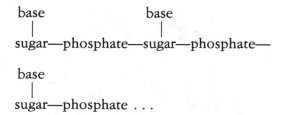

The DNA sugar is deoxyribose and its bases are adenine (*A*), guanine (*G*), thymine (*T*), and cytosine (*C*). The complete DNA molecule consists of two molecular chains wound around each other in a form called a *double helix*:

A-T-T-G-C-A-A-C

. . . .

. . . .

. . . .

T-A-A-C-G-T-T-G

The dotted lines between the bases indicate hydrogen bonds, the weak chemical bonds that hold the two chains together. Opposite every *A* base in one chain is a *T* base in the other chain. The same is true for *G* and *C*. The order of the bases in the helix determines the message conveyed by that gene.

There is a one-to-one relationship between genes and proteins. The genes order the arrangement of the amino acids of proteins, and these orders are the genetic code.

The sequence in a DNA chain could be considered one alphabet of the four bases *A*, *T*, *G*, and *C*. The amino acid pattern would then be a second alphabet of 20 letters (representing the 20 varied amino acids). The coding is not one-to-one and the bases of the DNA chain set a single amino acid in the protein chain.

DNA: GTA / ATG / CCA / GGA / . . . . .

Protein: v - m - p - g -. . . . .

Every cluster of three bases (which indicates an amino acid) is identified as a *codon*, the term for a coding of an amino acid. With 64 types of codons ($4 \times 4 \times 4$)

there are enough to code the 20 kinds of amino acids. To signify the start and the conclusion of a "message" in these alphabets, three "blank" codons are placed before and after the identified chain.

The actual specification procedure is a complex chemical process. The DNA is transcribed into a major nucleic acid called *messenger RNA* (ribonucleic acid). One base of DNA specifies one RNA base. The RNA takes this genetic information and as a messenger, leaves the cell's nucleus, moves into the cytoplasm, and is translated into protein in that part of the cell.

Geometric Patterns, configurations used to align, transpose, or substitute alphabet letters with other letters, numerals, or special forms such as those of SYMBOL CRYPTOGRAPHY.

Some of the standard geometric designs include squares or rectangles with boxes (cells) of equal size. In fact, a few, such as the FREEMASONS' CIPHER and the ROSICRUCIANS' CIPHER, began with letters in an open-sided matrix and were varied with combinations of crossed lines, or dots, or both. Such forms permit an orderly alignment of letter position and identifying mechanisms for both the sender and the receiver of a concealed message.

Letters have also been placed in rectangle-shaped groups to create a ROUTE, or "directional" CIPHER. By moving in a planned direction, up one column of letters, down another, or diagonally, a different order of the letters results. The communicators know the directions, potential NULLS to make an even number of lines of letters, and other specifics.

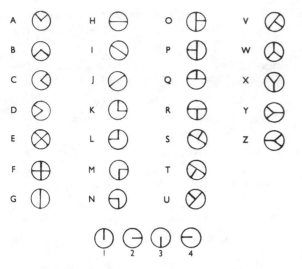

A directional code of circles. (Courtesy of Crown Publishers, Inc.)

Triangles, circles, and even trapezoids have proved useful to cryptographers. Circular designs have also been used in the CLOCK CODE and TIME CODE. An example of another type of "directional" pattern involves circles and their placement on paper that is itself turned according to directions (beneath the chart) for holding the paper: (1) straight up; (2) turned right, 90° clockwise; (3) turned upside-down; or (4) turned left 90° counterclockwise. These circles and lines can be used to form a CODE.

To misdirect a third party, a page position indicator can be placed among the circles, showing the recipient which way to turn the paper before reading the code.

Gouzenko, Igor (1919–1982), a CIPHER clerk in the Soviet embassy in Ottawa, Canada, who defected to the West in September 1945.

From cables he had seen, Gouzenko was able to provide a number of CODE-NAMES used in Soviet espionage in Canada:

Code Name	Actual Name
Gisel	GRU
Metro	Soviet Embassy, Ottawa
Lesovia	Canada
corporation	CCP (Canadian Communist Party)
corporants	CCP members
dubok	hiding place
nash	he/she works for us
neighbors	KGB
roof	front for espionage
shoemaker	passport forger

Gouzenko also divulged his knowledge of how the GRU (Soviet military intelligence) enciphered and used its ONE-TIME PADS, which gave valuable insight into the operations of the MGB (Soviet Ministry of State Security) and of Soviet agents in the United States.

Regarding the pads, the transmissions were first security-sealed with a CODE-BOOK and arranged in five-number groups. High priority, top-secret messages were given another layer of concealment by adding a random, once-used sequence of five-digit clusters to the first groups. The sum, attained by noncarrying addition, was the final CIPHERTEXT.

This process and the similar MGB system were of special interest to the United States where, in conjunction with a partly-damaged MGB codebook discovered in

Finland in 1944, Gouzenko's revelations helped FBI and Army Security Agency employees to solve KGB CABLES intercepted in 1944 and 1945.

As a result of Gouzenko's defection, several Canadians, including a prominent member of Parliament, were convicted of espionage and imprisoned. The treason of British scientist Alan Nunn May was also exposed amid the staggering revelations of the Soviet conspiracy to steal the secrets of the atomic bomb. This knowledge, in turn, assisted in the conviction of the Rosenberg Ring of atom bomb spies.

Gray Code, a transparent diplomatic CODE used by the United States from the conclusion of World War I through the early 1940s. A U.S. State Department system, the Gray used five-letter groups to represent commonplace terms and phrases. For example, *NADAD* was the frequently used equivalent for *period*. The code was so widely used and so transparent that it was the subject of amusement by the embassy personnel of other nations. It is said that a State Department staffer's retirement speech in Shanghai given in Gray was understood by the career diplomats in attendance.

It is also believed that Japanese cryptanalysts in the TOKUMU HAN department of the Imperial Navy broke messages covered by Gray after the *kempeitai* (military police) gathered scraps of telegram messages from State Department trash and that they even used a wax imprint of a key to enter the U.S. consulate in Kobe to remove CODEBOOKS from a safe, and copy them. Suspicions were apparently not aroused until a black bag mission was bungled at the office of the United States naval attaché in Tokyo.

Despite the demonstrated insecurity of the Gray Code, it was still in use in the late 1930s, as war clouds swirled over Europe and Asia. Even trans-Atlantic communications between Franklin D. Roosevelt and WINSTON CHURCHILL were covered by the Gray in 1940. Unknown to Allied officials, though, these messages were being handled in London by a clerk in the U.S. embassy who was an anti-Semite and a traitor.

Tyler Kent had had a promising diplomatic career until, under the influence of a pro-fascist group, he began to believe that the United States was being drawn into war by a Jewish plot. He fell victim to the charms of dressmaker Anna Wolkoff (also Wycoff) and provided telegrams and other documents to her and her group of Nazi sympathizers, including data showing that FDR had changed his neutrality position. Kent was ultimately convicted and sent to Dartmoor prison.

Green Cipher, a 1,418-page CODEBOOK, produced in 1910 by the Department of State and published by the Government Printing Office. (At this time, the State Department was still using *cipher* in the title of its codebooks.) The Green was the first book to be published since the Blue Code had been stolen overseas in St. Petersburg in 1905.

This 1910 version reflected a concern for transmission concealment, with some composition and design changes. The pages of the book were divided into five columns, as shown below:

| Dab | | | | |
101	Dab	101	Dab	A
Aa	da	00	ad	A
Aaben	fa	01	af	—treatise
Aach	ga	02	ag	—treaty
Aadord	ka	03	ak	—treaty port

The CODEWORD for the city *Aaben* was *Dabfa*. The PLAINTEXT Aaben was given this code term made from the top (Dab) and column letters (fa). This created a word with consonants for the first, third, and fourth letters. The plaintext phrase *A treaty* had the codeword *Dabag*, made similarly with consonants for the first, third, and fifth letters.

A process for dating telegrams was also revised.

| Month | Day | | Hour | |
	Tens	Units		
B Jan.	0 0	B 1	B 1	
C Feb.	A 1	C 2	C 2	
D Mar.	E 2	D 3	D 3	
F April	U 3	F 4	F 4	i—
				Forenoon
G May		G 5	G 5	and noon
K June		K 6	K 6	
L July		L 7	L 7	
M Aug.		M 8	M 8	y—
P Sept.		P 9	P 9	Afternoon
R Oct.		R 0	R 10	and
S Nov.			S 11	midnight
V Dec.			V 12	

The date and time were encoded with the alphabet letter representing the month, one letter each from the tens and units columns according to the day (for example, the fifth is *O* and *G*), and one letter each from the hour and forenoon or afternoon designation (such as *C* and *y* for 2 P.M.). Using this process, May 6, 1 P.M. becomes the date–time codeword *GOKBy*.

When used to conceal a communication's date and time sent, the date–time codeword was added to the first message word to make a 10-letter codeword.

For additional protection, the instructions restricted transmitting the plaintext of anything masked by the Green Cipher. Such communications had to be paraphrased and a copy sent to the State Department.

After May 1919, the Green had a slight title change, when Frank L. Polk, Acting Secretary of State, discarded the term *cipher* in reference to codebooks. With the inception of the new title *Department of State Code A1* for a new code list, the Green became the Green Code. It remained in use in combination with other codes through the 1930s, after which time World War II increased the need for security and necessitated several changes in diplomatic and military cryptosystems.

Grille, a form of STEGANOGRAPHY, or a concealment system that hides the presence of a message rather than its contents. Grilles can also be considered in the category of GEOMETRIC PATTERNS because of their structure and use.

The grille originated with GIROLAMO CARDANO, a 16th-century physician and mathematician who initiated the idea of hiding a message within innocuous phrases.

His grille was made of a piece of stiffened material or metal into which rectangular holes were cut. The message was written in the holes by letter, syllable, or word onto paper underneath the grille; then other letters and words were placed around these to create a seemingly normal missive. The planned recipient used a matching series of cutouts to read the hidden meaning (see below).

While this system was awkward to create and often revealed itself because of contrived phrases, it was used at high levels of European government into the 17th century.

In 1777, during the American Revolution, British general Sir Henry Clinton applied a crude form of grille in correspondence with his fellow officer Gen. John Burgoyne. At his headquarters in New York, Clinton sent a secret message to Burgoyne far up the Hudson River. The words were rather poorly concealed by what was called a dumbbell cipher because of its hourglass-shaped opening. Clinton's message was that he was unable to join Burgoyne in a plan to divide the colonies along the Hudson River. Historians have not concluded whether or not this correspondence reached Gen. Burgoyne or, if it did, that it actually affected his decisions. However, Clinton did not participate in the conflict, and Burgoyne was defeated by the colonists under Maj. Gen. Horatio Gates in the Battle of Saratoga, which was later recognized as the turning point of the war.

The revolving, or turning, grille was developed over time as a refinement on the fixed Cardano version.

The device was either square or rectangular in shape and was made of paper or cardboard. The square version seemed to have led to better spacing and thus easier operation. The 6×6 square was common.

And there was mounting in hot haste the steed
The mustering squadron and the clattering car,
And swiftly forming in the ranks of war;
And deep the thunder peal on peal afar;
And near, the beat of the alarming drum
Roused up the soldier ere the morning star
While thronged the citizens with terror dumb
Or whispering, with white lips, —'the
    foe! they come, they come!'

Openings were made in one quarter of the cells (nine in this case). The grille was placed on blank paper and the first nine letters of the message were inscribed in the holes. After a 90° turn of the grille, a second group of nine letters were written. This process continued until each of the 36 openings was filled. A longer message required repeating the procedure. The message sender then removed the grille and transcribed the transposed letters. This was usually done in columns from left to right to make the communication.

To decipher the text, the recipient needed a matching grille and knowledge of the 90° turns and the direction of the transcription (by columns or rows).

Gronsfeld Cipher, a CIPHER invented in the 17th century but used late in the 19th century by a group of French anarchists.

The method was named after the Count of Gronsfeld, an obscure 17th-century scholar, who described it to author Gaspar Schott. In 1659 the system was recorded for history in Schott's writings.

The cipher entered public awareness in France in 1892 when it was used by a group of anarchists. It was solved by eminent cryptanalyst ÉTIENNE BAZERIES and the plotters were arrested.

The Gronsfeld was an abbreviated version of the series of alphabets closely associated with Frenchman BLAISE DE VIGENÈRE. It used digits as a KEYNUMBER to initiate an encipherment, with the digits indicating a displacement in a standard alphabet from a given PLAINTEXT letter to its CIPHERTEXT equivalent. For example, the figure 8 above an *a* would be an instruction to count eight letters from plaintext *a* to get *i*, its cipher

replacement. With a chosen keynumber, a multi-alphabet encipherment can be attained (0 involving no change).

Keynumber: 5 3 1 6 2 8 0 7 9 4
Plaintext: a n a r c h i s t s
Ciphertext: f q b x e p i z c w

Keynumber: 5 3 1 6 2
Plaintext: a r i s e
Ciphertext: f u j y g

Ciphertext (five-letter groups):

f q b x e   p i z c w   f u j y g

The Gronsfeld method is not dependent on a specific alphabet to accomplish encryption or decryption. Furthermore, readily accessible numbers such as those of a telephone directory can be used as KEYS. The sender and addressee could use a phone number (at a certain page, column, and row) to encipher a given transmission.

GRU and HASP, the Russian military intelligence organization that preceded the KGB and a CRYPTANALYSIS operation involving its radio transmissions. With the rise of Joseph Stalin, the GRU (*Glavnoye Razvedyvatelnoye Upravleniye*) hierarchy was either replaced or thrown into confusion. Domestic mistrust and indecision spread to the overseas agents of the GRU, such as IGOR GOUZENKO, a CIPHER clerk who defected from the Soviets' Ottawa, Canada, embassy in 1945.

In addition to Gouzenko's disclosures, other GRU-related information was discovered in the KGB CABLES, World War II intercepts of Soviet communications that were partially deciphered due to the efforts of ROBERT LAMPHERE of the FBI and Meredith Gardner of the Army Security Agency (ASA, precursor of the NATIONAL SECURITY AGENCY). In 1959 Britain's Government Communications Headquarters (GCHQ) made a discovery that renewed interest in the World War II Soviet transmissions in England. GCHQ learned that the Swedish Signals Intelligence Service had intercepted some GRU radio exchanges between agents in Great Britain and their USSR headquarters. The Swedish authorities were persuaded to circumvent their standard neutrality policy and provide the data for analysis. Giving this project the CODENAME HASP, GCHQ analysts began to attack the GRU cryptosystems.

Following advances in COMPUTER-enhanced cipher solving, the first real breaks in HASP came in 1972, revealing that dozens of British journalists, technicians, and scientists provided information to the Russians during the war. Among them was a Cambridge cinema expert and freelance journalist named Montague, who passed facts releating to the Labor Party and other political groups. Even more jarring was the treason of J.B.S. Haldane, a respected biochemist who worked with Admirality submarine-related experiments.

Furthermore, the GRU decryptions finally revealed a long-operating spy ring that included the deep-cover agent Sonja (AKA Sonia), the atomic bomb spy Klaus Fuchs, and links with Alexander Foote (Soviet operative in Switzerland and a multiple defector). Most stunning in the HASP data was the realization that members of MI5 (British security, counterintelligence)

were either criminally negligent or riddled by Soviet moles, or both.

Gyldén, Yves (1895–1963), Swedish businessman and cryptologist. A native of Sweden, Gyldén was responsible for bringing a modern understanding of CRYPTOLOGY to his homeland, as well as an appreciation of its importance during World War I.

His father, Olof, had been a business partner of Arvid Damm, an inventor of CIPHER-making devices. The elder Gyldén and Damm started a company called *Aktiebolaget Cryptograph* to develop such devices for sale. The firm struggled because of financial and technical problems, and eventually a talented investor, BORIS HAGELIN, bought the company and changed its name to Aktiebolaget Cryptoteknik.

In the meantime, Gyldén had learned to work with the Damm machines and practiced techniques of CRYPTANALYSIS with them. Then, while employed at the pharmaceutical company founded by his grandfather, he made his first important contribution to cryptology.

Published in 1931, Gyldén's book, *Chifferbyraernas insatser i varldskriget till lands*, was an important study of World War I ciphers and CODES, revealing prewar misconceptions and showing the importance of the use of encrypted messages by warring nations. The expanded use of CRYPTOGRAPHY in radio communications also provided new opportunities for code and cipher solvers because of the increased volume of messages. The more communiqués, the more likely were revelations to be gained through such factors as unintentional errors, careless transmissions, repetition of standard phrases, and comparisons of previously intercepted orders with eventual battlefield results. The U.S. Army Signal Corps considered this text important enough to have it translated as *The Contribution of the Cryptographic Bureaus in the World War*.

Gyldén directly influenced Swedish and Norwegian cryptology with speeches that aroused curiosity about the methodology. When World War II began and the Nazis moved on Scandinavia's mineral wealth and strategic waterways, he was personally involved in cryptanalysis of intercepts gathered throughout the region. The findings from this work were shared with Nazi-opponents in occupied Norway. Sweden's cryptologic staff aided that country's military and diplomatic efforts and helped the government to balance successfully on the tightrope of outward neutrality while covertly assisting Hitler's enemies.

H

Hagelin, Boris (1892–1983), Swedish cryptologist and inventor. Boris Caesar Wilhelm Hagelin led a blessed life in the history of CRYPTOLOGY. Though not possessing the prescience and brilliance of WILLIAM FRIEDMAN or leading the boisterous life of HERBERT YARDLEY, Hagelin demonstrated his share of creativity, experienced danger, and achieved financial success. If Friedman was cryptology's modern genius and Yardley was its adventuresome rogue, then Hagelin was the golden boy who by all accounts remained untarnished through a long, productive life.

Born in Czarist Russia, the son of Sweden's consul-general, Hagelin studied in Russia and Sweden. After graduating from Stockholm's Royal Institute of Technology with a mechanical engineering degree, he worked for a Swedish electrical company and Standard Oil in America. After seven years, he joined a firm that made CIPHER devices, founded by Sweden's Royal Naval School Commander Olof Gyldén and inventor Arvid Damm.

The Gyldén-Damm company, *Aktiebolaget Cryptograph*, had a number of financial and technical problems, and Hagelin, backed by his father and a member of the Nobel family, bought the business and renamed it *Aktiebolaget Cryptoteknik*. Hagelin applied his engineering skills to develop and streamline new types of CIPHER MACHINES through the 1930s.

This decade saw grudging but growing recognition of security needs among peace-seeking nations that had been previously disillusioned by World War I. With the rise of fascism and the growing threat it posed, politicians and military men alike took an increased interest in all types of secrecy devices.

Hagelin was in the process of developing a machine for the United States when the Nazis invaded Norway in 1940. He and his wife then began an adventure that rivaled Yardley's best. The Hagelins left Sweden with blueprints and disassembled cipher devices in bags for a perilous train journey through Germany to Italy. From there they boarded a ship to America.

The design surreptitiously carried along the efficient German railway system was to become the U.S. Army's Converter M-209, the contract for which made Hagelin a millionaire. In the hands of skilled practitioners, the M-209 sent secret Allied messages throughout the war.

Hayhanen, Reino (1920–1961?), Soviet defector.

Carefully prepared in the late 1940s for an espionage assignment, Hayhanen was given the cover identity of Eugene Maki, an actual American who had disappeared in Finland. As Maki he was able to apply for and receive a passport to the United States.

After arriving in October 1952 in New York City, Hayhanen sent for his new wife. They lodged in different parts of the New York area before purchasing a home near Peekskill. But Hayhanen was not seeking Hudson Valley scenery; he wanted a fitting site for a radio transmitter. He had been given a very unwieldy pencil-and-paper cryptomethod called VIC, after his CODENAME. Generally speaking, it combined a SUBSTITUTION table and two TRANSPOSITION tables to encrypt messages. While awkward and time-consuming, it did manage to fool American intelligence (see VIC CIPHER).

In 1952 Hayhanen began drop site contact with Soviet deep-cover agent Rudolph Ivanovich Abel, whom Hayhanen had been sent to help as a courier and communications lieutenant. Abel was an experienced operative who was equipped with top-notch training and encryption systems. Beginning in Canada in 1948 with aliases such as Andrew Kayotis and Emil Goldfus, Abel eventually made his way to New York City. Posing as a retired photofinisher and artist, among other covers, he kept a radio receiver in his Latham Hotel room, where he tape-recorded communications from Moscow and later decrypted them. He replied to his spymasters with a radio transmitter in Brooklyn and concealed these transmissions with CIPHERS made from ONE-TIME PADS. These lists of nonsequential, often five-part groups of digits were top-rated among the shields against third-party decryption, since they had a random KEY used only once and thereby did not create any recurring patterns for analysis.

Hayhanen and Abel began their unseen contacts with a series of prearranged drops of microfilmed messages placed, for instance, in space behind a loose brick under a Central Park bridge. Communications were also hidden in hollowed bolts and flashlight batteries (see STEGANOGRAPHY). In fact, some historians believe that the problems in the Hayhanen–Abel relationship began when a newspaper boy discovered a hollow nickel and turned its contents, microfilmed paper with numbers on it, over to the FBI.

However, others say that the rift occurred gradually over a long period. After the pair had finally met, it was Hayhanen's careless work habits and weakness for liquor that finally alienated Abel. He ordered Hayhanen to return to Moscow for a "rest" in 1957. Hayhanen traveled as far as Paris, where he defected to the U.S. embassy and divulged his association with Abel as well as facts about their cryptosystems. (Hayhanen also exposed the treachery of U.S. Army sergeant Roy Rhodes, stationed at the U.S. embassy in Moscow, who in 1951 had been blackmailed and bribed into providing cryptographic information to the Soviets. Rhodes was court-martialed and sentenced to five years' imprisonment.)

Abel was arrested in his Latham Hotel room in June 1957. A one-time pad was found hidden in a hollow block of wood, along with other incriminating material. He was held as an illegal alien and convicted of espionage, attempting to obtain defense secrets, and failure to register as a foreign agent. Sentenced to 45 years' imprisonment, he was exchanged for U-2 pilot Francis Gary Powers in 1962.

Hayhanen's last years were shrouded in mystery. After being given political asylum in the United States, he is reported to have succumbed either to an automobile accident or to alcohol.

Hebern, Edward (1869–1952), American businessman and inventor of an early ROTOR.

A native of Illinois, Hebern made a living building and selling homes in California. At some point near the middle of his life, he became involved in designing and making cryptographic devices. Soon he was filing patents and developing the wiring patterns for the creation that gained him acceptance to CRYPTOLOGY's hall of fame: His early web of wire connections provided the first strands in the electrical fabric of a crucial invention called the *rotor*.

This wheel-like device had contacts on its outer edge. These points represented PLAINTEXT letters on the message input face and CIPHERTEXT letters on the output face. The various wire links between these contacts composed a MONOALPHABETIC SUBSTITUTION, a CIPHER alphabet feasible for concealment purposes. For example, electric current sent into the rotor at the input point representing plaintext *H* moved through the wire maze to the output point for ciphertext *Q*. In this way, single-letter substitutions were made.

In a fully constructed machine, the rotor was placed between plates with circular contacts with the rotor's studs. Typewriter keys represented plaintext. When a key was touched, current passed through the plate, rotor, and the opposite plate and a different letter appeared on a ciphertext-indicating device such as illuminated glass printed with letters. Furthermore, the rotor itself shifted a notch, thus changing the pattern and introducing another alphabet to the process. When other shifting rotors were added alongside the first, much greater complexity was possible and POLYALPHABETIC SUBSTITUTION was the result. This was an important step toward better concealment.

Hebern also initiated the "interval method" of rotor wiring, in which specific contacts were chosen rather than being established randomly. This resulted in a polyalphabetic distribution that kept enemy analysts from making an easy FREQUENCY study of common English letters.

Input Contact

A B C D E F G H . . . Z

Output Contact

K O G N J U P W . . . I

The difference or shift between input contact *A* and output contact *K* was called a displacement value. It measured the shift of the electrical current as it moved through the wire web of the rotor. The displacement in this example from *A* to *K* is 10; from *H* to *W* it is 15.

In addition, Edward Hebern's machine contained four other rotors. They were similarly wired to have one displacement value omitted from the possible total of 26. Each also had one value repeated twice. This was done because of the practical consideration that with an even number of studs it was not possible to have every displacement represented exactly once.

By 1921 the U.S. Navy seemed quite interested in Hebern's "Electric Code Machine." Buoyed by the military's enthusiasm and envisioning a dream come true, he began the first company for the manufacture of cipher machines in America, in Oakland, California. But his Hebern Electric Code company quickly experienced financial difficulties. Overeager investors became impatient when they didn't see immediate returns on their stockholdings. An investors' revolt, an investigation, struggles for controlling interest, and charges of securities violations eventually drove the fledgling company into insolvency and foreclosure.

Edward Hebern continued to try to sell his invention to the navy, failed, and became embroiled in more lawsuits. After World War II, he attempted to sue the armed forces for using his ideas without compensation, but these claims were eventually rejected. At the time of his death, he was still involved in litigation.

HFDF, high-frequency direction-finding, nicknamed "huffduff" during World War II.

Direction-finding involves locating radio transmission points. Antennas scan wide arcs to locate the position of the sender. When such antennas pick up the signal, their directional angles are traced to an intersection point on a map, indicating the location of the transmitter.

The U.S. Navy's direction-finding stations that scanned the Atlantic Ocean during World War II were an important part of the huffduff network. Their successes in communications intelligence (COMINT) resulted from the skill of the American personnel and the German navy's carelessness with its own communications security (COMSEC). The wolf packs' leader, Grand Adm. Karl Dönitz, favored close communications between his Berlin base of operations and the *Kriegsmarine* commanders at sea. But their early successes against Allied convoys had made the U-boat captains and crews overconfident and careless with their radio messages.

U.S. listening posts took advantage of everything from overused CIPHER concealments to radio operators' FISTS, or their personal styles of sending signals. Direction-finding data were collected at a Maryland control center, and rapid alerts were conveyed to antisubmarine forces.

An HFDF system was also in operation across the Pacific before World War II. At bases such as those in the Philippines and Guam, listening stations sent bearings for fixes and also provided intercepted messages for traffic analysis and CRYPTANALYSIS. This information was gathered at Station Hypo in Hawaii.

At Hypo were Joseph Rochefort; his cipher-solving team, including Thomas Dyer and Wesley Wright; and a series of IBM punch-card machines for categorizing and tabulating their findings. From huffduff they tried to chart the courses of Imperial Navy ships. Traffic analysis of Japanese communications involved identifying the message senders and the call signs of addressees, trying to find chains of command by determining patterns of radio contact, and noting increases in airwave use as indicators of impending military actions. The messages were then studied for clues such as repetitions or errors, in the hope of breaking through their encryption shields. Thus, files were built up on a wide variety of data that seemed to give a broad view of the Pacific scene.

But the Japanese counteracted this entire operation with meticulous communications security when it most counted, with a strike force called the *Kido Butai*. When this powerful armada entered the northern Pacific, the U.S. HFDF system did not pick it up because total radio silence was maintained. The *Kido Butai* achieved its objective—the surprise attack on Pearl Harbor.

Spurred on by this debacle, the U.S. armed forces initiated rigorous intelligence-gathering programs in every sector, including better direction-finding procedures and more stations. This was coupled with increasingly better interception and solution of major Japanese cryptomethods, including the JN25 series. As Allied forces began to move along the Pacific island chains, mobile direction-finding units went with them.

With the demise of the Tripartite Pact and the beginning of the Cold War, the United States and the West turned their electronic ears toward the Soviet Union, and after 1949, communist China. Various listening posts were set up from Bremerhaven, West Germany, to Karamursel, Turkey, and Wakkanai, Japan. These bases and many others maintained a variety of signals intelligence equipment as 24-hour electronic sentinels.

Today's HFDF sites are like science-fiction visions made real. At locations such as Kincardineshire, Scotland, a network of four circles of antennas, ranging from eight to a hundred feet high, ring a central operations building. Known as *Wullenweber* and *CDAA* (circularly disposed antenna array), the equipment snares low-band submarine signals and high-band radio—telephone communiqués with multidirectional accuracy. The term *huffduff* now has a quaint quality alongside the new vocabulary of deflector screens, folded and sleeved monopoles, coaxial cables, log periodics, and rhombic arrays.

Hill, Lester (1891–1961), U.S. professor and cryptographer. The New York native and mathematics expert entered the realm of cryptographic fame with a paper published in 1929, when he was an assistant professor of mathematics at Hunter College in New York City. His "Cryptography in an Algebraic Alphabet," printed in the June–July issue of *The American Mathematical Monthly*, was noteworthy because it was the first really practical method linking algebra and secret writing. Hill's system gave numerical values to KEYS and PLAINTEXT letters. It was quite different from other concealment styles in that there were an equal number of letters and equations in a form called polygraphic. Encryption resulted from solving the equations.

He used the numbers 0 to 25. This was called *modulo 26* and meant that any digit above 25 had to be reduced by deleting multiples of 26 from it. The remainder was equal to the number *modulo 26*. For example, 28 is 2 *modulo 26*, since $28 - 26 = 2$. 88 is 10 *modulo 26* because there are three multiples of 26 for a total of 78 in 88; then $88 - 78$ is 10. The number 110 is 6 *modulo 26*. There are four multiples of 26 (equaling 104) in 110, and $110 - 104$ is 6.

Hill made a SUBSTITUTION using a set of four equations with x representing plaintext letters: x_1 was the first letter, x_2 the second, x_3 the third, and x_4 the fourth. The ys indicated CIPHERTEXT letters.

$$y_1 = 8x_1 + 6x_2 + 9x_3 + 5x_4$$
$$y_2 = 6x_1 + 9x_2 + 5x_3 + 10x_4$$
$$y_3 = 5x_1 + 8x_2 + 4x_3 + 9x_4$$
$$y_4 = 10x_1 + 6x_2 + 11x_3 + 4x_4$$

The first encipherment step involves a standard English alphabet and a plaintext message converted into numbers that are randomly equated with the letters.

Plaintext: dusk   sign
Alphabet/Numbers:

a	b	c	d	e	f	g	h	i	j	k	l	m
2	24	11	18	3	16	9	5	17	23	21	8	15

n	o	p	q	r	s	t	u	v	w	x	y	z
4	1	14	19	7	12	20	6	10	25	13	22	0

Then the number values of the first four message letters, $d(18)$, $u(6)$, $s(12)$, and $k(21)$, are placed in the equation as y_1, y_2, y_3, and y_4.

$$y_1 = (8 \times 18) + (6 \times 6) + (9 \times 12) + (5 \times 21)$$
$$y_2 = (6 \times 18) + (9 \times 6) + (5 \times 12) + (10 \times 21)$$
$$y_3 = (5 \times 18) + (8 \times 6) + (4 \times 12) + (9 \times 21)$$
$$y_4 = (10 \times 18) + (6 \times 6) + (11 \times 12) + (4 \times 21)$$

The multiplications and additions within every equation are done in the *modulo-26* style, as in the first multiplication for y_1: 8×18 (144) = 14 *modulo 26*, since there are five multiples of 26, or 130, in 144. $144 - 130 = 14$.

$$y_1 = 14 + 10 + 4 + 1 = 29 \ (3 \ modulo \ 26)$$
$$y_2 = 4 + 2 + 8 + 2 = 16 \ (\text{no multiple of 26 here})$$
$$y_3 = 12 + 22 + 22 + 7 = 63 \ (11 \ modulo \ 26)$$
$$y_4 = 24 + 10 + 2 + 6 = 42 \ (16 \ modulo \ 26)$$

Then the numbers 3, 16, 11, and 16 are put in literal form and become the cipher letters *e*, *f*, *c*, and *f*. This process is repeated with the values for the second message word *sign* (12, 17, 9, 4).

$$y_1 = (8 \times 12) + (6 \times 17) + (9 \times 9) + (5 \times 4)$$

$$y_2 = (6 \times 12) + (9 \times 17) + (5 \times 9) + (10 \times 4)$$

$$y_3 = (5 \times 12) + (8 \times 17) + (4 \times 9) + (9 \times 4)$$

$$y_4 = (10 \times 12) + (6 \times 17) + (11 \times 9) + (4 \times 4)$$

With modulo 26:

$$y_1 = 18 + 24 + 3 + 20 = 65 \ (13 \ modulo \ 26)$$

$$y_2 = 20 + 23 + 19 + 14 = 76 \ (24 \ modulo \ 26)$$

$$y_3 = 8 + 6 + 10 + 10 = 34 \ (8 \ modulo \ 26)$$

$$y_4 = 16 + 24 + 21 + 16 = 77 \ (25 \ modulo \ 26)$$

Complete ciphertext: *e f c f x b l w*

Decipherments followed specific numerical sequences. The previously mentioned encryption was also decrypted by an equation.

$$x_1 = 23y_1 + 20y_2 + 5y_3 + 1y_4$$

$$x_2 = 2y_1 + 11y_2 + 18y_3 + 1y_4$$

$$x_3 = 25y_1 + 20y_2 + 6y_3 + 25y_4$$

$$x_4 = 25y_1 + 2y_2 + 22y_3 + 25y_4$$

Hill had another article published in *The American Mathematical Monthly* in 1931, in which he described the use of multiple matrices for encryption. These squares of numbers had their own procedures for addition and for multiplication. The matrix numbers indicated plaintext characters and several letters could be included in a few matrices. This is possible because, mathematically speaking, a matrix can be considered a single number. Therefore, a few matrices can encrypt more letters with fewer equations overall.

$$x_1 = \begin{pmatrix} w & a & i \\ t & t & h \\ e & r & e \end{pmatrix} = \begin{pmatrix} 1 & 8 & 20 \\ 7 & 7 & 2 \\ 16 & 5 & 16 \end{pmatrix}$$

This special type of multi-alphabet encipherment was very secure in terms of hiding letter pairs, repeating letters or words, and other factors that give solution seekers an angle. Yet, like his algebraic alphabet proposal, the matrices did not prove viable for practical applications. Their complexity and their solution time by intended addressees relegated them to their niche as admirable theoretical achievements in the annals of CRYPTOLOGY.

Hitt, Parker (1877–1971), U.S. Army Signal Corps officer and cryptologist. A native of Indianapolis, Indiana, Parker Hitt was a veteran of the Spanish-American War. He attended the Army's Signal School at Fort Leavenworth, Kansas, and became interested in CRYPTOGRAPHY. In 1916, he published the *Manual for the Solution of Military Ciphers*, which was printed by the Army Service Schools Press at Fort Leavenworth. The first such book of its length (101 pages) published in America, the manual increased interest in the subject, particularly in light of the war being fought at the time in Europe. Yet his text was soon rendered obsolete by the increasing need for better concealment methods for battlefield transmissions.

Not long after the United States entered the war, Hitt went to Europe as a part of Gen. John J. Pershing's staff, where he worked on encryption procedures for the American Expeditionary Forces. As the chief signal officer of the A.E.F.'s First Army, Hitt worked with

Parker Hitt. (Courtesy of the National Archives.)

such men as Capt. Howard Barnes and Maj. Frank Moorman. It was Barnes who put together the first wartime CODEBOOK for the U.S. Army, the AMERICAN TRENCH CODE. Moorman, head of the Radio Intelligence Section of the General Staff, also made important contributions to encoding procedures. Both consulted Hitt about CODES used in A.E.F. operations such as the important battle at Chateau-Thierry.

Concerned about the dangerously poor quality of U.S. codes and CIPHERS, Hitt also proposed variations for cryptographic devices. He developed a variation of the BAZERIES cylinder whereby he "unrolled" the alphabet letters, jumbled them, and placed them on strips of paper. With numbers added to them, they were mounted in a 7 × 3¼-inch holder and arranged according to a chosen KEYNUMBER. The strips were then moved up or down to spell the letters in a message. The other mixed lines of letters served as the CIPHERTEXT, with more than one line being used, depending on the length of the communication.

Hitt's friend JOSEPH MAUBORGNE, a Signal Corps officer, liked the method. He had it returned to a cylindrical form, and it eventually became the U.S. Army's main cipher device, the M-94, in 1922. A version of Hitt's original strip system was also adopted by the Army and the State Department in the 1930s and designated the M-138A (see M-138). Thus Hitt's few strips of paper resulted in reams of encryptions over a span of two decades.

Hoboes' Codes, a type of secret language long used by hoboes to communicate among themselves.

Hoboes' signs are functionally similar to some symbols in early CODES. They are also ideographic in nature because they represent an object or an idea without expressing the sounds forming its name.

Written with chalk on fence posts and sidewalks or carved in tree trunks on the outskirts of town, these symbols and variations of them form a type of CRYPTOGRAPHY within the hoboes' own range of interests and life-styles (see following page).

The knights of the road also developed a specialized vocabulary that fits the definition of JARGON CODE:

Hobo Term	Definition
boodle	a crowd, a bribe, robbery loot
catch back	return by the same rail freight route
jungle	camp, welcome shelter
homeguards	tramps who don't like to travel
nose divers	rescue mission regulars
open	friendly, as a town or home
sally	Salvation Army, the sanctuary for many

no alcohol	tell sad story	not kind	safe camp	unsafe place	night lodging
town awake	sick care	gentlman	don't give up	lend yourself	dishonest man
go	woman	railroad police	next, right	food for chores	stay away
danger	judge	be quiet	handout	town asleep	man with gun
kind lady	halt	alcohol	officer	sleep in hayloft	very good

Hoboes' symbols. (Courtesy of Crown Publishers, Inc.)

HUMINT (human intelligence),

intelligence gathered through human means, as contrasted with solely technological methods.

Human intelligence has been involved with aspects of CRYPTOLOGY since ancient times. The eyes, ears, and intuition of spies helped gather information that was transferred either orally or by writing, the presence of which was often hidden in clothing or innocent-looking objects (see STEGANOGRAPHY).

The early Spartans used a concealment device called a SKYTALE. Later, Roman agents used primitive signaling systems (*e.g.*, torches) to convey their secrets. Middle Ages court intrigue involved cryptic writing, INVISIBLE INKS, and BLACK CHAMBERS where such messages were unmasked.

In the modern age, long-range surveillance by cameras, listening devices, and satellites combined with encrypted data transmissions by COMPUTERS, may sometimes seem to render cloak-and-dagger espionage obsolete. However, even today, the individual agent is still needed to make sense of events amid rapid political and social change.

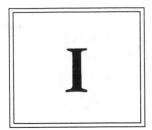

Invisible Inks, special fluids or chemicals used for concealment of writing, symbols, or other means of communication. Invisible inks were invented in ancient times. Because the purpose of such substances has been to render a message unseen by the unaided eye, this method is considered a form of STEGANOGRAPHY, or hiding the presence of a message without altering its content.

The inks are generally of two types, chemicals called sympathetic and organic fluids. The former are chemical solutions that become invisible as they dry. When other chemicals, called reagents, are applied to them, the hidden terms are again visible. The organic group consists of commonly obtainable substances such as fruit juice, milk, and vinegar. Generally these are made visible by heat. The parchment or paper with the message is placed near a candle flame or other heat to make the writing stand out again.

As early as A.D. 600, the Arabs were using such methods to communicate throughout their flourishing empire. Invisible inks were also used in Europe in the Middle Ages and were the subject of several treatises, ranging from the fanciful and heretical to the scholarly and scientific. The latter became more common during the Renaissance. In the 1400s, LEON BATTISTA ALBERTI's important texts about CIPHER making and solving (CRYPTANALYSIS) included references to invisible inks. Later, the French satirist François Rabelais humorously discussed concealed writing in his classic *Pantagruel* (1532). Amid his witty comments about life, he described making invisible ink from such substances as the juice of white onions, ammonium chloride, and alum.

By the late 1700s, knowledge of such methods had crossed the Atlantic and was being applied during the American Revolution. George Washington and his spies, led by BENJAMIN TALLMADGE, used inks that they called "stains." These inks as provided by a London physician named James Jay, brother of patriot John Jay. The agents, including the so-called Culpers (Abraham Woodhull and Robert Townsend), passed important information about British troops, ships, and armaments in occupied New York, writing their reports in a book on seemingly blank pages. At his headquarters, Washington recovered the words by applying a "counterpart liquid" to the parchment.

Invisible inks were increasingly applied as advances in chemistry made them even more effective. The most sought-after substance was one that reacted with very few chemicals and was therefore designated a "specific" ink. Well-hidden messages were sometimes also encoded or enciphered, making decryption extra difficult.

However, detection methods also improved as the cover breakers applied technology. They "striped" letters with developer on brushes in order to find the necessary reagent for a specific ink. Ultraviolet light was used to detect words spelled with starch, while infrared beams identified messages written with ink of the same color as the material (usually paper or cloth) on which it was placed.

The need to convey ever more detailed information with increasing speed eventually led to the shelving of most vials of secret ink. Technological advances replaced them with the ingenious product of microphotography, the MICRODOT.

Islands Coastwatching Service, a group trained to guard Australia's lengthy shoreline. The Australian intelligence services and their cryptologists made their mark on history during World War II. The foundation for this success was set in place in 1919 with the establishment of the Islands Coastwatching Service. The fishermen, planters, farmers, and local civic officials, among others, who did the observing used radios to coordinate their reports. By the time World War II began, these Royal Australian Navy watchers were ready.

The Coastwatching Service became a part of Australian naval intelligence and the Allied Intelligence Bureau, which directed and supplied the espionage and intelligence-gathering missions of combined Australian, U.S., British, Dutch, and other resistance forces in the Southwest Pacific. These operations were coordinated with U.S. general Douglas MacArthur's Far East command.

Many coastwatchers lived a moment-to-moment existence as they hid on islands that had been captured by the Japanese. Their radio links connected a region that included Port Moresby, New Guinea, through the Solomon Islands. Using CIPHERS such as the PLAYFAIR CIPHER, they supplied vital facts about Imperial Navy locations, troop carriers, convoys, and enemy landing sites, and their information contributed to important successes in the Solomons (Guadalcanal) and in New Guinea that laid the groundwork for the Allies' ultimate victory.

"J" Series, the U.S. designation of CODES for transmissions of the Japanese Foreign Ministry, its embassies and consulates in the 1930s and 1940s. The J-coded exchanges were given extra concealment by a TRANSPOSITION that was arranged by a KEYNUMBER. The cryptosystem had a sequence of blanks that changed the standard length of the column segments and further covered the PLAINTEXT. These transpositions and spaces were named "K" plus a numeral by U.S. analysts, who documented their changes as well.

With spaces represented by asterisks, the keynumber 4153267, and the message *all east asia co-prosperity spheres*, an abbreviated example of the method follows:

4	1	5	3	2	6	7
a	*	l	l	e	*	a
s	t	a	*	s	i	*

a	c	o	*	p	r	o
*	s	p	e	r	*	i
t	*	y	s	*	p	h
e	r	*	e	*	s	*

The encryption was made by writing it in columns according to the keynumber and bypassing the blanks to read *tcsr espr lese asate laopy irps aoih*. These were placed in five-digit groups along with designators for the method and KEY before being sent by radio.

U.S. code solvers gave the J group numbers in sequences along with K transposition identifiers such as J17K6, J18K8, and J19K9. The J codes did not include the Imperial Navy's encryption method for flag officers, a four-character code with a transposition SUPERENCIPHERMENT. Nor was the high-level JN25 fleet cryptographic system a part of this series.

Jargon Codes, open methods of linguistic concealment. A type of OPEN CODE, the jargon code is not hidden by symbols or transposed letters. Rather, an innocent word or words replaces another term in a sentence constructed in an innocuous fashion. For example, *She met him that afternoon* could actually mean "The enemy agent retrieved the package on Wednesday." Or the entire group of words could be a signal to initiate an action with no direct link to any single word.

The British Broadcasting Corporation broadcasted crucial jargon codes to the French resistance during World War II. The most important of these messages were the ones that announced the D-DAY invasion, which was signaled by phrases from the poem "Chanson d'Automne" by Paul Verlaine, as follows in English: "The long sobs of the violins of autumn" announced on June 1, 1944, that the Allied invasion of Europe was imminent. Then on June 5, "Wound my heart with a monotonous languor" told the freedom fighters that the attack would begin within 48 hours. The Maquis and other resistance groups then knew to initiate a number of actions to help ensure the Allies' success on June 6, 1944.

Jefferson, Thomas (1743–1826), third president of the United States, statesman, and amateur cryptographer.

As America's third president, primary author of the Declaration of Independence, architect, and inventor, Thomas Jefferson's life was filled with many varied and significant accomplishments. Among this multitalented man's numerous achievements, his CRYPTOLOGY-related interests are rarely mentioned.

In fact, Jefferson's best-known contribution, a device he called a "wheel cypher," wasn't recognized in his lifetime. However, he did use a combination CODE-and-CIPHER system called a NOMENCLATOR during the period 1785–1793.

In 1781, U.S. Secretary of Foreign Affairs Robert Livingston created a nomenclator that contained an alphabetized group of words and syllables on one side and a list of the numbers 1 through 1,700 on the other.

Jefferson and James Madison built their own private security screen using the Livingston system. It was practical because its flexibility permitted the numbers to be paired with the PLAINTEXT, or the letters to be concealed, in any pattern chosen by the sender and addressee. Some examples of the Jefferson–Madison method included:

nal	1190		527 P		941 qua		103
name	717 oa		746 pa		290 quest		1386
nant	42 oach	559 pan			381 question		799
nar	60 oad	217 paper			207 quin		1202

While this did not look very complicated, the following missive would be just so much ink on parchment without matching lists between the intended correspondents:

Don't 799 anyone. Look for the 717 on the 207.

The recipient would know not to *question* (799) anyone, but to find a *name* (717) on the *paper* (207).

As the whims of chance would have it, the sage of Monticello developed a very practical cipher device that had no record of actual use. Yet, though undiscovered for nearly a century after his passing, this creation earned Thomas Jefferson the title "Father of American Cryptography."

He proposed using a cylinder of wood two inches in diameter and six inches long. He would cut a series of wooden disks, each 1/6-inch thick. He decided upon a total of 36 disks with alphabet letters placed in mixed order on the periphery of each disk. Each section was numbered and placed in numerical order on an iron axis (spindle), with the assemblage held together by a metal head at one end of the spindle and a screw and nut arrangement at the other.

To send the message "Meet us in Virginia," its letters would be placed in line along the iron spindle. After securing their position with the nut and screw, the transmitter looked to any of the other various alignments for a CIPHERTEXT. He then chose one of these lines from the cylinder and wrote it in his communication.

When the letter arrived, the addressee would use his device to position a matching row of these same letters. Then by looking at the other alphabet rows, he would find the intelligible line of plaintext.

Curiously, after going to the effort of creating a very good method for its day, the third president apparently put the idea in a side drawer or shelf and eventually forgot about it. Ironically, versions of this device were created independently by Frenchman ÉTIENNE BAZERIES in 1890 and by PARKER HITT during the period of 1914–1917. Hitt's strip-cipher series of alphabets were also made in a cylinder form and became the M-94 of the U.S. Army in 1922.

Jewels, CODENAME for CIPHER MACHINES used by U.S. diplomats in the Soviet Union. Some of the best of their kind ever built, the closely guarded, top-secret machines had advanced encryption and decryption capabilities. They had magnetic strips with KEYS of numbers developed by the NATIONAL SECURITY AGENCY (NSA), which were used to send double-encrypted messages through two machines. There was an aura of invincibility about the Jewels that was later found to be false. Security at the United States' Moscow embassy and Leningrad consulate was thoroughly compromised, and the cipher machine data was stolen by high-tech "jewel thieves" from 1984 through the spring of 1987.

In 1987 news reports carried a series of accounts implicating some U.S. Marine embassy and consulate guards in treasonous activities committed after their having been seduced by female Soviet agents. Moreover, as documented by correspondent and author Ronald Kessler in his book *Moscow Station*, the Soviets had also managed to clandestinely alter the "clean" power line to the cipher machines, so that electronic security filters had been bypassed and signals were being diverted from the Jewels. Circuit boards and silicon chips had been replaced in the printers for the cipher machines, allowing KGB operatives to pick up and record signals from the unencrypted side of the communications circuits and printer processes. With the PLAINTEXT in hand, they could then proceed to make comparisons with encrypted messages and reproduce the crucial cipher keys. The top-secret encryptive equipment in Moscow and Leningrad had been turned into huge listening devices.

The result was a security nightmare, with CIA agents revealed and expelled, NSA eavesdropping practices revealed, U.S. negotiating positions compromised, and the arrest and execution of Russian informants for the CIA. The United States' own cryptographic secrets were used to cause extensive and perhaps still undocumented damage on a global scale.

JN25, a United States designation for a primary Japanese navy encryption method initiated in June 1939.

The name JN25 was chosen because it was the 25th Japanese navy cryptosystem studied by U.S. Navy cryptanalysts, including those headquartered at OP-20-G in Washington, D.C. As Japanese conquests in Asia began to threaten U.S. interests in the region, special attention was focused on the Japanese fleet's activities. The solution of Imperial Navy message concealments was thus a primary goal of U.S. intelligence.

Military and general history texts alike have variously described this system as a CODE or a CIPHER. The concensus of CRYPTOLOGY experts is that it was a TWO-PART CODE containing 33,333 five-digit groups. Every one of the groups was purposely arranged to be divisible by three, such as 36876, to make it easier to detect transmission errors. The entire two-part code was further covered with SUPERENCI-PHERMENT, accomplished with an ADDI-TIVE, *i.e.*, a sequence of digits added to the code's numerals.

AGNES DRISCOLL of OP-20-G is credited with breaking through the additive to find the primary CODENUMBERS and their

PLAINTEXT equivalents. This important achievement received an apparent setback in December 1940, when the Japanese introduced a new concealment named JN25b by U.S. analysts. It was a larger enciphered code with more additives. However, the Imperial Navy's communications security was flawed when JN25 additives were kept in service even as the new ones were initiated. The solved additives gave OP-20-G a wedge to break into the new shield, and portions of JN25b began to be understood in the winter of 1941.

The JN25 discoveries and partial recovery of JN25b data did not reveal enough valid intelligence to avert the attack on Pearl Harbor in December 1941. However, the solid base of JN25 and subsequent cryptomethod solutions provided real dividends for the United States at the Coral Sea and Midway battles in May and June 1942, which turned the tide of the Pacific conflict.

Jutland, Battle of, a naval battle between Great Britain and Germany in May 1916.

CRYPTOLOGY and radio listening posts were important factors in this confrontation of dreadnought battleships off the coast of the Jutland peninsula of Denmark. Britain's ROOM 40 intelligence staff had obtained copies of the *Kreigsmarine*'s naval CODEBOOK from the wreck of the German light cruiser MAGDEBURG in 1914. CRYPTANALYSIS of these documents enabled the British to understand intercepted German radio dispatches. Direction finding (see HFDF) helped to pinpoint the Kaiser's High Seas Fleet, and a decisive engagement seemed imminent on May 31.

However, a series of errors including a mistaken location of a German radio call sign and distrust in CODE-solving skills, caused Britain to lose a crucial opportunity. A sequence of all-night exchanges led to losses for both sides. But the Royal Navy was unable to use its best advantages to sweep her mortal foe from the waves.

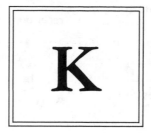

K

Kasiski, Friedrich (1805–1881), Prussian army officer and cryptanalyst.

A career military man, Kasiski rose to the rank of major in the Prussian army. Amidst this spartan, rigid life, he found time to study CRYPTOGRAPHY. In 1863 his 95-page book *Die Geheimschriften und die Dechiffrir-kunst* (Secret Writing and the Art of Deciphering) was published in Berlin. It is noteworthy in the history of CRYPTOLOGY in that it addressed a problem that had stumped would-be CIPHER-breakers for years: how to solve a message rendered secret by polyalphabetic ciphers that have repeating KEYWORDS.

A sending party might use the keyword *fly* to encrypt a PLAINTEXT. The KEY term is repeated, and an interesting pattern emerges in the CIPHERTEXT:

Key:	f l y f l y f l y f l y f l y
Plaintext:	t o b e o r n o t t o b e t h
Ciphertext:	*q a w m* a e x a p *q a w m y l*

Key:	f l y f l y f l y f l y f l y
Plaintext:	a t i s t h e q u e s t i o n
Ciphertext:	k z r g *y l* h v c j x p d a u

When the repeating key letters *f*, *l*, and *y* contact the repetitious letters in the message *t*, *o*, *b*, e and *t h*, a repeated sequence is found in the encryption *q*, *a*, *w*, *m*, *y*, l. This tells a cryptanalyst that a keyword has to repeat one or more times for a segment of it to encrypt two identical parts of the message that are separated by other letters. Such a discovery led Kasiski to notice patterns of repetitions and spaces between these groups.

This space factor is exemplified by the

letters between that don't repeat (*a*, *e*, *x*, *a*, *p*) and the next segment containing *q*, *a*, *w*, *m*. This sequence from the first letter of the series through the next time it repeats is called an interval, nine alphabet letters in this case. Kasiski found that this total revealed the number of times the keyword repeated. Letters aligned with this interval indicated three repetitions of the keyword (three letters × three). This finding enables the analyst to locate other points in the encryption where the keyword appears and thus begin to discern its own letter total. With knowledge of the key term's length, its actual letters and those of the alphabets it controls can be revealed.

The total number of letters in the keyword indicates the number of alphabets in the encipherment. The cryptanalyst can then attempt to find all the letters encrypted by the first keyletter and then the second, third, and so on. Such collections of letters, each enciphered by one letter, are known as MONOALPHABETIC SUBSTITUTION. This discovery can then be used to learn about the cipher's polyalphabetic aspects.

The message is examined for repeated letters, and the FREQUENCY of these is measured. Once the repetitions are found, the analyst tries to discover the numerical distance separating them. When this has been determined, the next step is to find this interval's factors. The factor most often located is the number of letters in the key.

This process is called a *Kasiski examination* and has a pattern that the analyst follows as exemplified by this random series of totals to display the procedure.

| repetition | Positions | | | factors |
	first	second	interval	
h q w c	3	163	160	$2 \times 2 \times 4 \times 10$
i d h	6	186	180	$2 \times 3 \times 3 \times 10$
w l k	20	220	200	$2 \times 2 \times 5 \times 10$
· ·	·	· ·	· · ·	· · · · · ·
· ·	·	· ·	· · ·	· · · · · ·

Though 2 already appears to be the most numerous factor, it is also one that is present in each even interval. Thus it is not a good candidate. Since very short keys have proven to be rather unlikely possibilities, analysts look for those of more length. Solvers also have to consider accidental repetitions as well as genuine key-induced repetitions.

Suppose the best potential factor is 8. This means that the number of letters in the key is eight. The analyst would then write out the message in lines eight letters wide. Beneath them he or she places the characters assumed to be encrypted with the same keyletter. Then in these columns more trial-and-error searches are made for plaintext equivalents. A frequency count is developed from this step.

It is important at this point to discover a monoalphabetic substitution, which will prove that the key length (8) is valid. Unexpected results, such as an unusual frequency profile, would indicate a mistake. For example, the regular English profile (outline) of the more rarely used plaintext letters has expected areas of low frequency at segements such as *pqr* and *uvwxyz*. A marked deviation from this outline would be a warning of something atypical and most likely a problem.

Normal profile:

```
≡        ≡      = ≡
          
a b c d e f g h i j k l m

≡ =      _    _   _
_         
n o p q r s t u v w x y z
```

Atypical:

```
         =   _    = =  _
_ _      ≡   _    _ ≡ _
a b c d e f g h i j k l m

  =    _       = = = _ _
_      _       ≡
n o p q r s t u v w x y z
```

In the example above, each stroke above a letter indicates how many times that letter appears in the ciphertext. It should be noted that in brief examples, more clues can sometimes be gained from the letters found in the "low" segments of such outlines than in the expected "highs." Nevertheless, there are rules of normal frequency that prevail.

A solution seeker would like to find an alphabet and a profile that could be identified as being generated by a known method. This would cause a number of tools to become available from documented practices. When an alphabet is found with no recognizable system basis, the analyst resorts to linguistic clues, CONTACT CHARTS, and more detailed frequency guesswork.

Kata Kana ("borrowed words"), Japanese ideographic writing arranged as syllabic lists of roman letters and developed for telegraphic purposes because the Japanese language was difficult to transmit by the standard international MORSE CODE. Syllables such as *na, hi, mu*, and *re* were equated with Morse dots and dashes.

In his controversial 1931 book THE AMERICAN BLACK CHAMBER, U.S. encryption expert HERBERT YARDLEY described his difficulties and eventual triumph in solving this syllabary style. He did it with the help of personnel from MI-8, the BLACK CHAMBER described in his book.

Yardley and this small but ambitious group learned that *kata kana* had about 73 syllables that had their own signs with roman letter eqivalents. They also discovered that this script had a characteristic FREQUENCY of letter use, just as have other languages. The *kana n*, as well as *i, o, ni*, and *to*, had patterns of position and repetition that were quantifiable with the help of frequency tables. This knowledge made it possible to find combinations of letters such as *ari, gyoo*, and *shi*. Locations of syllables then led to the decryption of words and sentences.

This phonetic syllabary was placed in CODE form, with the messages segmented and mixed in order to cover typical letters at the beginnings and ends of words as well as salutations and closings of communications. Still, the MI-8 staff managed to solve the messages, and the resulting information was of great value to U.S. negotiators at the 1921–22 Washington Disarmament Conference. Knowing the contents of Nippon's exchanges with her negotiators gave the United States a crucial edge in obtaining a favorable ratio of ship tonnages during the conference. Thus America gained status and military advantages.

After Yardley revealed these facts in his book and in articles in *The Saturday Evening Post*, the outraged Japanese initiated new security procedures. Yet the *kata kana* remained in use due to telegraphic necessities.

When Japan invaded Manchuria in 1931, its "brass-pounding" radio telegraphers used *kata kana* in messages with different levels of concealments. Even in 1940, with war a daily fact of life in other parts of the world, the method was used in a simple code like the *LA*.

Named for the indicator group that appeared before its CODETEXTS, the *LA* used *kata kana* in roman-letter form for telegraphic efficiency and CABLEGRAM financial savings. It had two-letter CODEWORDS of vowel–consonant or consonant–vowel pairs. Four-letter codewords indicated special terms, such as diplomatic phrases, monetary amounts, place names and so forth. CRYPTANALYSIS of such *kata kana* applications revealed crucial facts, such as that syllables ending in *e* had code replacements that started with *A*. This repetitive pattern aided ongoing decryption successes by providing familiar equivalents in many exchanges.

When recounting these solutions in the early 1940s, CRYPTOLOGY and military historians alike describe *kata kana* as having around 50 syllables. Yardley's *The American Black Chamber* contains a chart (p. 254) of 73 syllables. However, World War II–era documents clearly indicate 50 plus the nonsyllabic *N*. Apparently the method had undergone some streamlining even as the analysis became more precise.

Kerckhoffs, Auguste (1835–1903), Dutch educator and cryptologist. Born of a prominent family, Auguste Kerckhoffs became interested in languages at an early age. Travels through Europe increased his proficiency in German, Greek, Italian, and other tongues. After he married and took a teaching job near Paris, his keen mind and linguistic interests kept him involved in various unusual pursuits. These included promoting his dream of a world language called *Volapük*.

While expanding his knowledge and earning his Ph.D., Kerckhoffs worked as a tutor and began writing. After completing books on Flemish and English grammar, he wrote one of the true classics of CRYPTOLOGY. Published in 1883, his 64-page *La Cryptographie militaire (Military Cryptography)* took message concealing and revealing into a new era.

He discussed the known parameters of the field, then brought his readers into the modern times of enciphered CODE (see ENCICODE) mechanical encryption devices, the telegraph, and military message secrecy. Wartime CRYPTOGRAPHY, he said, had to be easy to understand and efficient. Furthermore, it should have a KEY that could be changed, be capable of telegraphic transmission, be portable, and be usable by one person without complicated steps of operation, among its more important prerequisites.

Kerckhoffs is credited as the first to distinguish between a general crytographic system (such as a CODEBOOK or CIPHER DISK) and the specific key used with it. While the general method might be surmised or discovered by an enemy, if the specific key were kept secret, a message concealed by it would be very difficult to uncover. Thus the real protection was to be found in the keys.

Kerckhoffs also introduced two important tools, *superimposition* and *symmetry of position*.

Superimposition is a primary way to solve POLYALPHABETIC SUBSTITUTIONS. The solution seeker tries to find a number of communications hidden by the same key. One cryptogram is arranged on top of the other. This sets up a series of columns whereby encrypted letters and their potential keyletters can be sought. For example, a short key that repeats to encrypt each communication conceals the first character of the first PLAINTEXT message with the first key letter, the second character with the second key letter, and so forth. As the key repeats, this is also true for the second message's first letter and second letter, to its completion. Kerckhoffs set up a chart that is briefly exemplified as follows:

Column

Cryptogram	1	2	3	4	5	6	7	.	.	.
1	b	g	j	d	x	c	r			
2	b	g	n	d	a	z	u			
3	b	c	m	i	x	z	q			
4	h	g	n	y	e	r	v			
5	b	l	c	d	h	p	r			
6	b	g	o	q	n	h	r			
.										
.										
.										

Kerckhoffs demonstrated that since all the letters were encrypted from the same source of key characters, then each of the letters in the first row had the same single keyletter. This was true for each column and each key element in turn. Thus each plaintext letter, concealed by the visible encrypted letter, will have its own CIPHERTEXT equal. With this one-to-one relationship established, each column can be considered a MONOALPHABETIC SUBSTITUTION. It can then be probed with such analytical tools as letter FREQUENCY counts, typical letter pairs and associates (see CONTACT CHART) and presumed common nouns and verbs.

Kerckhoffs developed a second major decryption tool, "symmetry of position." This can be exemplified with the words for his dream, *a world language* (letters used once), inserted into a cyclical alphabet in a table (see top of next page).

Characteristics and patterns of location can be found in such tables. The letter *b* is five places from the letter *a* throughout the alphabet sequences, as is the letter *h* from *p*. Eight cells are always found between *l* and *c*. Such constant intervals exist between letters at different points in the table.

This benefits analysis in a very important way. Assume that a transmission made from this table has been solved and it is known that cipher characters *r* and *n* conceal PLAINTEXT *c* and *g*. The cipher letters have an interval of four. When the solver discerns *r* in a different alphabet, he can find the location of the second letter in this alphabet because of the known number of places between them. Thus if *r* is found to be plaintext *h*, an interval

Plain:	a b c d e f g h i j k l m n o p q r s t u v w x y z
Cipher:	w o r l d a n g u e b c f h i j k m p q s t v x y z
''	o r l d a n g u e b c f h i j k m p q s t v x y z w
''	r l d a n g u e b c f h i j k m p q s t v x y z w o
''	l d a n g u e b c f h i j k m p q s t v x y z w o r
''	d a n g u e b c f h i j k m p q s t v x y z w o r l

of four aligns cipher *n* with plain *l*. This symmetry of position produces a new cipher equivalent that can be located throughout the new alphabet and create other breaks in its shield.

These discoveries made Kerckhoffs's *La Cryptographie militaire* a prominent text in the library of cryptology. Another achievement of note was his work on a multialphabet method called the SAINT-CYR SLIDE, named after Saint-Cyr, the national military academy of France, where it was used in courses. Furthermore, he made a linkage that others had missed. He found that the polyalphabetic functions of the slide were very similar to the alphabet table of BLAISE DE VIGENÈRE and a CIPHER DISK like that of GIOVANNI PORTA.

While his dream of a global language failed to become a reality, Kerckhoffs's findings directly benefited French cryptology in World War I (see ADFGVX, GEORGES PAINVIN).

Key, a set of instructions governing the encryption and decryption of messages. In CRYPTOGRAPHY, a key sets up a particular method of message concealment and controls the variable aspects of a given CODE or CIPHER system. The chosen key is provided to the addressee by prearrangement in order to unlock the shield covering the communication.

A key may consist of numbers equated with alphabets, words that have been replaced by symbols, the alignment of digits on a CIPHER DISK, the order by which groups of letters are to be read, or the position of ROTORS in an electromechanical cryptograph. The COMPUTER age and its security needs have necessitated the creation of more complex keys for encryption purposes (see PUBLIC KEY and TWO-KEY CRYPTOGRAPHY).

Keynumber, a series of digits that serves as a KEY for encryption purposes. A cryptographer uses a keynumber to control such functions as the sequence of letters in sentences, the pattern of words developed with TRANSPOSITION columns, and the generation of CIPHER letters from a standard alphabet to make a POLYALPHABETIC SUBSTITUTION.

A keynumber can initiate a displacement process with an alphabet (see GRONSFELD CIPHER). This involves counting forward from the position of a given PLAINTEXT letter to the new alphabet location of its CIPHERTEXT replacement (for example, 4 above *m* means count forward 4 places to *q*). The numbers 0 to 9 mixed and repeated demonstrate this, as in the example below:

Keynumber:	7 6 1 2 4 8 9 0 5 3 7 6 1 2 4
Plaintext:	s e n d c o u r i e r f i v e
Ciphertext:	z k o f g w d r n h y l j x i

A keynumber can also indicate the order of letters in a single word. For example, the keynumber 41532 can be an instruction to put the fourth letter of a plaintext word first, the first letter second, and so forth, in order to encipher the given word. Thus *begin* becomes *ibnge*.

Keynumbers may be found in a handy source such as a telephone directory. Another long sequence of numbers can be developed from *pi* (π) using its value to 24 decimals. The previously described displacement process could then be applied.

Key:	31415	92653	58979
Plaintext:	docum	entin	diplo
Ciphertext:	gpqvr	npznq	iqysx

Key:	32384	62643
Plaintext:	matic	pouch
Ciphertext:	pcwqg	vqagk

Keyphrase Cipher, CIPHER in which a phrase forms the KEY.

When EDGAR ALLAN POE was editor of *Graham's Magazine* in Philadelphia, he asked his readers to challenge him by sending him cryptograms to solve. He described a method purportedly used by the Duchess of Berry, who was a monarchist opposed to the then French ruler in 1832. Her secret correspondence to a group of anti-monarchists in Paris was supposedly written in CIPHER. The system reportedly used the keyphrase *Le gouvernement provisoire* as a SUBSTITUTION. In a 24-letter alphabet (with x and z removed), it can be arranged as follows:

```
ABCDE FGHI J KLMNO PQR S TUVWY
l e g o u v e r n e m e n t p r o v i s o i r e
```

The keyphrase is not a letter-for-letter substitution, but rather a polyphonic one whereby a CIPHERTEXT letter can replace more than one PLAINTEXT letter. In this example, cipher *e* conceals *B*, *G*, *J*, *L*, and *Y*. Cipher *o* masks *D*, *Q*, and *U*, while cipher *r* hides *H*, *P*, and *W*. With *n* replacing *I* and *M* and *i* covering *S* and *V*, there would probably be some ambiguity, even for the intended addressee, which suggests that careful instructions may have accompanied the keyphrase.

The Carbonari of Italy and France apparently used a type of keyphrase for their secret messages. Founded in 1811, this anti-monarchial revolutionary group was named for the charcoal burners among whom they met and from whom they acquired some of their jargon.

Their method was similar to the one Poe described. However, repeated letters were each given separate identities (and thus separate cipher varieties) with numbers. The Italian phrase that translates as *Good evening friends of liberty* could have concealed a dangerous vow as follows:

Alphabet:	a b c d e f g h i j k l m n o p q r s t u v w x y z
Keyphrase:	b u o n a s e r a a m i c i d e l l a l i b e r t à
W/numbers:	b u o n a s e r a^1 a^2 m i c i^1 d e^1 l l^1 a^3 l^2 i^2 b^1 e^2 r^1 t $à^4$
Ciphertext:	l^2 r a o l^1 d e^2 i^1 e^2 a^1 i i u a d i^2 l^1 a^3
Message:	t h e c r o w n w i l l b e o u r s

Keyword, a word used as a KEY for an encryption system. Other keywords are chosen for their own length and lack of repeating letters, ideal examples of which are *blackstone*, *democrat*, *republican*, *absolute*, and *watfoldshire*. These words are then used as bases upon which to build encryptions. The name *watfoldshire* can be used to form a 12-column matrix by which a PLAINTEXT message can be transposed into CIPHERTEXT. This is accomplished by assigning numerals to the letters in sequence according to their positions in the standard English alphabet:

w	a	t	f	o	l	d	s	h	i	r	e
12	1	11	4	8	7	2	10	5	6	9	3
s	h	e	i	s	t	h	e	n	e	w	e
m	p	l	o	y	e	e	w	h	o	i	s
s	t	e	a	l	i	n	g	t	h	e	m
i	c	r	o	c	h	i	p	d	a	t	a
a	t	r	a	p	m	u	s	t	b	e	s
e	t	b	y	i	n	i	t	i	a	t	i
n	g	p	l	a	n	e	l	e	v	e	n

The letters under number 1 can then be read vertically and continued into the column under number 2 and on through the column, under 12 creating the enciphered message in standard groups of five: *hptct*, *tghen*, *iuiee*, and so forth.

Decryption is accomplished with possession of the keyword that gives the order of columns and the size of the matrix in which the letters are placed. By reading from left to right, discernable words begin to appear, such as *she is the new employee. . . .*

Keywords have been an important part of polyalphabetic ciphers for many years. In the early 1780s, MARIE ANTOINETTE and her paramour, Swedish Count Axel Fersen, applied keywords in a method using lists of capital and lower-case letters. The keyword was located among the capitalized letters. In a horizontal line beginning with a capital letter were lower-case pairs that served as plaintext and ciphertext.

KGB Cables, secret cables sent by Soviet agents during World War II. They began as intriguing, seemingly unsolvable transmissions sent between U.S. cities and Moscow in 1944–45. For a time transcriptions and/or copies of these messages languished on paper in a safe at the espionage section of FBI headquarters in Washington, D.C. However, thanks to a clever, hard-working FBI agent and a skilled Army analyst, the CIPHERS were broken and spies were revealed.

The FBI special agent was ROBERT LAMPHERE, an Idaho native who had risen through the ranks with proven ability and a talent for counterespionage work. The Army Security Agency philologist was Meredith Gardner. Gardner had gotten a start on the cables' philologist with the help of a partly burned Russian CODEBOOK found by Allied agents in 1945. While Gardner applied letter FREQUENCY counts and other analytical techniques, Lamphere delved into the FBI's information network, where he found a collection of Soviet cipher material that had been secretly photographed by agents in 1944.

Gardner recognized the basic forms of Soviet ONE-TIME PADS, which should have been totally secure. But USSR intelligence groups had run short on cipher material during World War II and had sent duplicate pads with ADDITIVES to both their Soviet Purchasing Commission and MGB (Ministry of State Security) agents in New York. Furthermore, the fire-singed pages of the 1945 codebook had given Gardner code groups for common radio message terms such as "spell" and "end spell" needed to do letter-by-letter spellings of unusual names or odd words not in a codebook's limited vocabulary.

Gardner began looking for chinks in the armor of five different Soviet global communications systems: ambassadorial; KGB; GRU (military intelligence); naval GRU; and trade traffic (for military equipment shipments). He learned that there were encryption repetitions across some of the channels, indicating that duplicate one-time pads had been used.

The Lamphere–Gardner effort developed into an operation that was given various cover names, including BRIDE and VENONA. The latter was especially used by England's GCHQ (Government Communications Headquarters) after they were informed of the cable decrypts by U.S. authorities. This information-sharing was an extension of a 1943 arrangement that was expanded in 1947 with the pact known as UKUSA.

The GCHQ staff applied Gardner's clues to the KGB cables on a Moscow-to-London channel, of which the following is an example:

Your communication of 48315 and 37282 15361 61527 50359 23813 involving spell majen endspell 35188 49231 78143 95104 83621 complete secrecy when found 61056 92705 34298 47016 spell parwick endspell 27241 59125 weekly until verified.

In the United States, with the solving of ciphers, the FBI's investigative machinery was put into action. News-making arrests and resulting convictions included those of:

1. Judith Coplon (Justice Department employee), who passed documents to contact Valentin Gubitchev (Soviet U.N. mission).
2. Klaus Fuchs (British scientist), who divulged several atomic bomb secrets.
3. Harry Gold (U.S. chemist), who conducted industrial espionage and acted as a courier of atomic bomb secrets.
4. The Rosenberg ring (Julius and Ethel Rosenberg, David Greenglass, and their associates), who were atomic bomb spies.

Investigations of other Soviet agents in the United States led to some lesser convictions as well.

In England, the results were less spectacular, due to infiltration of British intelligence by the Cambridge spy ring and other Soviet agents. U.K. intelligence did have some successes with cable decryptions, however (see GRU and HASP).

Kinsey Code, a CODE developed by U.S. zoologist Alfred Kinsey to protect the identities of his respondents during his pioneering studies of human sexuality. Kinsey developed a code to record their answers. Only four staff personnel were permitted to know the PLAINTEXT of the code, which disguised intimate replies by a combination of abbreviations, Xs, dashes, and checks that were placed in columns. The precautions helped to persuade people to share their thoughts and actions, and Kinsey was able to collect enough material for publication.

Knock Cipher, an audible cipher in which taps or similar noises represent letters.

The originators of this secret communication were inmates who languished behind bars in jails and dungeons throughout the centuries. Whether criminals or prisoners of conscience, they developed an audible method whose visual foundation was a checkerboard such the one below (with *u* and *v* combined):

	1	2	3	4	5
1	a	b	c	d	e
2	f	g	h	i	j
3	k	l	m	n	o
4	p	q	r	s	t
5	uv	w	x	y	z

Beginning with the left-hand column, one tap followed by another would signify *a*, the letter located at 1 across and 1 down. Two taps followed by three was the letter *h*. Thus the knocks or taps, interspersed with pauses, indicated the column and row positions, respectively, of the letters comprising the message.

The system became the basis for more elaborate methods that changed a KEYWORD into numbers and then, by a process of addition, elicited a CIPHERTEXT (see NIHILIST CIPHER).

Kullback, Solomon (1907–), U.S. cryptologist. A native of New York City, Kullback had earned an M.A. in mathematics from Columbia University by 1929. In 1930 he was hired by WILLIAM FRIEDMAN to work for the Signal Intelligence Service (SIS) within the U.S. Army Signal Corps. Having a knowledge of Spanish, he began as a junior cryptanalyst.

During the 1930s, the SIS developed encryption systems for the army, solved foreign cryptomethods, and continued research in cryptologic areas. As the armed forces of Japan and Nazi Germany grew more formidable, greater effort was directed toward their encryption systems. Due to U.S. interests in the Pacific, SIS paid special attention to Japan as its empire expanded in the late 1930s.

Solomon Kullback was one of a group of young cryptanalysts who met the difficult challenges of the Japanese language and cryptosystems (see "J" SERIES and KATA KANA). Others who took on the challenge with William Friedman were FRANK ROWLETT and ABRAHAM SINKOV. These men built upon AGNES DRISCOLL's pioneering foundation of CIPHER MACHINE solving. It was largely Kullback and Rowlett who unraveled a Japanese machine called RED by U.S. analysts. This breakthrough, in turn, was important in the solving of a machine called PURPLE, which was used for Japan's diplomatic traffic. The Friedman team launched an attack on Purple with the help of the U.S. Navy's OP-20-G staff directed by LAURENCE SAFFORD.

Solomon was thus involved in one of the greatest decryption achievements of any era when this top-level diplomatic encryption system was broken in 1940, primarily with the help of a U.S. cipher machine, the Purple Analog. This breakthrough was to affect a number of cryptologic and military actions throughout the course of World War II (see MAGIC and BATTLE OF MIDWAY).

During the war, Solomon directed the SIS cryptanalytic branch. With the U.S. victory in 1945, his employment shifted to the Armed Forces Security Agency. In 1952, when the AFSA became the NATIONAL SECURITY AGENCY, Solomon became chief of its Office of Research and Development. He retired in 1962 and later taught at George Washington University in Washington, D.C., Florida State University, and Stanford in California.

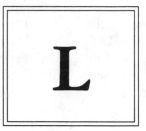

L

Lamphere, Robert (1918–), an FBI agent during World War II who was directly involved in some of the most noteworthy counterespionage cases of the COLD WAR era.

Lamphere had worked with the FBI in Alabama before being transferred to New York City. After investigating violations of the Selective Service Act for three-and-a-half years, he joined the FBI's Soviet Espionage Squad in early 1945. It was here that he played a primary role in the investigation of Gerhart Eisler, an Austrian-born member of Soviet Intelligence who had taken advantage of Russia's wartime alliance with the United Stastes to practice espionage.

By 1947 Robert Lamphere had become a supervisor in the FBI's Espionage Section in Washington, D.C. Here he studied a file of enciphered cables between Mos-

cow and sites in the United States, such as the Soviet consulate in New York City, that had been clandestinely gathered by the FBI in 1944 and 1945 (see KGB CABLES).

Lamphere coordinated CRYPTANALYSIS of these communications by U.S. Army intelligence, and enough of the transmissions were solved to expose Judith Coplin, an employee in the Justice Department. She had had access to documents from the Foreign Agents Registration offices and was providing information to Valentin Gubitchev, a Russian employee of the United Nations. Both were arrested by the FBI and convicted of espionage conspiracy. However, Coplin's 15-year sentence was overturned because of technicalities, and Gubitchev was deported.

Lamphere persevered with the decipherment project and made even more important revelations, including the infiltration of the Manhattan Project by Soviet agent and physicist Klaus Fuchs in 1944. Lamphere and the Espionage Section were able to trace Fuchs to the Rosenberg ring of atomic bomb spies.

Robert Lamphere concluded his FBI employment in 1955. His later work included executive positions with the Veterans Administration and a major insurance company.

Literary Codes and Ciphers, secret communications that have been both described by and incorporated into literature for centuries.

The flourishing Arab culture that expanded across the Mediterranean region in the 7th century had an advanced literature that included poetry, riddles, and imaginative puzzles with concealed terms and phrases. In his classic *Pantagruel* (1532), Renaissance author François Rabelais combined fact and fancy in a humorous description of real and imaginary secret inks. However, it was not until the 1800s and the full development of the novel that message masking and revealing found a permanent place in literature.

In 1843, EDGAR ALLAN POE added his name to the hallowed halls of hidden writing. In his story "The Gold-Bug," the hero, William Legrand, uses heat to expose INVISIBLE INK on a parchment. The ink hides a cryptogram that when solved leads to a fabulous pirate's treasure. Several critics have found flaws in both the overall plot and specific details. However, generations of readers have been captivated by the story's energetic prose and have been challenged to solve the cryptogram. Thus Poe brought an exciting light

to a heretofore murky realm and piqued the curiosity of a growing readership.

Other writers took heed and found their own fortunes in the aura of mystery that enveloped hidden communications and their solution. Jules Verne put hidden messages in his prescient novels. For example, in *Journey to the Center of the Earth* (1864), he used a three-stage cryptogram written in what appears to be characters similar to Scandinavian runes. Eventually, after some clever delays, which produce anticipation for the reader, it is discovered that the writing is actually a reversed Latin text. The decryption reveals the crucial directions leading to the earth's center.

H. Rider Haggard, the author of *King Solomon's Mines* (1885), has a hero solve a cryptogram to find a treasure and true love in the book *Colonel Quaritch, V.C.* (1911). Love also benefits from a specially designed CIPHER solved by Westrell Keen in *The Tracer of Lost Persons* (1906) by Robert Chambers. Faced with a series of rectangles crossed with diagonals and still smaller lines, Keen discovers that the various marks form a type of number system that equates with letters, revealing a message that helps him to bring a couple together.

Sir Arthur Conan Doyle's Sherlock Holmes solves his share of cryptic messages, as befits a sleuth of his vast talents. In "The Adventure of the Red Circle" he is not fooled by an elementary series of signals using flashes of light. Nor does a book CODE puzzle him for long in "The Valley of Fear." From a numerical code, he brilliantly deduces that the text forming its basis is *Whitaker's Almanac*. In the "Adventure of the Dancing Men," dangerous gangster Abe Slaney sends threatening messages by means of stick figures drawn with chalk. These threats are meant for Elsie, wife of an English squire. Holmes discovers the encryptic meaning of the positions of the stickmen's arms and legs, and then sends a missive to Slaney with some of the same figures. Tricked into returning to the squire's country home, Slaney is arrested and confesses.

Twentieth-century fiction has also seen wide use of codes and ciphers. In Ian Fleming's James Bond novel *From Russia with Love*, the *Spektor* CIPHER MACHINE figures in the plot but is not described in detail (see MOVIE CIPHERS AND CODES). A 1960s spy novel entitled *Cipher* (the basis of the movie *Arabesque*) describes a cryptographic method that uses symbols similar to hieroglyphics which actually conceal a form of MICRODOT. An atypical and fascinating cryptographic theme was presented in a 1983 book that depicts a monastic mystery. In *The Name of the Rose* by Umberto Eco, a traveling monk with detective skills solves a secret message, finds hidden passageways, and reveals murder by poison.

Lovell, James (1737–1814), Continental

Congress delegate and cryptologist. A Boston teacher at the outbreak of the Revolutionary War, Lovell had gained his first public notice as an orator. After the battle of Bunker Hill, he was arrested by the British for spying, based on unsubstantiated charges. Sent to Halifax, Nova Scotia, he was exchanged in November 1776 for a British officer.

Becoming a delegate to the Continental Congress, Lovell worked with the Committee on Foreign Affairs. Its espionage-related activity and his personal interest in intrigue apparently brought forth his latent analytical skills in a way that was extremely advantageous for CO-LONIAL CRYPTOLOGY. He was equally skillful in building message shields for the rebels and in solving the English encryptions. From 1777 to 1782 he worked tirelessly for the Foreign Affairs Committee.

One of his primary CIPHERS, involving a combination of letters and numbers, was based on the first two or more letters of a KEYWORD. Under each keyletter, a 27-part alphabet (ending in an ampersand) was compiled. The numbers 1 to 27 were placed in the left margin.

This can be illustrated with the word BRAVELY. The first three letters, *B R A*, are arranged at the top of vertical columns, with 27 letters in sequence from *B* to *A* in the first column, *R* to *Q* in the second, and *A* to *&* in the third, as is partially shown below:

```
 1   B   R   A . . .
 2   C   S   B . . .
 3   D   T   C . . .
 4   E   U   D . . .
 5   F   V   E . . .
 .   .   .   .
 .   .   .   .
 .   .   .   .
24   Y   N   X . . .
25   Z   O   Y . . .
26   &   P   Z . . .
27   A   Q   & . . .
```

Encipherment is accomplished by the following procedure: The letters of the message word are found under the keyletters, beginning with *B*, then *R* and *A* in a cyclical pattern. At the point where the message letters are found, the cipher maker looks to the number in the left margin that is aligned with a given letter. This digit then becomes the cipher for that letter. In the abbreviated version seen above, the letters *D, U,* and *E* happen to align with 3, 4, and 5, respectively. The word *ANY* becomes 27, 24, 25.

Lovell included some particular rules, such as that regarding an unciphered word or phrase. If either of these was used, the cyclical pattern returned to the first key letter of the sequence (*B* in this example) to begin again. Numbers beyond 27 were used as NULLS (also known as *baulks*). A combination of the digits 28 and 29 in regular order at the beginning of a message indicated that the letters were to be encrypted in the standard order; 29 before 28 signaled a reversed order. All these elements combined to make a polyalphabetic cipher.

However convenient and concise Lovell may have considered this and similar methods, his fellow correspondents had numerous problems with them. At various times his encryptions sent to BENJAMIN FRANKLIN and John Adams in Paris led only to confusion for their recipients. Lovell did not encipher every message correctly, and even the erudite Franklin seemed awkward in his attempts at decryption.

In spite of these vexing situations, Lovell persevered at a most opportune time for the colonies. In autumn of 1781, Colonial agents intercepted papers including exchanges between Gen. Charles Cornwallis, who was leading a successful campaign in the Carolinas and Virginia, and his junior officers. Colonial Gen. Nathanael Greene forwarded the intercepts to Congress, and Lovell made some interesting discoveries.

Some of the cryptograms were cloaked in MONOALPHABETIC SUBSTITUTION (that is, masked with a single alphabet). Others combined aspects of single and multiple alphabets, with digits serving as encipherments. Lovell noticed that these styles appeared to be in general use among the enemy commanders. He also discovered that when changes in the cryptomethods occurred, the resulting differences were only ones of position in the same alphabet. He informed Gen. Washington of these findings.

An even more important revelation occurred when a British water-borne courier and his dispatches were captured *en route* from Gen. Henry Clinton in New York City to Lord Cornwallis. By this time Cornwallis had led his army to Yorktown on the Virginia coast to await reinforcements and resupply from New York. Gen. Washington had laid seige to the town. The intercepted dispatches were sent to Lovell who deciphered them and revealed a British plan to relieve Cornwallis by sea.

With this information, Gen. Washington and Adm. de Grasse, his French ally, closed a land and water ring around Yorktown and the Chesapeake Bay. Cornwallis surrendered on October 19, 1781, and when Adm. de Grasse chased the Royal Navy from the area on October 30, the colonial victory was complete.

In 1782 James Lovell left Congress to become a customs collector and later a naval officer in Boston, the cradle of the revolution that he had helped to victory.

M-94, developed in early 1917 by the U.S. Army Signal Corps Engineering and Research Division, a cylindrical cipher device. The officer in charge of this project, Maj. JOSEPH MAUBORGNE, was a personal friend of PARKER HITT, who had created a design for a CIPHER cylinder. Hitt's design became the basis for the M-94.

In 1922 the M-94 was officially accepted for use by the U.S. Army. It was made of aluminum alloy with a 4¼-inch shaft that held 25 disks similar to silver dollars. The assemblage was tightened by a thumb nut at one end of the shaft. Each metal circle had identity markings of letters *b* through *z* and the numbers 1 through 25. The position sequence became the KEY for both the concealment and the solution.

On the edge (rim) of the disks, a varied series of alphabet letters were stamped.

When the disks were rotated, they fulfilled the need for multiple alphabets and thus were part of a polyalphabetic device. After the cipher maker placed the various disks in a predetermined sequence, he revolved them until the first 25 letters of the communication were arranged horizontally. A choice from any of the other rows provided a line of nonsensical letters that became the CIPHERTEXT. This pattern was continued with groups of 25 letters until the entire message was enciphered.

Decryption was accomplished with knowledge of the key arrangements of the disks. Once assembled, the disks were turned until the same line of jumbled ciphertext letters was formed. A glance at the other rows of letters would eventually reveal one that made sense (the intended message).

In a historical context, the M-94 had

precursors in two similar cylinder designs. One was the 20-disk device of French army major ÉTIENNE BAZERIES. Each disk's circumference contained 25 letters, and he called it the "cylindrical cryptograph." Maj. Bazeries presented it to the French Association for the Advancement of Science in 1891, but it was refused by French military officials. Thus his device did not gain acceptance in his native land.

The second mechanism was the very credible "wheel cypher" developed by THOMAS JEFFERSON in the 1790s. It had 36 disks containing 26 alphabet letters each. President Jefferson's description of his creation went unnoticed among his papers until it was discovered at the Library of Congress in 1922. Ironically, this was the same year that the U.S. Army officially accepted the M-94 for its encryption needs.

The M-94 entered a period of widespread use from its inception through the 1930s. With the identification *CSP 488*, it was provided to the Navy in 1927 for message exchanges with the Army. Other applications involved military attachés (1929), naval attachés (1930), and the U.S. Coast Guard (1930).

Advanced electromechanical and electrical cipher inventions, developed to satisfy the increased need for secrecy brought on by World War II, displaced the M-94 by late 1943.

M-138, a CIPHER device that was the brainchild of PARKER HITT, a U.S. Army officer and cryptanalyst. Alarmed by the primitive, virtually unprotected condition of the army's communications, Capt. Hitt developed a hand-operated system of al-

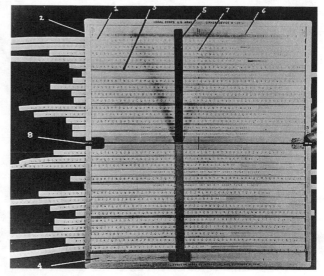

M-138 A strip cipher. (Courtesy of the National Security Agency.)

phabet strips that he introduced to his superiors in 1914.

Hitt based his method on one created around 1890 by the brilliant French army commandant ÉTIENNE BAZERIES, who had made a series of alphabets on disks that were placed on a rod to form a cylinder. Hitt unrolled the disks' letters and placed them on 25 slips of paper in a different arrangement. On each piece, he put mixed alphabets that were repeated twice, and numbered them. Then he arranged these papers in a $7 \times 3\frac{1}{4}$-inch holder.

The strips were not used at random; a KEYNUMBER governed their position in the holder. Encipherment was achieved by moving the strips up or down until the message letters of the first line were aligned horizontally. Then another row of letters was chosen at random as the CI-PHERTEXT. This method was repeated to encrypt the entire communication. The recipient of the message reversed the process once the alphabet slips were arranged according to the keynumber coordinated with the sender. The process became known as the "strip system."

In early 1917, Hitt's friend at the Army Signal School, Maj. JOSEPH MAUBORGNE, made improvements in the device. Mauborgne reintroduced the cylinder form with disks on a rod for the U.S. Army, and gave the alphabets more varied arrangements than did the Hitt original. In 1922 this version became the M-94 and remained in active service until early in World War II.

Another adaptation of the M-138 was the M-138A used by the U.S. Army in the 1930s. It also functioned on the principle of mixed, sliding alphabets. The M-138A had 100 sliding strips with as many as 30 in service at one time. The slides were placed in horizontal grooves in a hinged board, and the grooves were filled with the alphabet slides according to a KEY. Encipherment was accomplished by aligning the PLAINTEXT letters to read vertically in line with an attached guide rule. The ciphertext column was then selected and the guide rule was moved in and placed beside it for easy copying. The process was continued for any additional parts of the message. Decryption involved using the preset key to arrange the strips, then reversing the procedure, to pass from unintelligible letter groups to recognizable words.

The U.S. State Department and Navy were using the M-138A as World War II began. All of these applications from Parker Hitt's idea made it one of the most frequently applied U.S. concealment systems.

M-209, a CIPHER MACHINE used by the U.S. Army and espionage units from World War II through the early 1950s.

The M-209 was originally called the *Hagelin C-48*, after its creator, Swedish entrepreneur BORIS HAGELIN. He had developed it from a series of mechanisms produced at his Stockholm business, *Aktiebolaget Cryptoteknik*, in the 1930s. When the Nazis invaded nearby Norway in 1940, Hagelin and his wife left Stockholm with blueprints and two dismantled cipher machines and made a perilous train journey through Berlin to Genoa, Italy, where they boarded a ship for the United States.

The U.S. Army became interested in the Hagelin device, and after passing a number of tests, the C-48 was given the designation *Converter M-209* and was activated for medium-level cryptographic concealment in military units as large as divisions. The contract with the government made Boris Hagelin a wealthy man. The M-209 also gave U.S. forces better transmission protection than they had had with the majority of World War I–era cryptosystems. However, the M-209 did not have the security of a ONE-TIME PAD, and it had some weaknesses.

The machine was primarily a gearlike mechanism that used varied teeth to move a CIPHER alphabet through multiple positions to achieve POLYALPHABETIC SUBSTITUTIONS. The substitutions were built on a running KEY with a period of $26 \times 25 \times 23 \times 21 \times 19 \times 17$ that was equal to 101,405,850 letters.

The machine's works appeared to be a maze of metal to the casual observer. Yet there were really just a few primary aspects of the mechanism's function:

1. A cylinder (the "cage"), containing 27 horizontal sliding bars. These bars revolved on the cylinder, and each was a sextuplet of 1s and 0s. The 1s were projections, also known as lugs, with two per bar. The lugs could be fixed in two of eight possible positions on the bar (two inoperative and six operative). The bars could be put in positions (1 through 6) that corresponded with six key wheels. When the bars were moved to the left and engaged, they form the cogs (teeth) of a gear with a varied number of teeth.

2. Guide arms (vertical rods controlled by the keywheels). These could be nonoperational or moved into one of six active positions. In an active mode a guide arm contacted lugs as long as the lugs were also in an active position. If either guide arms or lugs on a bar were in an inactive position, no contact would occur. The guide arm was positioned to meet an active lug turned downward by the cage apparatus. The angle of the arm pushed the lug to the left, whereby a tooth was added to the gear. The number of teeth thus engaged set the displacement number (shift in the alphabet sequence) for each encryption.

3. Six-letter KEYWORDS, arranged as an external setting to create a starting point for another major part of the

device called the keywheels. The keywords, made from the letters on the wheels, were varied for each communication and sent along with the transmission to the intended receiver. The beginning position of the wheels was an integral part of a series of encipherment stages.

4. Six keywheels, each of which directed a guide arm and had a varied number of letters on its rim. These letters had no common divisor (such as 17, 21, 25). Projections (pins) on the periphery could be active or inactive, as they indicated a letter on one of the half-dozen keywheels. The total number of pins was 131, with each wheel having 17, 19, 21, 23, 25, and 26.

The keywheel pins could be inactive (0) or active (1). On each wheel was a pin that could affect the encipherment of a letter. Called the current pin, it was one of six such projections, collectively called the current sextuplet. With the encryption of a letter, each wheel moved forward one place, and the next character was enciphered with a new group of inactive and active pins. The first keywheel returned to its starting point after completing 26 such actions, as did the others with their differing numbers of letters and pins. Thus, character by character, the message was concealed, with each PLAINTEXT letter being hidden in an ongoing alphabet displacement.

5. Printing mechanism. A knob on the left-hand side moved an indicator

disk having 26 plaintext characters. The turning of this knob also moved a typewheel that printed the output letters on paper tape. The knob also was connected (through a gear in the typewheel and an intermediate gear) to the ends of the slide-bars that became the teeth of the variable gear. A plaintext character was thereby set for encryption.

Decipherment was very similar to encipherment. The lugs' prearranged key locations and the preset key arrangements for the pins had to be positioned to match those of the sender's mechanism. When the encrypter moved the half-dozen keywheels, the letters on the rims were his indicator. He then placed their arrangement at a planned place in the message to give the recipient the necessary beginning position; otherwise the CIPHERTEXT would be a jumble.

The cipher alphabet was the same as the plaintext, only reversed. With a key displacement of 0, $a = z$, $m = n$, $q = j$, and so forth.

Plaintext: a b c . . . m n o . . . x y z
Ciphertext: z y x . . . n m l . . . c b a

Because the two letter sequences were reversed, the concealment process was reciprocal. As can be seen in the previous example, a was encrypted as z and z as a. During concealment, spaces were placed to section the ciphertext into five-character groups. In deciphering, compensation for the spacing was made by not printing the letter z. The resulting words were complete except for the z, which appeared infrequently anyway.

The M-209 had weaknesses similar to those of ROTOR-based machines. Keywheels might be set close enough to cause message letter overlaps, permitting analysts to compare letters and parts of words. The discovery of similar or matching ciphertexts could lead to plaintext revelations.

Also, the key settings were vulnerable because of the periodic nature of their pins. For example, a mistaken pin setting on the 21-letter keywheel would result in an incorrect letter surfacing every 21 letters and would also have caused the guide arm to initiate other lugs in a chain reaction of mistakes. This knowledge of the machine, algebra equations dealing with known and unknown factors, and trial-and-error displacement sequence arrangements each help the solution solver to find the chink in their armor.

Yet, though deemed to have provided only moderate security, the M-209 proved itself many times under battle conditions around the globe. The M-209 remained sturdy in elements while issuing many millions of enciphered characters. More complex mechanisms and even electrical devices have no better service record.

Madison, James (1751–1836), fourth president of the United States. From the early years of his public service, Madison had first-hand experience with secret writing methods. As a member of the Virginia delegation to the Continental Congress, he used a NOMENCLATOR of about 846 items to send private messages to Governor Benjamin Harrison of Virginia. This system consisted of a list of digits, alphabet letters, syllables, and place names such

as *vienna* (not capitalized in this usage), as in the following excerpt:

27	public	101	rhode island
28	found	112	carolina
29	perhaps	118	america
30	ing	144	britain
42	only	437	§ section
43	farther	764	¶ paragraph
44	at	782	- hyphen
45	ci, cy	846	" quotation

News from the Continental Congress regarding foreign and domestic affairs was conveyed by such means to interested persons in Virginia.

Madison also exchanged coded messages with other members of the Virginia delegation, including Edmund Randolph, as well as with THOMAS JEFFERSON, who went to Paris in 1784 as BENJAMIN FRANKLIN's successor.

When Madison was Secretary of State (1801–1809), he used a 1,700-element nomenclator to correspond with Robert Livingston, who had been chosen in 1801 as minister plenipotentiary to France. More than 40 communiqués were encoded in the style exemplified here:

118	could	551	place
119	council	552	plai
120	count	553	plan
121	country	554	play
302	monarch	689	with
303	monday	690	within
304	money	691	without
305	month	692	wn

The method had many number/word combinations, but the alphabetical organization weakened its masking potential. U.S. representatives had not kept pace with the advances in CRYPTOGRAPHY that were being achieved by other nations.

By 1803, when the United States was negotiating with France for the Louisiana Territory, Madison communicated with his representatives James Monroe and Robert Livingston using a new CODE of some 1,600 parts that came to be called the "Monroe Cypher." It still had general nomenclator characteristics, and its 1,600 elements were still arranged alphabetically:

118	consider	551	those
119	constitu	552	thought
120	consul	553	thousand
121	cont	554	thr
302	fa	689	arp
303	fab	690	art
304	fac	691	ary
305	fact	692	as

No attempts to intercept or solve these methods were recorded. With patience and skill, Madison and the others successfully negotiated the Louisiana Purchase, doubling the size of territory in the United States.

Magdeburg, a German light cruiser of World War I, source of an important CODE.

In September 1914, the *Magdeburg* ran aground in the Baltic Sea. Its commanding officer tried to scuttle the ship with explosive charges to prevent capture, but these were only partially successful. When the

Russian Navy closed in on the scene, they found at least one, and possibly two, *Kriegsmarine's* codebooks in the chart-house and passed this data to the British Admiralty.

The text was not solved immediately. But steady effort by a group of inexperienced analysts (known as ROOM 40, after their location in the Admiralty Building) eventually led to the breaking of Germany's naval cryptomethods. Additional cryptographic material was obtained from sunken U-boats. As solutions increased, the Room 40 staff were able to reveal German diplomatic communiqués as well.

The *Magdeburg* decryptions were to have direct effects in naval engagements such as the BATTLE OF DOGGER BANK and the BATTLE OF JUTLAND. Even more crucial was the Room 40 decryption of the ZIMMERMANN TELEGRAM and its secret plan to give U.S. territory to Mexico in exchange for that nation's entry into the war. The revelation stunned the United States and tipped the divided Congress toward a declaration of war in 1917.

Magic, the COMPARTMENTATION CODE designation given to intercepts of Japan's diplomatic messages solved by U.S. cryptanalysts in 1940.

The solutions were achieved by groups called SIS and OP-20-G in Washington, D.C. (later the SIS moved to quarters in Arlington, Virginia). WILLIAM FRIEDMAN and his staff at the Signal Intelligence Service were part of a branch of the U.S. Army and OP-20-G was a section of U.S. Navy intelligence directed by LAURENCE SAFFORD. One of these two groups' greatest achievements was the analog mechanism built to decrypt Tokyo's PURPLE diplomatic messages which had become operational in February of 1939 (see ALPHABETIC TYPEWRITER 97). After an extraordinary pencil-and-graph-paper effort to chip away at the shield, one of Friedman's civilian technicians, Leo Rosen, had the breakthrough realization that telephone selector switches could help enhance tests of decryption techniques. This gave rise to a different way of viewing the entire problem of electrical connections and processes, and a month later, in August 1940, Friedman and his associates had drawn up a blueprint for their own analog mechanism. The first working device was a maze of wires and clicking relays built by Rosen at a cost of $685. By the latter weeks of autumn 1940, U.S. analysts were using the Purple Analog to decrypt Japan's secret diplomatic communiqués.

Friedman's own nickname for his staff was "magicians." As military people began to see the decryptions produced by their creation, the word *Magic* became more broadly applied to other cryptographically produced intelligence. Yet as U.S. differences with Japan escalated, the dissemination of the Magic decrypts became a point of divisive and lasting controversy. The information was made available to President Roosevelt, some of his cabinet members, and high-ranking military officers. However, a few of these officers chose not to distribute parts of this intelligence to distant outposts. Declassified documents later revealed that two such base commanders were Adm. Husband Kimmel and Gen. Walter Short at Pearl Harbor. In the wake of that disaster, better analysis and distribution of the Magic and similar information became standard procedure.

Maria Theresa (1717–1780), Austrian empress and supporter of CRYPTOLOGY. Queen of Hungary and Bohemia and archduchess of Austria, she was an active and innovative monarch.

As a hub of European commerce, Vienna was a center for diplomacy and mail transfer, and the empress was not at all averse to meeting with the directors of Vienna's expert postal interceptors, the GEHEIME KABINETS-KANZLEI. However, her real contribution lay in her support of the chamber employees and her appreciation of their work. Financial rewards, career advancement, and honors were freely bestowed upon talented cryptanalysts. Maria is said to have been knowledgeable enough about cryptographic practices to have advised Austria's envoys to change their NOMENCLATORS and encryption KEYS lest they be overused and thus vulnerable to other skilled practitioners.

Maria Theresa made a myth of the pretty but frivolous crowned head cliché. With her shrewd foresight, she was ahead of her time.

Marie Antoinette (1755–1793), queen of France from 1774 until her death by guillotine. Often described as a foolish, giddy squanderer, this queen of French king Louis XVI is nevertheless credited with sending some rather cleverly enciphered missives.

Her mother, Empress MARIA THERESA of Austria, had a keen interest in secret correspondence, and this seems to have influenced Marie, who used one CIPHER similar to that of GIOVANNI PORTA and one based on a popular novel. Concealment took on added importance for her *billets-doux*.

Many of Marie's amatory notes were intended for Count Hans Axel Fersen. This handsome Swede, a hero of the American Revolutionary War, was her lover and cryptographic advisor. When unrest in France boiled into revolution against the Bourbon regime, Marie dispatched letters requesting help from monarchist relatives and friends throughout Europe. Axel provided a concealment system for a number of these letters; it was a POLYALPHABETIC SUBSTITUTION with KEYWORDS. The keyword letters were in capitals aligned in columns. The PLAINTEXT and CIPHERTEXT letters were placed in pairs horizontally alongside the capitals in an arrangement similar to this:

M kn or sv wz ad eh il mp qt ux yb cf gj

N ab cd ef gh ij kl mn op qr st uv wx yz

O pr su vx ya bd eg hj km np qs tu wy zb

Suppose the KEY *M* (for Marie) is chosen to hide the word *SAY*. According to the pairs, *s = v*, *a = d*, and *y = b*. *SAY* becomes *vdb*. If key *N* is used, *s* is replaced by *t*, *a* by *b*, and *y* by *z*. With this key, *SAY* is *tbz*.

In spite her clever efforts, Marie and King Louis XVI met their fate in the Reign of Terror. Though he escaped the anarchy of Paris, Axel Fersen was falsely accused of poisoning Sweden's crown prince and murdered by a Stockholm mob in 1810.

Maru Code, Name for Japanese supply ships' CODE during World War II.

Before the outbreak of the war, Allied listening posts and cryptanalysts had concentrated on the Imperial armed forces' cryptosystems and the Japanese government's diplomatic concealments. Once a number of these were revealed, the same teams turned their attention to the supply vessels that were vital to continuing a major conflict.

The *maru*s used a four-number code called the *S Code*. From 1942 through early 1943, the five-month effort to break this system was accomplished by the Station Hypo intelligence team based in Hawaii. Knowledge of the code enabled the Pacific Fleet intelligence center to track Japanese convoy routes from their position reports, made on a precise basis at regular time intervals. By 1943 the unmasked communications were providing a wealth of information, including timetables, routes, and destinations of the *maru* convoys. With this knowledge, along with improved submarine tactics and better torpedoes, the rate of *maru* sinkings increased substantially. As of January 1944, U.S. subs were destroying enemy merchant ships at a rate of almost 330,000 tons a month. By 1945 over 8.5 million tons had been relegated to the deep, helping to hasten the end of World War II.

Mary, Queen of Scots (1542–1587),
Mary Stuart, queen of Scotland from 1542 through 1567. The star-crossed life of Mary Stuart has been the subject of debate over the centuries. A frequently studied and romanticized figure, she became the victim of a series of devious intrigues that included CIPHER messages.

As the cousin of the childless Elizabeth I, Mary was the direct heir to the throne of England. After the death of one husband, the murder of a second, and the flight of a third, Mary was forced by influential no-

bles to leave Scotland. When she sought protection from her Protestant cousin, the Catholic Mary found herself in ever closer custody that became imprisonment.

One individual who feared Mary's Catholic supporters in England was Sir Francis Walsingham, Queen Elizabeth's secretary of state and a master of intrigue. Sir Francis was kept aware of real and rumored plots to overthrow Elizabeth through his highly efficient personal spy system. Eventually deciding that Mary was too dangerous to be allowed to live, he endeavored to implicate her in a scheme whereby she could be convicted of a high crime and executed. The result of his intricate maneuvering with CRYTOLOGY expert Thomas Phelippes came to be known as the Babington plot.

The 1586 conspiracy was named for a primary participant, Anthony Babington, a wealthy Catholic squire from Derbyshire. He and his friends, including a priest named Ballard, sought overseas support from France and Spain for a scheme that would free Mary and perhaps assassinate Elizabeth. The latter aspect of the plan has been questioned by some historians. It may have been a part of Walsingham's provocations inserted by his own people in the plot. What is certain is that Gilbert Gifford, a confidant of the conspirators, was also a double agent acting for Sir Francis.

Gifford was an expert linguist who had once trained for the priesthood. As Walsingham's *agent provocateur*, he interrupted Mary's correspondence from Chartley Hall, her current place of confinement. With a sympathetic brewer acting as courier, the messages had been wrapped in leather and then placed in a corked tube in the stoppers of beer casks (a form of STEGANOGRAPHY). Gifford helped to exchange these packets and made sure that cryptanalyst Phelippes had a chance to decipher them. The encryptions of the Scots queen, an obvious mixture of Greek letters, numerals, and SYMBOL CRYPTOGRAPHY, were no challenge for the clever Phelippes.

In a fateful letter of July 14, 1586, Babington sent details of the conspiracy to Mary. On July 17, she replied in cautious agreement and in so doing clearly implicated herself. As an added strike against the plotters, Walsingham apparently had Phelippes pen a CIPHER postscript on the letter making it appear that Mary sought the names of the six would-be assassins of Queen Elizabeth. Babington and the other conspirators were arrested, forced to confess, and were gruesomely executed. In a separate trial, the evidence of the cipher missives also weighed heavily against Mary, and she was found guilty of high treason. On February 8, 1587, at Fotheringhay Castle, she was beheaded.

Mata Hari (1876–1917), World War I spy for Germany who was captured through wireless intercepts and CRYPTANALYSIS.

Margaretha Gertrude Zelle was a Dutch woman of only average attractiveness. As Mata Hari ("Eye of the Dawn"), she had spiced her stage act with exotic costumes and choreography reputedly adapted from Javanese and Indian temple dances. When World War I broke out she was recruited by Germany as a secret agent operating in Spain and France. She was given some professional training that included the use of INVISIBLE INKS.

Curiously, in spite of her legendary reputation, espionage histories give mixed accounts of Mata Hari's specific successes. (This is in sharp contrast to the highly successful work of "Cynthia" [Amy Thorpe], who helped obtain important CODEBOOKS for the Allies during World War II.) Mata Hari's efforts on behalf of the Kaiser involved her designation as agent *H-21* with activities in France and Spain that included affairs with influential men. During December 1916, the German naval attaché in Madrid sent radio communiqués to Berlin requesting money and new orders for Agent H-21.

By this time, England's ROOM 40 staff had deciphered wireless intercepts along the Madrid–Berlin connection. They had exchanged their knowledge with their Triple Entente allies, the French, who applied this information and uncovered a SUPERENCIPHERMENT. The DECIPHERED transmissions included those involving agent H-21.

Later arrested in France and confronted with evidence of the financial requests made on her behalf, Mata Hari claimed these were payments from her paramours. She was convicted nevertheless and sentenced to death. Though a debatably successful spy, Gertrude Zelle was, by all accounts, a courageous woman. She refused a blindfold and bravely faced a firing squad near Vincennes, France, in October 1917.

Mauborgne, Joseph (1874–1971), U.S. army general and cryptologist. Joseph Mauborgne's early claim to cryptanalytic achievement derived from his solving a PLAYFAIR CIPHER in 1914. At that time

Joseph Mauborgne. (Courtesy of the National Archives.)

this encryption method (actually created by Englishman Charles Wheatstone) was considered a difficult one, and Mauborgne is credited with the first documented third-party solution of this standard British army field CIPHER. He further enhanced his reputation in cryptologic circles by writing a 19-page booklet in 1914 about the procedures he used, *An Advanced Problem in Cryptography and its Solution*, the first such material published by the U.S. government.

One of his primary contributions to CRYPTOGRAPHY was his important im-

provement in the security method devised by AT&T engineer GILBERT VERNAM. According to historian David Kahn (*The Codebreakers*, 1967) Mauborgne saw a weakness in the Vernam security system, which used the BAUDOT CODE and paper tapes of different lengths to encipher messages on the printing telegraph (teletypewriter).

Mauborgne saw that heavy use of the system might bring about repetition of the chosen KEYS even though two loops of tape were used. This repetition in turn might make the cipher susceptible to analysis by superimposition (see AUGUSTE KERCKHOFFS). Mauborgne eliminated the possibility of repetition by combining the random key of Vernam's tape system with the nonrepeating key developed by the Army Signal Corps. The combination was called the "one-time system," and barring an accidental repetition, the method was considered unsolvable (see UNBREAKABLE CIPHERS).

His second major achievement was in his role as chief signal officer for the U.S. Army Signal Corps. As a major general, in 1937, he promoted an increased interest in and funding for U.S. cryptographic efforts. He arranged for the Signal Intelligence Service to have more training, staff, and eavesdropping stations, a difficult task during the Depression. From a few dozen often undecipherable intercepts, the amount of usable decrypted data increased manyfold under Mauborgne's careful leadership. In this regard he also deserves special credit for his encouragement and support of WILLIAM FRIEDMAN, a master analyst. It was Friedman, SIS staffers, and Navy OP-20-G members who made the crucial attack on the top-level Japanese diplomatic encryptions named PURPLE by U.S. experts. Though Mauborgne retired in autumn 1941, his legacy served the United States well through World War II and beyond.

Microdots, miniature copies of documents used for the secret transmission of information. They were "the enemy's masterpiece of espionage" according to FBI director J. Edgar Hoover. In January 1940, the FBI received its first warning of the dots' existence and it was not until August of 1941 that an example was sighted, when a lab technician happened to notice a glint of light on an envelope that had been taken from a suspected German agent. The gleam came from a microdot masquerading as a typewritten period.

The product of German science, the microdot was developed by the following series of steps: A secret communication was photographed and printed no larger than a postage stamp. This in turn was photographed with a reversed microscope, reducing the image to .05 inches in diameter. After the negative was developed, a hypodermic needle was used to raise the microdot from the photographic emulsion. Finally, the dot was inserted into an innocent-looking text in place of a period or dot where it was held with an adhesive substance such as collodion. A number of the "dots" were made in very small film squares as the system progressed.

This technology improved to the point where the process could be performed in a trunk-sized device. Additional advances enabled the image to be fixed but not developed. This kept the film clear and less noticeable on shiny surfaces such as the gummed edges of envelopes. Soon these improvements enabled Nazi spy rings to hide greater numbers of dots in telegrams and letters and minute film strips under postage stamps.

Alerted by a warning from a double agent in 1940, Allied postal censors, lab technicians, and counterespionage agents combined their talents to break Nazi spy rings, succeeding even where the microdot messages were encrypted as well as reduced and concealed.

After the end of the war in 1945, microdots were used widely by Soviet agents operating worldwide, including Rudolph Abel, who relied on them in the 1950s to back up his radio message encipherments while doing espionage work in the New York City area. Abel made microdots by reducing 35-millimeter film negatives with a lens of a short focal length. After preparing the dots, he placed them in the loosened binding of U.S. magazines and then sent these innocent-looking issues to a general delivery address in Paris.

Because of German and Soviet successes with microdots, this method, as well as microfilm strips, was widely used in novel and movie plots (see LITERARY CODES AND CIPHERS, MOVIE CIPHERS AND CODES).

Midway, Battle of, pivotal battle fought in June 1942 between U.S. and Japanese navies, that validated the importance of signals intelligence for the U.S. armed forces. The confrontation itself proved to be one of the most amazing reversals in the annals of military history.

Even as U.S. and Japanese ships were fighting in the Coral Sea near Australia in May 1942, the Imperial General Headquarters in Tokyo issued Navy Order No. 18, setting in motion Operation MI, the invasion of Midway Island and the occupation of points in the western Aleutian Islands. The Japanese strategy was to destroy the U.S. Navy in a decisive engagement, thus forcing the United States to a peace conference to end the Pacific conflict.

However, by this point the U.S. had broken the Japanese fleet's cryptographic system (labeled the JN25). The designating letters *AF* were discovered among parts of the revealed messages. Such letters were important because the Japanese had been giving the coordinates of their geographic locations in a CODE called the *Chi-he* system. Previous clues had been pieced together to interpret some of these letter pairs. For example, *AK* was believed to be Pearl Harbor, while *AG* was Johnston Island (located 500 miles to the southwest of the Hawaiian Islands). There was a strong indication that *AF* was Midway.

Commander Joseph Rochefort and the Station Hypo team in Hawaii put the final pieces together in May, when they found the decrypted words *koryaku butai* ("invasion force") followed by the designator *AF*. Also, the Japanese Second Fleet command had sent messages to its air units about advancing landing-base equipment and ground crews to AF.

For still more verification, Rochefort created a scheme with fleet intelligence officer Edwin Layton and Lt. Comdr. Jasper Holmes. The Midway headquarters was told to transmit a plain-language message that its fresh-water distillation plant was incapacitated, in the hope that this CLEARTEXT would be heard by Japanese listening posts. Within days, the Japanese response was overheard and decrypted, showing AF being used as Midway's location code.

Thus forewarned, Adm. Chester Nimitz and his staff reacted with an imaginative plan. Task Force 16, commanded by Rear Adm. Raymond Spruance, was made up of the carriers *Enterprise* and *Hornet*, supported by five heavy cruisers, one light cruiser, and nine destroyers. On May 28, this force sailed for a location named Point Luck, 350 miles northeast of Midway Island. At the same time, a radio deception plan was initiated, involving the seaplane tender *Tangier* at Efate in the New Hebrides and the heavy cruiser *Salt Lake City* in the Coral Sea. These ships sent radio signals in patterns similar to carrier task forces conducting typical air operations, and it was hoped that Japanese traffic analysts would therefore believe that U.S. carriers were far from the Midway region.

While this radio fog screen continued, Task Force 17 steamed toward Point Luck. Commanded by Rear Adm. Frank Jack Fletcher, it consisted of the repaired carrier *Yorktown* (damaged at the BATTLE OF THE CORAL SEA), two heavy cruisers, and six destroyers.

The Imperial Navy squadrons opposing them were massive but spread out from the Marianas Islands to the Aleutians. For example, planes from two carriers of the Northern Area Force were to attack Dutch Harbor in Unalaska, which was to be followed by the occupation of the western Aleutian Islands of Attu and Kiska. The next day, Midway would then be bombed by planes from four carriers of Adm. Chuichi Nagumo's *Kido Butai* (mobile strike force): the *Akagi, Hiryu, Kaga*, and *Soryu*. The following day, Second Fleet transports would send troops ashore to occupy the strategic island. Three hundred miles to the west, Adm. Isoroko Yamamoto (on the Combined Fleet Flagship *Yamato*), with two other battleships, a small carrier, and support vessels, awaited the expected Pacific Fleet counterattack from Hawaii.

Before the battle began, the Japanese initiated a long-expected change in the JN25 naval operational cryptosystem. By May 28 they had switched to a new version that was not immediately decipherable to the Allies. However, the change had come too late to hide the plans for Midway. The American fleet intercepted the Japanese force, and the resulting battle, which occurred from June 3 to 6, 1942, was a stunning defeat for Japan, as seen in the following totals:

	U.S.	Japan
Personnel	347	2,500
Aircraft	147	322
Carriers	1	4
Support Vessels	1 (destroyer)	1 (cruiser)

Beyond the tonnage and men lost, the Imperial Navy suffered a severe psychological setback. Its vaunted position as ruler of the Pacific waves was swept away in those early June days, never to be regained.

Mind Reading, a form of entertainment that applies cryptomethods in its presentation. Mind readers and their assistants communicate with a variety of CODES, including physical actions, number–word combinations, and CODEWORDS.

Body positions, especially of the head and arms, are sometimes used to convey prearranged signals between the mind reader and the assistant. Even putting weight on one leg, shrugging, or leaning to one side could convey a meaning to the mentalist. The head positions used in a "glance" code are especially useful for passing silent messages in the midst of company. There are 12 clear directions in which one can be seen to glance without looking straight ahead: With the head in each of three positions, lowered, level, or raised, one may look to the extreme right, slightly to the right, slightly to the left, or to the extreme left.

These positions can represent letters, numbers, or words. For example, the first 12 letters of the alphabet, *a* through *l*, can be indicated by performing the 12 head positions with the eyes partially shut. The second group of 12 letters, *m* through *x*, can be represented by the same positions with the eyes fully open. A straight-on glance with slightly closed lids can be *y*, and the same position with eyes closed, *z*. Double letters can be shown by blinking, and a steady, straight-ahead look can signify that the message is concluded. The same pattern of head movements can be used to convey words or numbers.

Mind reading number/word codes are memorized by the mentalist and his or her assistant before a performance in order to imbed messages in apparently innocent dialogue with the audience and each other. Here is a sample list of codewords and their numerial equivalents:

1	give	6	show
2	look	7	move
3	rapidly	8	stop
4	speak	9	answer
5	now	10	please

An extra word such as *next* could indicate "repeat." The performers may also extend their code to numbers that represent letters: 1 = *a*, 2 = *b*, 3 = *c*, and so forth.

When the blindfolded mind reader is asked to determine the value of a playing card, for example, the medium might say, "*Give* me this object *rapidly. Now* tell me, oh wise one." The three italicized key words indicate the numbers 1, 3, and 5. These in turn are matched with the letters *a*, *c*, and *e*, which spell the value of the card in question. The particular suit could be revealed in the same way. Of course, the partner does not specifically emphasize the clue words.

Code number and word lists can be extended to include common items that audience members might normally possess, such as purses, keys, wallets, and money. For instance, the number seven could be chosen to represent a dollar bill, 71 could be a 10-dollar bill, 75 a five, and 77 a 20. This same type of system can also be used for the names of people, places, and events. Experienced secret communicators can make the apparent probing of others' minds seem all too real.

Monoalphabetic Substitution, a cryptomethod in which a single CIPHER al-

phabet is used to conceal the letters of a PLAINTEXT communication.

Plaintext: a b c . . . m . . . z
Ciphertext: b c d . . . n . . . a

The equivalent letters remain an alphabet even if their order is jumbled.

Plaintext: a b c . . . m . . . z
Ciphertext: w l x . . . q . . . h

At times a single alphabet can supply several substitutes for a letter. For example, plaintext *v* could be represented by a number such as 7 or by a series of numerals such as 21, 28, 36, and 46. Such replacements are called homophones because, though they are a plural set in order to increase concealment complexity, they replace only *v*, not any other alphabet characters. Also, a monoalphabet can use SYMBOL CRYPTOGRAPHY, whereby special art or characters can serve as alternates. Designs, letters, and numerals that signify nothing but are included to puzzle potential interceptors are called NULLS.

Symbols, characters, and similar factors are also used in multialphabet systems. But when two or more lists of equivalents are applied to hide the plaintext, the method is described as being polyalphabetic (see POLYALPHABETIC SUBSTITUTION).

One-alphabet ciphers are often called simple SUBSTITUTION ciphers and the alphabet a substitution alphabet. An ancient example of this basic form was the CAESAR SUBSTITUTION, in which (expressed in modern English) the letter *a* was represented by *d*, *b* by *e*, and so forth, in a pattern of displacement by three alphabet spaces.

Monoalphabetic substitution was also found in Renaissance CIPHER DISKS, on which the engraved or printed letters, numerals, or symbols on an inner ring were aligned with those on an outer one. As LEON BATTISTA ALBERTI showed, once letters and numerals had their alignments changed within a given encryption procedure, new alphabets were activated and the method became polyalphabetic. The early NOMENCLATORS of the Italian city-states also had monoalphabetic letter substitutions in their cipher sections. The nomenclators combined this form with a CODE-like list of words, name alternatives, and syllables.

Morse Code, a CODE of dots and dashes that facilitated telegraph and radio communications. Samuel Finley Breese Morse's early electromagnetic telegraph device underwent a series of developmental stages, and so did the methods for the messages sent on it. An early model had 10 symbols denoting 10 numerals; Morse created a vocabulary of numbered words in order to send phrases with these digits. Later, this style was replaced by the familiar dash-and-dot code that proved to be far more practical. In 1851, as the use of the telegraph spread, a convention of nations met and agreed upon an International Morse code (with some variations), an example of which appears below.

Soon thereafter, a number of *word lists* appeared, with such titles as *Telegraph Dictionary* or *Secret Corresponding Vocabulary*, to help businessmen improve the economy of their telegraph messages.

During the U.S. CIVIL WAR, Morse code

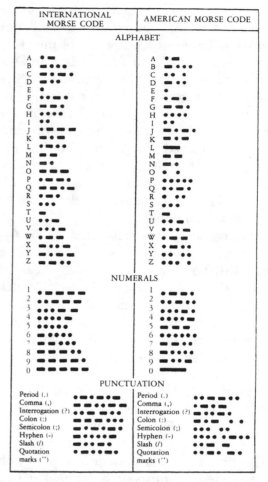

Morse code. (Reprinted with permission of *Encyclopedia Americana,* 1990 edition, Grolier, Inc.)

was used to transmit encrypted military dispatches by telegraph. Later, during World War I, the code's dots and dashes were used to send secret transmissions via wireless.

Movie Ciphers and Codes, crypto-methods as depicted in film.

Over the years, CODES and CIPHERS have figured into the plots of a number of movies. Three early instances of this were *Dishonored* (1931), in which Marlene Dietrich played a spy whose music carried a secret message; the 1942 serialized melodrama *The Secret Code*; and *Murder on the Blackboard* (1934), in which a code of musical notes named a murderer. Yet like the plots of RADIO SERIALS, these movies focused more on action and last-minute escapes than on concealment processes or solution techniques.

A cryptanalyst was featured in *Rendezvous* (1935), which was based on a book entitled *The Blonde Countess* by real-life code and cipher expert HERBERT YARDLEY (this particular cipher solver was dissatisfied with his office assignment and yearned to see battle). The important work of CRYPTANALYSIS was yet to receive its due.

Sherlock Holmes and the Secret Weapon (1942) was an improvement on this state of affairs in that, in this film, greater emphasis was placed on hidden messages. The famous sleuth became involved with threatened scientists, a bombsight device (the secret weapon), and a code using stick figures (reminiscent of Holmes' case "The Adventure of the Dancing Men"). (In an interesting example of fact mirroring fiction, the United States' own Norden bombsight was actually stolen in 1937 by Nazi agents, one of whom hid blueprints rolled up in an umbrella and successfully smuggled them aboard an ocean liner sailing for Germany.)

Many other wartime movies featured codes or secret signals of some type; among these were *Night Train to Munich* (1940), *The Saint's Vacation* (1941), *Powder Town* (1942), and *Ministry of Fear* (1945). However, in these films, the concealment methods were rarely described in detail. In 1945 the fine semidocumentary *The House on 92d Street* did depict a cryptographic alphabet table similar to that associated with BLAISE DE VIGENÈRE, which was used by fictional Nazi agents, whose schemes were successfully foiled by FBI counterintelligence.

Codes and ciphers became more numerous in 1960s spy movies, such as the James Bond series. Along with their sophisticated science fiction–type gadgetry, the Bond films also employed encryption devices or methods, with varying degrees of detail:

From Russia With Love (1964)—The *Spektor* CIPHER MACHINE was one of Bond's objectives.

Diamonds Are Forever (1971)—A coded cassette tape controlled ground-based equipment that in turn operated a satellite with a powerful laser.

For Your Eyes Only (1981)—The *St. Georges*, a British platform for sea-based signals intelligence, was sunk by a mine off the coast of Albania. An on-board code transmitter became a search objective.

Never Say Never Again (1983)—Highjacked cruise missiles with atomic armaments that had to be deactivated by a series of numbers revealed in a solved encryption.

Two other films about different characters are noteworthy here as well:

Sebastian (1967)—This remains one of the few celluloid dramas devoted almost entirely to an encryption solver's life. Unlike Yardley's discontented hero, Sebastian was a debonair gentleman who was quite comfortable with COMPUTERS and was fascinated with word and number puzzles. Cryptographic terms were mentioned frequently, and a primary goal was to solve some intercepts of Soviet satellite communications.

The Amateur (1983)—A CIA cryptologist seeks terrorists. In his spare time he tried to solve a cipher that was similar to a cryptomethod of SIR FRANCIS BACON.

Murray Code, one of two noteworthy communications methods involving CRYPTOGRAPHY that have had the name Murray. The first was a series of CODES designed by William Vans Murray in the late 1700s; the second was a telegraphic code developed by Donald Murray in 1903.

William Vans Murray was a Federalist member of Congress from Maryland. A statesman concerned with the status of the United States in the world, in 1797, he was appointed U.S. Minister Resident to the Batavian Republic, which had been established by France in 1795. Thus William Murray served at a crucial period in relations between France and the United States (see XYZ AFFAIR).

At the time of his appointment, he had been given a code using nonsequential digits with mixed words and syllables. Thirteen of the numbers had two of these code elements; for example, 12 could mean either *1* or *-lation* as an attempt to have better concealments. In The Hague for important negotiations with the French, Murray felt the need for a more

William Vans Murray, by Mather Brown. (Courtesy of the Andrew W. Mellon Collection, the National Gallery of Art, Washington, D.C.)

secure means of covering his communications. He therefore enlarged this code to include terms needed specifically for the negotiations, such as 2008 for *Jacobin*, 2063 for *Talleyrand*, and 2042 for *Neufchateau*. At this same time, Murray created the secret symbols in an 11-element code.

Murray's caution was well founded, as skilled British agents did manage to intercept some of the U.S. messages and DECODE them. But he and his associates, including John Quincy Adams, did not use only one encryption system; they used a NOMENCLATOR believed to be made up of some 1,600 elements, with digits such as 536 for *the* and 1092 for *they*. Near the end of 1798, Adams sent Murray a type of strip CIPHER whereby different alphabets were aligned with each other. This cipher concealed messages about the sale of a Swedish island, a speech by England's king, the actions of the Holy Roman Emperor in Vienna, and a treaty dispute involving Austria. Thanks in part to the efforts of William Vans Murray, U.S. differences with France were resolved and the standing of the United States among other nations was measureably improved.

The other Murray code involved inventor Donald Murray, who around 1901 developed an improved communications method for the British post office that was an adaptation of the BAUDOT CODE for teleprinters. The Baudot process involved a device that made marks (holes) and spaces in paper tape that corresponded to alphabet letters, numerals, and keyboard functions. Murray studied the Baudot system and streamlined it by assigning the combinations with the fewest holes to the alphabet letters and keyboard functions used most often in telegrams. Murray also introduced a "start" signal element at the beginning of each letter and a "stop" signal at its conclusion for improved transmission process. To overcome transmission garbles, a seven-unit error-detecting code was used on busy circuits; an error could be detected when this 3-mark-and-4-space sequence was altered by a mistake.

To send a telegraphed message with this Murray code, the operator typed on a keyboard. When each key was depressed, five long bars moved to form the code for that letter. Spaces occurred when the bars were held in their places by tabs located on the letter keybar. Marks resulted when the bars moved to the left and protruded beyond the space bars. The extended bars closed electrical switches, which sent current through the line as a mechanism called a rotating cam linked a battery to each of the bars in their turn.

At the recipient's teletype, each mark caused an electromagnet to depress one of five bars and thus form the five-unit code that represented each of the arriving characters in turn. The depressed bars (marks) and unmoved bars (spaces) caused a corresponding cut latch to drop and stop a turning typehead. The back of the character was then hit with a hammer mechanism that printed the letter on paper.

The Donald Murray code was improved with duplex, multiplex, and time-division systems whereby messages moved in different directions and time intervals on the transmission circuit. Thus Emile Baudot and Donald Murray's five-unit code proved adaptable even to the modern era of alternate-current signaling and frequency-division techniques.

Myer, Albert (1829–1880), U.S. Army surgeon and cryptographer. To finance his medical studies, Myer worked as an operator for the New York, Albany, and Buffalo Telegraph Company. After entering the army, he developed a visual signaling method in 1856 and called it flag telegraphy. (Two British officers, Sir Francis Bolton and Vice Adm. Philip Colomb, independently developed a similar system at about the same time.) Though it was approved for use in 1860, the year Myer became chief signal officer, the system was not fully appreciated until the outbreak of the U.S. CIVIL WAR in 1861. Myer's technique then came to be known as "wigwag," from the motions of its hand-held flags or disks for daytime signaling and torches or lanterns for sending messages at night.

In this code, alphabet letters were equated with three positions of the flag, disk, or torch. The flags measured two, four, or six feet square and were generally either red or black banners with white square centers or white banners with red square centers. The disks were 12 to 18 inches in diameter and were made of metal or wood frames with canvas surfaces. Somewhat easier to handle than the flags, they provided a different method for daylight communications. Each torch was a metal cannister filled with a flammable liquid attached to a staff. A second "foot torch" was placed on the ground before the signalman as a fixed point of reference, making it easier for the recipient to follow the torch's movements.

Each letter consisted of a combination of three basic motions. All began with the flagman holding his device vertically and motionless above his head. The first motion was initiated by bringing the device downward on the signalman's right side and then quickly returning it to its upright position. Motion number 2 involved bringing the device down on the left side and then returning it to the starting position. The third motion required lowering the device in front of the signalman, then restoring it to its vertical position.

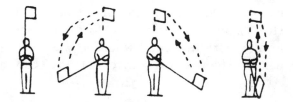

Flag telegraphy. (Courtesy of Crown Publishers, Inc.)

The chart below indicates how letters and directions were conveyed. For example, *a* (112) would be signaled by motion 1, motion 1, and motion 2 in rapid succession. The periods signified a written pause in a sequence of movements. In action, this was also a pause, unless concluding the message.

a—112	h— 312	o—223	v— 222
b—121	i— 213	p—313	w— 311
c—211	j— 232	q—131	x— 321
d—212	k— 323	r—331	y— 111
e—221	l— 231	s—332	z— 113
f— 122	m—132	t— 133	
g—123	n— 322	u—233	

MYER'S SIGNAL DIRECTIONS

3—End of a word

33—End of a sentence

333—End of a message

22.22.22.3—Signal of assent: "I understand," or general affirmative

22.22.22.333—Cease signaling

121.121.121.3—Repeat

211.211.211.3—Move a little to the right

221.221.221.3—Move a little to the left

212121.3—Error

The method was first applied in combat by the Confederacy. A former Myer trainee, one Lt. Alexander, sent flag signals at Bull Run to warn the South's Gen. Beauregard of a Union flanking movement.

Union forces successfully used flag signals in September 1862, when Gen. Burnside was alerted to an attack by Stonewall Jackson's cavalry at the Battle of Antietam in Maryland. But at Chancellorsville, Maj.

Gen. Joseph Hooker met disaster at the hands of Robert E. Lee in May 1863 due in part to very poor command links with his troops.

Two months later, the pivotal Union victory at Gettysburg, Pennsylvania, was directly influenced by signalmen who scaled the strategic heights of Little Round Top. Their presence is credited with delaying an early Confederate assault there, the failure of which affected the tactics of the entire battle.

Another Union success, Adm. David Farragut's naval victory at Mobile Bay, Alabama, in August 1864, benefited from signals exchanged between Northern ships and land forces. Several reports indicate that a flagman conveyed Farragut's legendary command, "Damn the torpedoes, full speed ahead!"

While a number of banner exchanges succeeded, others were intercepted by experienced observers on both sides. Always security conscious, Albert Myer applied for a patent for a CIPHER DISK intended to accompany the wig-wag system. The disk used only the numerals 1 and 8 in various combinations on its outer ring and a randomly placed alphabet on its movable inner ring. Myer specified that those exchanging messages each have one of his disks and a prearranged plan to coordinate it with the flags or other visual signals. His goal was to give better protection to the observable aspects of a system like wig-wag by sending signals with numbers that could only be decrypted with the disks.

With a planned starting point such as A = 118, the transmitter would send the

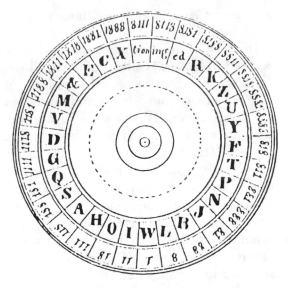

Albert Myer's cipher disk. (Courtesy of the U.S. Patent Office.)

numbers 8881, 888, 11, 18, and 888. The recipient would have his disk set at A = 118, and a brief check of the other alignments would reveal the letters of the word *union*.

In 1863, Myer's disk did improve the security of wig-wag. However, wire telegraphy had obvious advantages, and that became the predominant system for long distance communication. Myer, meanwhile, developed yet another signaling system, using rockets and Roman candles to signal alerts and to provide artificial illumination during night assaults (see VERY LIGHT). His inventiveness, foresight, and loyalty were rewarded when he was twice named chief signal officer of the U.S. Army.

N

Napoleon (1769–1821), French emperor (1804–1815). As the "little corporal" became a military giant bestriding Europe for a generation, he depended on a *petit chiffre* (little cipher) to communicate with his commanders and their huge armies.

In his early campaigns, Napoleon sometimes used Claude Chappe's AERIAL TELEGRAPH to convey orders for troop movements. As his conquests extended throughout Europe, the emperor replaced this visible semaphore-type system with a more secretive means of communication.

His *petit chiffre* was a NOMENCLATOR, a list of CODE-like names, words, and syllables combined with a CIPHER alphabet and printed on large folded pieces of paper. According to historian David Kahn, Napoleon's particular system consisted of some 200 word groups.

During the invasion of Russia in 1812, the fire that swept Moscow around Napoleon's occupying forces also destroyed copies of his *petit chiffre*, forcing him to write a number of command messages "in clear." It is thought that some of his unconcealed orders were intercepted and used against his already decimated Grande Armée in its disastrous retreat across Russia.

National Security Agency, the successor to the Armed Forces Security Agency in 1952 and the center of U.S. CRYPTOLOGY. The top-secret NSA develops concealment methods for various U.S. government departments as well as ways to solve the CODES and CIPHERS of other nations. The NSA has created and maintained a number of signals intelligence-gathering systems around the globe, from outer space to the oceans' depths. Its headquarters are located at Fort Meade, Maryland, near Washington, D.C.

The NSA's professional cryptanalysts usually begin their training with pencils and graph paper, learning techniques such as FREQUENCY counts of letters, CONTACT CHARTS, and CONSTRUCTION TABLES to discover the PLAINTEXT of concealed messages. The solution seekers also apply high-tech tools and methods, such as COMPUTERS, teleprocessing, electrical engineering, and physics.

A global intelligence network has evolved to supply the NSA with data. This network combines human intelligence (HUMINT), provided by CIA and military intelligence agents, among others, and land-based listening posts, and sea and airborne platforms. Information gathered from these sources is sent to various NSA departments based on factors such as its type, level of encryption complexity, and region. Developing nations' communications are the most vulnerable to decryption because these countries do not often have sophisticated concealment methods. The NSA analysts do not claim high rates of success for solving the encryptions of advanced nations. Nevertheless, they maintain their vigil, hoping for a miscue of repeated CIPHERTEXT, an accidental transmission in CLEARTEXT, and new computer enhancements for even quicker electronic analysis. Defectors with encryption secrets are certainly, though warily, welcomed.

Naval Signals, any of a wide variety of cryptosystems used by maritime forces for communication.

For centuries, navies have used signals such as trumpets, drums, torches, and flags to communicate with other ships and with land forces. It was not until the mid-1600s, however, that ship-to-ship communications were formalized by the British using the proposals of Adm. Sir William Penn. His single-flag method made it possible to send 30 to 40 commands, as well as alphabet letters, throughout the fleet. The world's leading military force, the Royal Navy continued to pioneer in naval communications throughout the 18th and 19th centuries. In the early 1780s, Adm. Baron George Rodney developed a system wherein signals were transmitted by clusters of lanterns attached to yardarms and raised with hoists.

At about the same time, Adm. Richard Kempenfelt's flag system was adapted for general use. This process equated banners with letters of the alphabet. Adm. Kempenfelt produced what was considered the first scientific naval signal book during this period.

Between 1803 and 1812, Rear Adm. Sir Home Popham made some improvements in the banner system with a series of numerical flags; his uses of flag combinations increased the available vocabulary.

Capt. Frederick Marryat wrote the first book applicable to international codes in 1817. In his *Code of Signals for the Merchant Service*, colored banners signified numbers assigned to words compiled in a 9,000-item book.

In 1857 the British Board of Trade adopted a system of 18 colored flags. The Board published these as part of a CODE of more than 70,000 elements, *The Commercial Code of Signals*. Hoists of flags signified every consonant except *x* and *z*; the vowels (except *y*) were deleted. Flags also represented particular naval terms, among others.

Semaphore (Greek: *sema*, "a sign" + *pherein*, "to bear") was the name given a two-flag, hand-held system developed around 1880. In this alphabetic code, flag positions were equated with alphabet letters. A more rapid technique than the wig-wag system of ALBERT MYER, semaphore was well-suited to deck-to-deck communication.

After this series of improvements, flag signals were generally accepted by seagoing nations, who adapted such systems to their own needs. Lanterns or lamps were generally used at night, while whistles and horns served for fog warnings and alerts for vessels that were off course. The need for a night signal that could be seen at great distances was satisfied by the American pyrotechnic method known as the VERY LIGHT. Similar to a Roman candle but fired from a pistol, Edward Very's device consisted of a cartridge that exploded approximately 200 feet above ground. Its "star bursts" could be shot in timed patterns with color variations to constitute a visual code. The Very Light entered widespread use in the latter third of the 19th century.

The introduction of electricity profoundly improved naval communications. When current could be generated aboard ship, whale-oil lanterns were replaced by electric lamps with green, red, and white glass covers that could indicate alphabet letters and numbers. In the late 1800s, this brought a new generation of codes to the fore, including the German *Conz*, the

Semaphore. (From *The Blue Jackets' Manual*. U.S. Naval Institute. Annapolis, Maryland, 1990.)

French *Ducretet*, the Austrian *Sellner*, and the French *Ardois* (see ALBERT NIBLACK). Louvered blinker lights were also introduced to flash MORSE CODE over the waves.

The development of wireless telegraphy (radio) created another level of naval communications. The visible, basically NONSECRET CODES of banners and lights, were partially supplanted by a method with much secrecy potential. In December 1912 the U.S. Naval Radio Service commenced operations. With the advent of World War I, the necessity of concealing messages with CRYPTOGRAPHY increased dramatically. In World War II, encryption methods played a major role in naval actions such as the BATTLE OF THE ATLANTIC, the BATTLE OF THE CORAL SEA, and the BATTLE OF MIDWAY.

Today, naval signals remain a high-priority objective of espionage agents. The infamous John Walker spy ring, for example, were all convicted of passing to the Soviets over a 20-year period information ranging from U.S. Navy manuals to encrypted communiqués.

Niblack, Albert (1859–1929), U.S. naval intelligence officer.

This native of Indiana was a foresighted military man whose contributions ranged from signal systems to intelligence gathering.

A U.S. Naval Academy graduate, Albert Niblack served in both the South Pacific and Alaska early in his career. In the late 1890s he gathered data about signaling systems and sea-borne tactics from a variety of sources. In an era when dreadnoughts ruled the waves with big guns, Niblack's interest in the seemingly bland specialty of communciations must have appeared tame to his students at the Naval War College. Yet with the application of electricity to signal systems, Albert saw the growing importance of these developments and their potential contribution to warfare.

During this same period, the U.S. Navy had adopted a French light system known as *Ardois*. As described by Niblack, in his efforts to improve U.S. techniques, this method used either four or five lamps, each of which had a 32-candle-power incandescent light in both its upper and lower halves. Cover shades for the glass globes provided the two colors that became standard for this method in the United States (red for the lower half and white for the upper half).

Clusters of lights were arranged to make a CODE. Hoisted up masts with their current-supplying cables attached and controlled by a keyboard device, the lamps provided much clearer and more varied messages than the lanterns or pyrotechnic devices of past eras, though the latter were still used for night and emergency signals (see VERY LIGHT). With its patterns of red and white lights, the *Ardois* system conveyed messages in the familiar dots and dashes of international MORSE CODE. This made more alphabet letters and numerals practical for conveyance by illumination.

Niblack left the War College in 1896 to serve as an attaché in Europe. While stationed in Berlin, he reported on growing German militarism. His efforts reputedly involved a clandestine search of Kaiser Wilhelm's desk for details about battleships. He was also successful in acquiring data about German torpedo components. Returning to sea duty, Niblack saw action in both Cuba and the Philippines during the Spanish-American War.

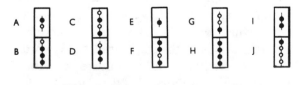

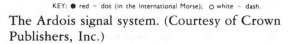

The Ardois signal system. (Courtesy of Crown Publishers, Inc.)

He was in China when the Boxer Rebellion erupted in 1900 and led a regiment of seamen during the U.S. occupation of Vera Cruz, Mexico, in 1914. In World War I, he achieved the rank of rear admiral and held a command in the Mediterranean theater. May 1919 found him in the key role of chief of ONI, the Office of Naval Intelligence, where he directed his energies toward gathering strategic intelligence about the increasing Japanese influence in the Pacific. Later in 1920, working as a military attaché in London, Niblack began to organize intelligence agents in Europe, before this operation was halted by the Navy Department. In July 1923, he left the navy with a foundation of much better signaling methods and strategic awareness.

Nihilist Cipher, a cryptosystem based on a traditional prisoners' CIPHER that was developed by the Russian Nihilists.

The Nihilists were a group of Russian anti-czarists who united in the 1850s and early 1860s. They sought the overthrow of the existing order by means of sabotage, terrorism, and assassination, but without the ideology of a Marx or the iron discipline of a Lenin, they were never as well organized as the Bolsheviks. To protect themselves from the Czars' dreaded *Okhrana* (secret police) and to pass their letters through the BLACK CHAMBER mail watchers, the Nihilists developed their own cryptosystems, including one based on the KNOCK CIPHER used by prisoners.

This system involved sequences of taps representing the rows and columns of a checkerboard of alphabet letters. One tap followed by two indicated row one, second column, or the letter *b*. Sometimes a square of six rows and six columns was used to include the 35 Cyrillic letters of the old Russian alphabet; at other times a 5×6 matrix was used, with some of these letters deleted.

The Nihilists applied a SUBSTITUTION method to this checkerboard. The PLAINTEXT was numerically enciphered and added to a KEYWORD, that repeated through the length of the communication, thus generating the CIPHERTEXT. With the English alphabet, the checkerboard matrix would appear as follows (*u* and *v* are combined in one space):

	1	2	3	4	5
1	a	b	c	d	e
2	f	g	h	i	j
3	k	l	m	n	o
4	p	q	r	s	t
5	uv	w	x	y	z

The keyword *unite* could be numerically enciphered by locating each letter first horizontally and then vertically and recording its coordinates. Thus *unite* would be 51 34 24 45 15.

Adding the repeating key, the finished ciphertext for the message *strike czar now* would appear as follows:

Plaintext	s	t	r	i	k	e
Digits	44	45	43	24	31	15
Repeating Key	51	34	24	45	15	51
Ciphertext	95	79	67	69	46	66

Plaintext	c	z	a	r	n	o	w
Digits	13	55	11	43	34	35	52
Repeating Key	34	24	45	15	51	34	24
Ciphertext	47	79	56	58	85	69	76

This method of adding a numerical key to a checkerboard-generated substitution outlasted the Nihilists. After the Bolsheviks seized power in the November 1917 revolution, they adopted this method and used it for a number of years to conceal exchanges among their clandestine operatives (see SOVIET CRYPTOLOGY).

Nomenclator, the predominant concealment system from the 15th to the mid-19th century, from the Latin *nomen*, "name," + *calator*, "caller."

Beginning as a list of names, the nomenclator developed into a collection of syllables, words, and names similar to a CODE, with a separate CIPHER alphabet having multiple substitutes for letters (known as *homophones*). The abbreviated names, parts of names, and syllables had come from a combination of personal secret writings and the concealments used by the scribes of popes and royalty.

The Renaissance trade rivalries of the Italian and other Mediterranean city-states increased the need for organized masking systems. With a growing number of names and phrases to encode, SYMBOL CRYPTOGRAPHY was incorporated into the nomenclators. Also used were meaningless symbols called *nihil importantes*, or NULLS, which were placed in the nomenclators to confuse would-be solution seekers. A portion of a 15th-century nomenclator similar to one from Siena, Italy, with twenty-three letters equated with symbols and names concealed by CODEWORDS, symbols, nulls (nihil importantes), and double letters complete the example on the following page.

The nomenclators became longer and filled larger pieces of parchment. However, they continued to list their plaintext words in alphabetical order until the superb French cryptologist ANTOINE ROSSIGNOL (1600–1682) recognized this as a weakness and developed the one-part and two-part nomenclators. The former kept the traditional alphabetical and/or numerical order. The two-part version had PLAINTEXT elements alphabetized and code elements mixed in one section. The second part had ordered code lists and mixed plain elements, thereby increasing its security. Although Rossignol's improvement was not always applied, nomenclators continued to grow, having as many as 3,000 elements by the 1700s. Nomenclators remained in existence as designed cryptosystems from about 1400 to around 1850 when the invention of the telegraph and its message partner, the MORSE CODE, superceded them. Rather than revising their nomenclators or creating new ones, governments phased out the long-used masking systems.

Nonsecret Codes, CODES that are used primarily for communicative rather than cryptographic purposes. This category includes a wide range of systems, from business codes to visual and audial signaling methods.

Commercial codes have been used mainly to save words (and hence toll costs) on telegrams and CABLEGRAMS. While some were specially created by private companies, others, such as the ABC CODE, were published, thus rendering these versions anything but secret.

The MORSE CODE, in both its U.S. and international versions, was not a mystery to anyone who took the time to learn its

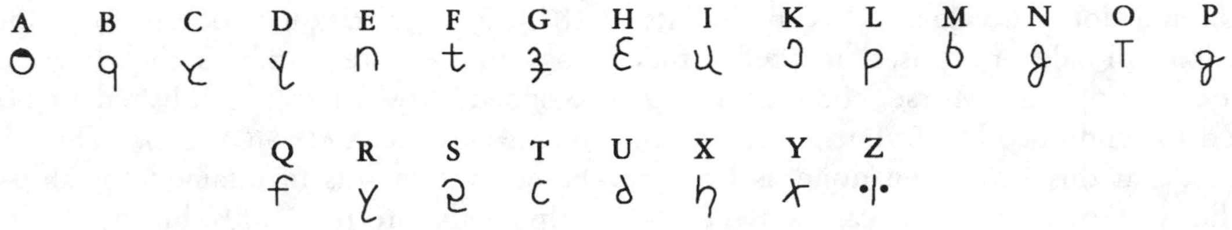

A	B	C	D	E	F	G	H	I	K	L	M	N	O	P

Q	R	S	T	U	X	Y	Z

ANTONELLO DA FURLI

CARDINALES

COMES URBINI

DUX CALABRIE

DUX VENETIARUM

FLORENTINI

GENTES REGIE

GENTES VENETORUM

MARCHIO MONTISFERRATI

NAPOLI

PITIGLIANO

SORANO

DOMINUS ALEXANDER STORZA

ILDIBRANDINUS

FORTE

FLORENUS

LUX

VENTUS

CELUM

TERRA

STELLE

ARENA

ARBOR

NOBILE

DURUM

FORTUNA

DUPLICES: BB   CC   DD   FF   LL   MM   NN   PP   RR   SS   TT

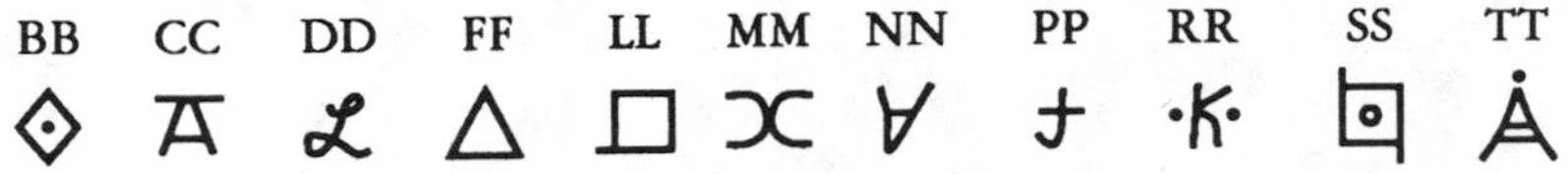

NIHIL . IMPORTANTES:

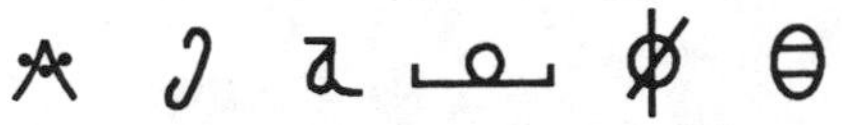

dash and dot equivalencies. Nor were its audible "di-dahs" purposely masked at the telegraph offices. Morse code could be used to send encoded or enciphered messages, and this was often done as by the military. However, great care was necessary here, since a misplaced dot or dash could easily garble the message.

The origins of nonsecret codes can be found in ancient times, when the first messages were sent over distances and required predetermined signals including shouts, horns, flags, drums, cannons, and smoke. The Romans erected an elaborate system of some 3,000 towers for torch communications throughout their vast empire.

In France in the 1790s, Claude Chappe developed his AERIAL TELEGRAPH. This semaphore-type system consisted of movable wooden arms mounted on posts and placed atop towers and hills. Except during heavy fog and in inclement weather, Chappe's invention could convey messages north from Paris to Lille in two minutes and south from Paris to Toulon in 20 minutes, remarkable time in both cases.

On the high seas, England introduced in the late 1700s a flag-based system of signals for the Royal Navy, which was eventually used by merchantmen as well. By 1817, an international code using colored flags to indicate numbers that had been assigned to words was published in book form (see NAVAL SIGNALS). The flag-based system was maintained for ship-to-ship needs into the 1800s, but by the mid-19th century the flags and the Chappe system had been rendered obsolete by the telegraph and transoceanic cables.

Null, a meaningless letter, symbol, or number purposely placed in a CODE list or a CIPHER alphabet. Nulls complicate the decryption efforts of unintended third-parties by disrupting anticipated sentence patterns, word lengths, and syllable groups (see FREQUENCY).

Null ciphers are a type of OPEN CODE in which only a few chosen words or letters are significant, such as the last letter of every other word, or the third word in every sentence.

The frequent use of nulls for covert purposes was impractical because it often resulted in stilted language that was obvious and vulnerable to analyses. However, servicemen from many countries and in many wars used similar methods to try to outwit the censors of homeward-bound mail.

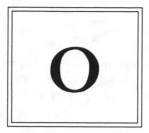

Observation Panel Codes, systems of ground-to-air communication first used during the early years of the airplane. Apparently independent efforts toward developing such signaling methods occurred in the United States and England in the period 1906–12.

The panels, also known as "strips," generally consisted of pieces of cloth placed on the ground in various configurations to convey messages to pilots. For ease of handling, the sizes and shapes of the cloth became standardized over time; bright white came to be preferred as the predominant color because of its superior visibility. In time, both the infantrymen who arranged the panels and their aerial observers felt the need for more numerous and more systematic configurations, and the panels were formalized into true CODES, although a high level of secrecy could not be maintained. The panel codes were collected in manuals, along with descriptions of MORSE CODE, pyrotechnic devices such as the VERY LIGHT, lamps, and other communication systems.

In World War I, panels were used to designate friendly camps, to direct aerial observation, and to transmit news near the front. With strips of 12×1-foot white cloth, coded messages were sent using a series of letters and symbols:

Am not receiving your signals	II
Battery receiving signals, but guns not ready to fire [With a bar underneath for every 10 minutes that will probably elapse before guns are ready.]	$\underline{\Delta}$
Message received	F
Observe for fire effect	V

147

Target not understood or not
   received   ▭

Wireless not ready   W

After the development of more ground-to-air radio, the use of strips diminished. However, during World War II, panels proved quite useful in airborne commando raids and in the resupply of resistance groups. In 1943, a combined operations manual for Britain and the United States listed nearly 100 configurations of strips, ranging from widely used messages such as "O.K. to land here" to a design applicable only once for a special spy mission.

Ogham, a type of ancient script (etymology uncertain). Its origins are with the Celtic peoples, and its inscriptions have been categorized as Primitive Irish, the oldest form of Irish. As unusual as this script was in its standard forms, some versions of it were also encrypted.

Ogham's alphabet has been standardized from inscriptions dating circa A.D. 350 to A.D. 600 and found on stones ranging from Cork and Kerry in Ireland to Wales and the Isle of Man.

The script can be arranged vertically or horizontally, but the basic pattern of the writing style is the same. The letters are

Examples of Ogham.

indicated by groups of one to five strokes or notches that are arranged along a center stem-line. These are considered to be in five configurations: above the line, below it, perpendicular above and below, diagonal above and below, and the fifth group of varied designs that have been interpreted as dipthongs with consonant-like values.

The 15th-century collection of history, genealogy, and folklore known as the *Book of Ballymote* lists a number of methods of enciphering *ogham*, including styles called *head of quarreling*, *interwoven*, and *well-footed*. These have concealment patterns involving, respectively, adding lines that join and/or intersect the *ogham* marks; adding straight and looplike extensions to the ends of the ogham marks; and placing a sequence of dots at the ends of the lines above and below the stem-line. Other encryption systems are listed below, along with their descriptions:

Ogham name	Description
host	each letter tripled
point against eye	reversed alphabet
serpent through the heather	an irregular line placed atop and beneath consecutive characters
vexation of a poet's heart	lines as brief strokes projecting just beyond a rectangle

In his 1937 book *The Secret Languages of Ireland*, the scholar R. A. Stewart Macalister proposed that certain aspects of alphabets and languages used by diverse groups such as the Greeks, Romans, Druids, and Celts all have links to the *ogham* script and the Old Irish language. Macalister believed that *ogham* was based on a phonetic rearrangement of earlier letter-pronunciation styles and that it was actually a system of notating hand gestures, with the inscribed series of marks derived from the positions of the fingers. He also suggested that *ogham* had been used among the Ancient Irish for secret communications with manual movements similar to a sign language.

On the Roof Gang, the human element in the U.S. chain of electronic ears that arced the northern Pacific in the years after World War I.

In the 1920s, a navy listening post had been placed in the U.S. consulate in Shanghai, where radio eavesdroppers attempted to intercept Tokyo's diplomatic messages. Then, during 1926 and 1927, the first U.S. Asiatic Fleet intelligence units were established at Guam and Olongapo (later Cavite Naval Base) in the Philippines.

In 1928 a special classroom was built atop the navy department building in Washington, D.C., where students, or "roofers," were taught by instructors of the navy's cryptologic organization, OP-20-G. One of the primary objectives of the four-month instruction period was to increase the number of radiomen who could understand KATA KANA, used in the Japanese version of MORSE CODE.

From the late 1920s onward, navy listening stations were established at such varied outposts as Bainbridge Island near

Seattle; Dutch Harbor, Alaska; and Heeia on Oahu, Hawaii. The *H* from Heeia soon became the basis of the CODENAME for the Pacific Fleet's intelligence unit in Hawaii, Station Hypo. Codenamed Station Negat, for the *N* in Navy Department, OP-20-G in Washington, D.C., was the "auditory nerve center" of each of these human and electric "eardrums." The post at Cavite Naval Base in the Philippines was Station Cast.

The OTRG members who passed the difficult training course went to duty posts in exotic and faraway locations. Along with the *kata kana* intercepts and translations used by navy encryption solvers, the "gang" worked with direction-finding and traffic analysis. While stateside citizens struggled with the Depression and hoped that the New Deal would revitalize the economy, the "roofers" listened for the Japanese dashes and dots that eventually spelled danger on the horizon.

One-part Code, a CODE in which the PLAINTEXT words or numbers and their concealment equivalents are alphabetically or sequentially in a parallel form. This is a less complicated form than the TWO-PART CODE, where code terms or numbers are not alphabetical or sequential and a second part or section is needed for decoding.

One-part codes have been used by both businesses and governments. The GREEN CIPHER (the State Department once used the word CIPHER for its CODEBOOK titles) was an example of a one-part code whose minimal concealment was provided by five-letter codegroups made up of consonants and vowels. The Green and others like it did not prove secure for top-level embassy communiqués, but businesses did continue to use similar codes to reduce telegram and cable costs.

A Segment of a One-Part Business Code

cebai	Send	
cebco	"	as follows
cebeh	"	as usual
cebgl	"	cheapest route
cebif	"	newest route
cebkm	"	quickest route
cebmu	"	rail route
cebok	"	road route
cebqx	"	water route

One-time Pad, A special CIPHER method with a nonrepetitive KEY of letters and/or characters that is used just once. This technique is directly associated with two U.S. citizens. While researching security procedures for the printing telegraph (teletypewriter) in 1917, AT&T engineer GILBERT VERNAM originated a method of imprinting paper tape with electromechanical pulses to create a CIPHERTEXT. Vernam worked in association with U.S. Army Maj. JOSEPH MAUBORGNE, who is credited by historian David Kahn with improving this process with a random, nonrepetitive unmarked key.

CRYPTOGRAPHY experts in different countries were conducting similar research, and between 1918 and the early 1920s other, independently developed one-time techniques appeared. In Germany during this period, a single-use system was formalized and became known as the one-time pad. The German Foreign Office developed the process, whereby two pieces of paper were typed with a series of random numbers, which became the KEY. A group of these pages were formed into two identical collections that came to be known as pads. The transmitter and the recipient each had an identical copy of the pads.

During World War II, U.S. agents of the Office of Strategic Services (OSS) and their allies in Britain's Special Operations Executive (SOE) had one-time methods that combined alphanumeric grids and numerical KEY sheets. The grid form was often made of easily disposed silk and contained 26 alphabet letters with both columns of sequential numerals and cyclical alphabets aligned beneath them. The sheets of five-digit groups were printed on paper or a very flammable synthetic material. By 1944 technicians had developed pages made of film that were read with a hand-held magnifying device.

By the early 1960s, pads had become the size of postage stamps or scrolls the size of large pencil erasers (see SOVIET CRYPTOLOGY). Some, like the VIC CIPHER, were printed on paper that was photographed and sent as microfilm for extra concealment. Pads have been made of foil-like material and have had pages of extremely combustible cellulose nitrate for rapid destruction in case of emergency.

When properly prepared and distributed, one-time pads are considered UNBREAKABLE CIPHERS. Their randomness and lack of repetition prevent an analyst from gaining quick angles with any known solution techniques. Even an attempt to check every possible key would fail, because this trial-and-error method would produce an impractical number of possibilities, even for today's COMPUTER technology. Concerns about relevant "current time" data are always present too, as secrets can quickly become stale and irrelevant.

When an encryptor uses a pad for encipherment, he includes a prearranged means of indentification called an indicator group. The indicator changes with each transmission and identifies the new pad sheet to be used. The numbers on each page provide a random key that is added to a second group of digits formed from the PLAINTEXT words of the message.

The words of the communication can be changed into numerals by such means as a monome-dinome table, a checkerboard, or similar matrix that converts letters to numbers. The monome-dinome table aligns letters with single and paired numbers by using a KEYWORD to initiate and mix the alphabet. This style also has configurations of numerals at the top and side of the matrix to make the single and paired numbers possible (see STRADDLING CHECKERBOARD, UNBREAKABLE CIPHERS). To encipher a message, a checkerboard can also be set up with the frequently used English letters e, t, a, o, n, r, i, and s mixing the alphabet and top and side digits. A full stop (.) and diagonal (/) for letter/number shifts often appear in such checkerboards as necessary functional devices.

	0	9	8	7	6	5	4	3	2	1
	e	r	t	o	n	i	s	a		
1	b	c	d	f	g	h	j	k	l	m
2	p	q	u	v	w	x	y	z	.	/

In this example, the frequently used letters in the top row are replaced by the numerals above them. The letters in the other two rows are replaced by coordinates derived from reading the corresponding numbers from the side and then the top (for example, $d = 18$ and $v = 27$). The plaintext letters are each given number equivalents from this checkerboard until the message becomes a series of digits.

If an international security agent (CODENAMED ao) located a wanted weapons smuggler (given the CODENUMBER 20) he could send an encrypted communication with both digits in the number 20 being tripled for transmission clarity.

Plaintext: f o u n d / 2 0 / i n
Conversion: 17 7 28 6 18 21 22 22 00 00 21 5 6

Plaintext: p r a g u e . a o .
Conversion: 20 9 3 16 28 0 22 3 7 22

To these digits the agent would then add a series of nonrepeating numbers from the one-time pad using a noncarrying form of addition called *modulo* 10, or the Fibonacci system, in which the tens digits are not carried over. Thus, $9 + 2$ is written only as 1, not as 11. This increases the rapidity of encipherment and decipherment, helps prevent carrying errors, and permits encryption from left to right. An example is shown at the top of the following page.

Such a series of numbers is often sent in a standard form of five-numeral groups:

51860	99873	98950	83305
72549	78089	46801	

Even if agent AO's transmission is intercepted by the arms dealers, odds are that the dangerous smuggler known as 20

Conversion:	17728618212220002156209316280223722
Pad digits:	44142380527675081259526181628723189
Ciphertext:	51860998739895083305725497808946801

would be captured and convicted long before the pad-secured communiqué could be revealed—if ever.

Despite their resistance to solution, one-time pads are vulnerable on a few points—and thus aren't universally applied. By their very nature, the pads need huge quantities of continuous random digits. This can be accomplished with computers, but since the communicators cannot memorize the stream of numerals, the pads must be printed and distributed, rendering them vulnerable to discovery. The system has still not proven widely applicable as a military field cipher. For their part, businesses generally prize efficiency and economy over such high-level security. Thus, one-time pads have tended to be used only in the specialized worlds of the diplomat and the spy.

Open Code, a CODE concealed in an apparently innocent message. Open codes are a branch of linguistically masked communications, which includes NULL ciphers, geometric methods (see GRILLE), and JARGON CODES.

In a null CIPHER, only some letters or words form part of the cipher, such as the second letter of every word in the first three paragraphs, the last word before each new paragraph, or the third letter after each comma.

In a geometric code message, words or letters appear in certain positions or patterns in a diagram. These are sometimes made with the help of a grille, which is a piece of cardboard or other material with apertures cut in prearranged places. Another type of "position" code can also be created using the naturally irregular strokes of handwriting, such as the subtle break in a letter's loop or slightly more or less space between certain words.

An entertaining example of a jargon code comes from World War I. An alert English censor became wary of large orders for cigars wired each day from British coastal cities by two "Dutch businessmen." The censor initiated an investigation that led to the arrest of Wilhelm Roos and Heicke Janssen on charges of spying for the Kaiser. It was discovered that an order such as 6,000 Coronas for Dover was the code for six heavy cruisers in port. In July 1915 the pair faced a firing squad at the Tower of London, their stogie scheme going up in rifle smoke.

In the very clever orchestration of their espionage and diplomatic concealments prior to World War II, the Japanese used a series of open codes that can be classified as jargon. On November 26, 1941, Tokyo sent Japanese ambassador Kichisaburo Nomura and special envoy Saburo Kurusu (in Washington, D.C.) an open code for telephone calls to facilitate their reports on the difficult negotiations with the United States. The code contained such terms as *Miss Kimiko* (President Roosevelt), *Miss Fumeko* (Secretary of State Cordell Hull), The Marriage Proposal (negotiations), and *The Birth of a Child* (crisis imminent).

As the talks in Washington were reaching a critical stage, Tokyo sent other open codes to its embassies. One, the *Ingo Denpo* ("hidden word") code, was set up to conceal plain language messages in the event that obviously coded telegrams were banned. Some of its terms were *Arimura* (code communications prohibited); *Hattori* (relations with Japan and are at crisis level or on the verge of catastrophe); *Kodama* (Japan); and *Minami* (U.S.A.). These cables were indicated by completing them with the use of the English *Stop* instead of the Japanese *Owari* (end).

A second open code was formulated by Japan's Foreign Office for emergency notifications to its embassies. If diplomatic relations were about to be severed along with international communications, a warning phrase about weather conditions was to be placed in the daily Japanese language news broadcast. (See WINDS CODE.)

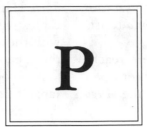

P

Painvin, Georges (1886–1980), French army cryptanalyst. A reserve officer on the French artillery staff, Georges Painvin proved to be a military genius whose CIPHER-solving skills saved thousands of Allied lives during World War I.

A prize-winning cellist and a graduate of the prestigious *École Polytechnique*, Painvin exhibited skills in CRYPTANALYSIS early in the conflict and was assigned to the Bureau du Chiffre (Office of Ciphers) in Paris. The first organization of its type, the office's duties included protecting French communiqués, intercepting enemy transmissions, and breaking encryption shields. The latter became Painvin's specialty.

Through 1916 and well into 1917, the Germans struggled with a number of methods to cover their many radio transmissions. One designated by the French as the *ABCD* was discovered to be a VIGENÈRE-type table with keyletters *a*, *b*, *c*, and *d* and a TRANSPOSITION. But further analysis proved this to be a kind of ciphering drill that even included portions of newspaper articles in its message text. Painvin and his associates decided that the ABCD was a deception and it did indeed fade from the airwaves.

However, a method called the ADFGVX was a different matter. It was a clever field cipher first transmitted with five letters, *A*, *D*, *F*, *G*, and *X* in March 1918. These letters had apparently been chosen because their International Morse code equivalents were less likely to be jumbled in transmission than those of the other letters. The five-letter CIPHER was overheard by French listening posts, but the cipher had not been solved by March 21, when the anticipated German spring offensive began.

This massive assault decimated front-line Allied defenses. Yet the very size of the operation and the resulting increase in radio usage gave Painvin more intercepts to study. The fact that only five letters were initially used in the ADFGVX made him think that this German encryption was based on a checkerboard process for rearranging letters. Painvin matched some segments of messages that provided clues to a KEY for a given day and eventually the key to the transposition of the checkerboard's letters. Other data enabled Painvin to begin comparing word endings, to find repetitions, and to make FREQUENCY counts. On June 1, a sixth letter (V) was added by the Germans. But then a comparison of intercepted cryptograms sent within a narrow time frame elicited enough information to allow him to make preliminary transposition and column-arrangement checks. He finally pried away the cover of the most recent ADFGVX messages by the early evening of June 2 and sent his news to French headquarters even as the Allies were bracing themselves for an onslaught that they feared would capture Paris and end the war.

Then early on June 3, Painvin's arduous work paid a huge intelligence dividend. General headquarters' analysts had used the keys he recovered to read an ADFGVX dispatch. It was an order regarding munitions, a telltale signal of an impending attack. Direction-finding identified the senders as the German high command and the recipients as commanders in a village near a possible point of assault. Airborne reconnaissance confirmed the movement of munitions and other supplies toward this area between Montdidier and Compiègne, 50 miles north of Paris.

French general Ferdinand Foch responded with defensive measures to absorb the expected onslaught. German general Erich Ludendorff launched the new attack on June 9; the French were ready. After a pivotal series of battles, the German offensive of the Marine was stopped. With the arrival of more fresh U.S. troops, the tide began to turn toward an allied victory.

Pepys, Samuel (1663–1703), English diarist and civil servant. For nine years and five months in the 1690s, Pepys kept his famous DIARY, in which more than 3,000 pages were written in a form of SHORTHAND called tachygraphy. A description of the method, which involved combinations of longhand, contracted words, characters, numbers, and dot patterns, was first published in 1620 by Thomas Shelton. For additional security, Pepys also included sections in foreign languages, including French and Spanish, and added some creative NULL symbols. Thus, his private thoughts remained hidden until 1819, when a student named John Smith of St. John's College, Cambridge, began a decipherment of the entire diary. Finally, in 1822, the task was completed, and Pepys's remarkable recollections were revealed for posterity.

Permutation, a form of TRANSPOSITION in which symbols or letters are rearranged but retain their original identities. Thus this method is not as secure as SUBSTITUTION, wherein letters or other characters have their identities changed.

An example of permutation is the blocking of a message into groups of eight and then the transposition, within each group, of the first and last and the fourth and fifth letters or characters.

Plaintext: HOLD•800•SHARES•OF•A
              CMO•INDUSTRIES.•NAT
              TE•SMITH.•

Permutation: 0OL•D80H•SHRAES.•F•C
              AMOOINDSUTRIES•N•A
              TE•SMTIH.•

As can be seen from some of the repeating positions of the characters, more location and identity changes would improve the security of the message.

Photography has had a supportive role in cryptographic practices as a field providing mainly physical concealments.

The process of microphotography joined hidden communications during the Franco-Prussian War (1870–1871). René Dagron, pioneer of miniature photos, and associates left besieged Paris by balloon and set up a message service from Tours, in west central France. Dagron reduced military documents on film measuring 30×55 mm. These miniaturized items were placed in tubes attached to homing pigeons' tail feathers. The information generally reached Paris safely and, though the Prussians won the war, the value of microfilm was established.

Dagron had accomplished a form of STEGANOGRAPHY, hiding the presence of a message without necessarily encrypting it. The best known aspect of such a process in the film world is the Nazi's masterpiece of espionage, the MICRODOT. There are also steganographic techniques that involve chemicals. Cryptophotography is the term that includes both image reduction and chemistry. The chemical processes included latent imaging, gelatin hardening, and bleaching.

In the first of these techniques, the apparently blank space of a seemingly innocent photograph was actually occupied by a latent image. To produce the image, the nonsecret negative was printed with ordinary chemicals. The secret negative was then placed in a white space within the other image and exposed. The photo was next put into a fixing bath. The intended recipient knew to put the photo in the necessary developer to reveal the hidden image. Before the invention of the microdot, this process was considered one of the better concealment systems.

Gelatin hardening, also known as tanning, took advantage of the changeable properties of gelatin. Its concealment potential depended on skilled application of solutions and type and quality of paper in one process, or the use of fixed films or plates in a more complicated procedure. In this paper-based system, a message was written with a solution of formaldehyde on gelatin-covered, high-quality photographic paper. After being permitted to harden, the surface appeared untouched to the casual observer and thus provided a level of concealment. The intended addressee recovered the message simply by placing the photo in tepid water or ammonia, allowing the gelatin to swell up, and examining the contents under low-angle illumination.

In the bleaching method, an exposed but undeveloped photographic image (either negative or positive) was placed in a chemical solution. The image was recovered by the recipient with a developer that reversed the effects of this solution. The following are examples of chemicals that were used in this process:

Solution	Developer
copper sulphate and sodium chloride	metol hydroquinone
potassium bichromate and hydrochloric acid	metol hydroquinone
mercuric dichloride	metol hydroquinone
mercuric chloride	sodium thiosulphate or ammonia

This method often left suspicious traces of images, visible especially in sunlight. A fixing bath helped with the masking aspects but made development and image recovery more difficult. Thus the process never achieved widespread use as a crypto-photographic technique.

Plaintext, a message either before it has encoded or enciphered or after it has been DECODED or DECIPHERED. The recovery can be made by the intended addressee who knows the KEY, or unintended third-party solvers with the processes of CRYPT-ANALYSIS. By contrast, CLEARTEXT is a message sent without being concealed by a CODE or CIPHER, and CODETEXT and CI-PHERTEXT refer to a message that has been encoded or enciphered, respectively.

Playfair Cipher, a SUBSTITUTION CI-PHER bearing the name of the man who popularized but did not create it. Invented by English scientist Sir Charles Wheatstone about 1854, the method was named for his friend, Lyon Playfair, the first Baron Playfair of St. Andrews. It was Lyon who presented the cipher to associates in the British aristocracy as well as in the Foreign Office. Because Playfair was better known in these circles, his name became linked with the cipher.

Developed for telegraph secrecy, it was the first literal digraphic substitution cipher. (GIOVANNI PORTA's digraphic table used symbols rather than letters.) In Wheatstone's method, two letters were enciphered, with the result depending on both. Eventually, the Playfair cipher came to be used by Britain's forces in the Boer War and World War I, and by THE IS-LANDS COASTWATCHING SERVICE in Australia during World War II, among others.

The system functions on the basis of letter position relationships in a 5×5 alphabet matrix. A KEYWORD sets the pattern of the letters, with the other letters entered in the cells of the matrix in alphabetical order (*i* and *j* are combined in one cell). For this example, we use Wheatstone's first name:

c	h	a	r	l
e	s	b	d	f
g	i/j	k	m	n
o	p	q	t	u
v	w	x	y	z

The message to be enciphered here is *the scheme works*. The PLAINTEXT is first divided into two-letter groups. If double letters occur, either an *x* is used to separate them or an *x* is added to make a complete pair (for example, *will arrive = wi lx la rx ri ve*). Thus the phrase ready for encipherment becomes: *th es ch em ew or ks*.

The letters in each pair have one of three possible relationships with each other in the matrix; they can be in the same column, in the same row, or neither in the same column nor the same row.

The corresponding rules of replacement are:

1. If two letters are in the same column of the matrix, use the letter below each plaintext letter as its CI-PHERTEXT (for example, *ab* becomes *bk*). The columns are cyclical: If the letter is at the bottom of a column, it is exchanged for the top letter in that column.
2. When two letters are in the same row, the one to the right of the message letter is its cipher equivalent (for example, *m* becomes *n* and *v* is replaced by *w*). The rows are also cyclical, with the last letter in a row being replaced by the first letter of the same row (for example, *l* becomes *c*).
3. If the letter pairs are in neither the same column nor row, each is exchanged with the letter at the intersection of its own row and the other's column. In this situation, a type of imaginary rectangle exists, with the unseen corners of the rectangle determined by the plaintext pair. For consistency, put the letter in the same row as the first plaintext letter as the first in the ciphertext pair (for example, *xi = wk, mb = ir, zc = vl*).

Plaintext	th	es	ch	em	ew	or	ks
Ciphertext:	pr	sb	ha	dg	sv	tc	ib

Decipherment follows these rules to restore the plaintext:

1. If both letters are in the same column, the letter *above* each ciphertext letter is the plaintext.
2. If both letters are in the same row, the letter to the *left* of each ciphertext letter is the plaintext.
3. Letters in neither the same column nor row are simply reversed—if *th* is *pr*, then *pr* becomes plaintext *th*.

Pletts' Device, a cryptographic device developed by J. St. Vincent Pletts, of England's bureau for CRYPTANALYSIS at the beginning of World War I. He had been an engineer employed by the Marconi Wireless Telegraph Company before the outbreak of hostilities.

Pletts joined a section known as M.I.-1(b) in the Military Intelligence Division of the War Office. In time, he and his associates were making contributions to cryptanalysis worthy of their Admiralty cohorts, who were known collectively as ROOM 40.

Pletts's radio and engineering background enabled him to construct a device of his own, an updated version of the WHEATSTONE CRYPTOGRAPH developed by scientist and inventor Sir Charles Wheatstone and first demonstrated publicly in 1867. The British authorities hoped to use Pletts's adaptation as a field CIPHER in the later stages of the war.

This device consisted of two brass disks arranged to function as a stator, or outer disk, and a rotating inner disk. They were held together by an eccentric that was turned around the pivot. White rings on both rotor and stator were divided into sectors, 26 on the rotor and 27 on the stator, on which alphabets could be written (leaving one blank space on the stator). An arm, fitting over both stator and rotor, had an aperture through which two letters could be aligned. Each revolution of the handle and eccentric moved the rotor one letter position in relation to the stator, thus providing the possibility of POLYALPHABETIC SUBSTITUTION.

Directions for using the device have apparently not survived. However, it appears likely that a PLAINTEXT letter was located on the stator. The arm was then moved to bring this character into the aperture. The aligned CIPHERTEXT letter was then read from the rotating disk. Using a known KEYWORD, a fixed beginning position on the mechanism, and a predetermined sequence of movements (such as clockwise), the user could complete an encryption. The intended addressee, using an identical device, would begin at the given starting point and reverse the process to recover the plaintext.

British officials presented Pletts's invention to U.S. experts for testing. WILLIAM FRIEDMAN, with the help of his wife, ELIZEBETH FRIEDMAN, discerned the keywords and broke the encipherment. As a result, the device was rejected for use as a field cipher.

After the war, J. St. Vincent Pletts apparently made no further attempts to broaden his niche in the archives of CODES and ciphers.

Poe, Edgar Allan (1809–1849), U.S. author and amateur cryptologist.

A very early example of Poe's interest in secretive writing can be found in *The Narrative of Arthur Gordon Pym.* In this tale, strange words of Arabic and Ethiopian origin are spelled in chips from cave walls and in map outlines. Poe gave a more detailed description of cryptologic principles in 1839 with a Philadelphia newspaper article. The *Alexander's Weekly Messenger* story, entitled "Enigmatical and Conundrum-ical," dealt with riddles, enigmas, and methods to solve puzzles. He briefly described how alphabet letters could be replaced with marks and other characters, and he invited readers to send their own examples in the mail.

First from the Philadelphia area and later from as far west as Iowa, the replies began to stack up. Poe solved the submissions but refused to reveal his methods, thereby tantalizing subscribers and attracting new ones for the paper as word of the articles spread.

By 1841 he had left *Alexander's* for a position at *Graham's Magazine* and made a new offer to DECIPHER cryptographic submissions from his readers. Having learned about a concealment system used by a French duchess, he solicited to messages using the KEYPHRASE CIPHER. While he was able to unmask some of these cryptic missives, he did not have complete success. Nevertheless, his ongoing articles about CRYPTOGRAPHY earned him a reputation as a genius in this field. With clever comparisons, references to previous studies, and writing his own versions of earlier findings, Poe kept up his self-promotion.

Poe next decided to write a story involving the solving of cryptograms. "The Gold-Bug" was the highly successful result. In 1843, he entered the story in a contest sponsored by the *Dollar Newspaper* and won a 100-dollar prize. The tale, acclaimed by critics as an irresistible read, was printed in the *Saturday Courier* and reprinted in the *Dollar Newspaper*.

The story tells how William Legrand, a nature enthusiast of Sullivan's Island, South Carolina, finds an unusual gold-hued beetle and makes a sketch of it for his friend, the tale's narrator, on a piece of parchment found on the beach. When the narrator happens to hold the paper near a flame, Legrand notices that there are cryptic directions hidden on the parchment in INVISIBLE INK. Legrand applies more heat to the paper to reveal the cryptogram. Then an alphabet FREQUENCY count enables him to recover the message. As the plot unfolds, Legrand, a servant, and the narrator go on an exciting search, at the end of which they discover a wonderful secret—the hidden treasure of pirate captain William Kidd.

Although the tale was criticized for plot inconsistencies, the great success of "The Gold-Bug" popularized cryptographic and cryptanalytic techniques. Its energy and proven appeal also inspired other writers to spread the word about these subjects.

Polyalphabetic Substitution,

a method of creating a CIPHER through the use of more than one replacement alphabet.

This type of concealment method gives cryptographers several levels of letters within which to hide their original words and sentences. From the point of view of the cryptanalyst, the multiple layers create many impediments. Analytical tools such as counting letter FREQUENCY and finding typical introductory terms or words associated with a particular field are rendered less effective by multiple alphabets.

Plaintext:	a b c d e f g h i j k l m
Cipher alphabet #1:	l m n o p q r s t u v w x
Cipher alphabet #2:	i j k l m n o p q r s t u

Plaintext:	n o p q r s t u v w x y z
Cipher alphabet #1:	y z a b c d e f g h i j k
Cipher alphabet #2:	v w x y z a b c d e f g h

Message word: t e c h n o l o g y
Alphabet #1: e p n s y z w z r j
Alphabet #2: b m k p v w t w o g

Polybius (ca. 203–120 B.C.), Greek historian and cryptographer. In addition to his historical writings, Polybius also made an interesting contribution to the field of CRYPTOGRAPHY, creating a method of signaling using torches and a square filled with letters that had numbered columns and rows. Each of the letters had a pair of numerical coordinates derived from the numbers of the row and column in which it was located. Using the English alphabet and combining *i* and *j* in a single cell, a 5 × 5 square could be arranged as below:

	1	2	3	4	5
1	a	b	c	d	e
2	f	g	h	ij	k
3	l	m	n	o	p
4	q	r	s	t	u
5	v	w	x	y	z

Polybius proposed the use of the torches to convey these numbers. For example, two torches in the left hand and one in the right would indicate *21*. The observer would then look at his own letter group and see that these numerals are the coordinates of the letter *f*. With a series of signal sites, including early telescope-like devices for viewing, Polybius hoped to transfer messages across great distances. However, there is no known account of his ideas being applied.

To later writers seeking methods to conceal their messages, the square became a type of checkerboard. It was used at different times and in various ways to turn letters into digits, generate SUBSTITUTION ciphers, and divide the coordinates into parts (FRACTIONATING CIPHERS), among other matrix variations (see KNOCK CIPHER, QUADRATIC CODE, and NIHILIST CIPHER).

Polygraphic, a concealment technique that encrypts two or more characters at one time. In this system, when a matrix of letters is enciphered, the matrix is considered as a unit. If any part of this unit is altered, the whole encryption is changed.

A primary example of a polygraphic CIPHER is the digraphic form PLAYFAIR CIPHER, in which digraphs (pairs of letters) were encrypted in a 5×5 square with their arrangement set by a variable KEYWORD.

Another digraphic example is a cipher using a pair of letter squares, each made with the letters of a keyword followed by the remaining alphabet letters in order (the letters *i* and *j* are combined). The keywords are *democrat* and *republican.*

r	e	p	u	b		d	e	m	o	c
l	i	c	a	n		r	a	t	b	f
d	f	g	h	k		g	h	i	k	l
m	o	q	s	t		n	p	q	s	u
v	w	x	y	z		v	w	x	y	z

Encipherment begins by finding the first PLAINTEXT letter in the first square and the second plaintext letter in the second square and mentally drawing a diagonal line from one to the other. The CIPHERTEXT equivalents of these letters are the letters on the ends of the opposite imaginary diagonal line. For example, the digraph *du* is on a diagonal from the third row of the first square to the fourth row of the second square. Its encryption equivalent is *lm*, the letters on a diagonal from right to left and in the same columns as *u* and *d*, respectively.

Decipherment is accomplished by locating the first cipher letter *l* in the second square and the second cipher letter *m* in the first square and then finding the letters that form the opposite diagonal, thereby reversing the original process.

A different approach to polygraphic encryption was achieved by a mathematics professor named LESTER HILL. Developed around 1929, the Hill system provided plaintext characters with numerical values. This was accomplished by equating mixed digits with an alphabet using the numbers 0 to 25.

a b c . . . i j . . . m n . . . q r s . . . z
5 9 13 . . . 6 17 . . . 8 21 . . . 1 15 11 . . . 18

Numbers higher than 25 in this process were subject to *modulo 26*, a method by which numerals were reduced by deleting multiples of 26 from their totals. For example, 56 is 4 *modulo* 26 since 56 minus 26 × 2, or 52, results in a remainder of 4. This procedure made it possible to use the equations of Hill's system without having to resort to unwieldy numbers and uneven totals.

The digits equated with the given plaintext alphabet were then put into a series of algebraic equations. A sequence of constant values became the KEY and served as the basis for each multiplication and addition equation. The plaintext was represented by xs and the ciphertext by ys.

$$y_1 = 8x_1 + 6x_2 + 9x_3 + 5x_4$$

When equations such as these were solved, encipherment was achieved. In the partial alphabet shown above, the word *aims* is assigned the numerals 5, 6, 8, and 11. These are placed in the equation as shown below.

In the alphabet above, 21 is *n*. Thus y_1 = *n*, the first ciphertext letter. Since the change of one letter's numeric value in the equation would alter the sum, poly- (multiple) encipherments were possible. Decipherment also required a fixed set of equations into which numeral values were placed and solved, for example: $x_1 = 23y_1 + 20y_2 + 5y_3 + 1y_4$. This permitted the encryption and decryption of larger polygraphs than would be possible in the standard graphic versions, and their built-in protection against solution was strong indeed. However, the method was too complicated for general application and was never adopted for widespread use.

Porta, Giovanni (1535–1615), Italian scientist and author. The erudite Neapolitan Giovanni Battista Porta was a true Renaissance man. His early travels and studies of earthly wonders enabled him to write his first book, *Magia naturalis*, at age 22. As an officer of an early scientific society called the Academy of Lynxes, he discussed many of the important issues of his day and met other farsighted men, including Galileo. His many writings included such topics as astronomy, architecture, distillation, meteorology, and pneumatics. He also expanded *Magia naturalis* to 20 volumes, including recipes for INVISIBLE INKS and techniques of STEGANOGRAPHY, or physically concealing the existence of messages.

These descriptions of secretive methods were expanded in the book that gained Porta his place in the library of cryptologic achievements. In *De Furtivis Literarum Notis*, Porta very capably summarized the known secrecy systems of his day, including ancient and current concealment processes, clues to their solution, and critiques of weak examples. He gave a very early classification of methods (letter changes and letter values) that was the precursor of later position shifts and alphabet exchanges (see TRANSPOSITION and SUBSTITUTION).

Among the new types of CIPHERS was one that was digraphic, the first known cipher wherein a single symbol represented two letters. This was an advance for CRYPTOGRAPHY because it expanded the ways

$$y_1 = 8(5) + 6(6) + 9(8) + 5(11)$$
$$y_1 = 40 + 36 + 72 + 55$$
$$(modulo\ 26) = 14 + 10 + 20 + 3 = 47,\ \text{which is 21 } modulo\ 26$$

that letters could be concealed and complicated matters for would-be solvers. (For the first literal digraphic cipher, see PLAYFAIR CIPHER.) Porta advised using lengthy terms and irrelevant words in a cipher KEY.

After describing how elaborate concealment systems could be created, he just as artfully explained ways to remove them. In 1563, Porta is thought to have published the first European solution of a MONOALPHABETIC SUBSTITUTION that contained neither real nor false word divisions. Up to that time, ciphers had been particularly vulnerable at such divisions.

Porta was also foresighted in discussing another analytic tool—the presence of one or more probable words in an encrypted text. For example, if the message in question was known to be about trade matters, words related to types of goods, money amounts, travel routes, port names, and so forth, might be expected to appear in the text. Knowledge of the spelling and syntactical usage of such words would help in isolating and identifying them.

The first to write about POLYALPHABETIC SUBSTITUTIONS, Porta's primary contribution to this field was in combining the best elements of preceding styles. He then proceeded to solve ciphers with mixed alphabets and keys of different letter lengths.

POTUS-PRIME,

the name for the communication system on which Franklin Roosevelt and Winston Churchill sent trans-Atlantic cables during World War II. (POTUS = President of the United States; PRIME = Prime Minister.)

Because their plans affected world history, the two leaders' messages had to be secure. Thus, early voice-scrambler methods were supplanted by a much more secure system that combined an advancement in CIPHER MACHINES and Western Union technology. The equipment that made it possible was called the zero machine.

Messages from Churchill to Roosevelt were conveyed by the U.S. Army, and U.S. Navy personnel handled the communications in the opposite direction. Thus neither department had full access to all of their contents. These exchanges were assigned the letters *xxxo*, which indicated a higher level of priority than did the "urgent" designation.

Communiqués were typed with on-line SIGABAs to produce CIPHERTEXT. They were linked by a relay box to a Western Union office. The encrypted signals from the SIGABA were brought through a transmitter distributor in this office and directly onto the trans-Atlantic cable on the first available free circuit. After the signals crossed the ocean, they were received by another SIGABA, which DECIPHERED the material and restored the PLAINTEXT.

In March 1943, the Western Union cable became a Variplex system, allowing more than one message to be sent at the same time. However, this improvement was offset by the diminished speed of transmitting any given message when the cable was in heavy use.

A problem arose because the SIGABAs at both transoceanic locations needed exact synchronization, since false pulses along the cable produced the wrong stepping order at the decrypting terminus, resulting in nonsensical text. This was fixed by a device called a "kick eliminator," the application of which enabled the zero machine to be the swiftest, best-protected transmission of its type.

ROTORS were at the core of SIGABA security. Therefore, indicators were sent with each message to tell the receiving personnel which rotor settings were necessary for decipherment. Along with the special priority designation *xxxo*, the sending operator applied indicator letters from a table.

AHY	JSGUF	OFA	XEMWR
ECA	ZKQBR	OGE	CLFZO
EDE	CNATB	OHI	XHTLF
EFI	RSPHJ	OJO	MPIGR
EGO	KGNGA	OKU	HZAFX
EHU	BPCIV	OLY	QUYNP
EJU	SKOJQ	UGA	EMDQH

From the list of three-letter groups the sender chose two, such as *OKU* and *ECA*, and combined them. In this case, the indicator would be *OKUECA*, the receiving SIGABA's control rotor setting would be *HZAFX*, and the alphabet rotor setting would be *ZKQBR*.

Public Key, a KEY published in a directory available to the public.

In a single-key system, the message transmitter and addressee both keep the key a secret. However, the distribution of such keys is a significant security problem, especially when more than two people need the same key.

In 1976 Professor Martin Hellman and researcher Whitfield Diffie, of Stanford University, proposed a new type of encryption method. Called a public-key cryptosystem, it avoided key distribution difficulties by having encryption keys published in a directory available to the public. Security was maintained by a second decryption key. Using the national directory, one person could send secret data to someone else's COMPUTER. Protection would be maintained since barring theft, only the recipient would have the decryption key. Because it is computationally impractical to recover the decryption key by possessing the encryption key, the encryption key does not need to be concealed. It should be protected from being covertly exchanged or modified, however, since a fraudulent encryption could be used, in conjunction with a decryption made for it, to steal data.

This Hellman–Diffie proposal was apparently anticipated by a similar version developed by the NATIONAL SECURITY AGENCY (NSA) a decade earlier. As the public key concept became well known, it led to new suggestions and methodologies. As with the DES (Data Encryption Standard), debates arose over whether universities and companies should be allowed to develop such systems, and whether organizations such as the NSA should be entitled to have knowledge of their mathematics and to approve their applications.

These techniques, also known as TWO-KEY CRYPTOGRAPHY, and ongoing improvements remain a subject of political debate and business competition into the 1990s.

Pulse Code Modulation, a speech security system, in which soundwaves are converted into a sequence of binary electrical impulses.

In a typical example, the speech is sampled several thousand times a second. Each sample is identified with one of a series of amplitude levels, represented by a multi-element binary pattern. The result is a sequence of binary digits. With advances in technology, streams of these binary signals have reached the level of 24,000-plus bits per second.

The binary impulses can be encrypted by a process similar to that developed for the teletypewriter by GILBERT VERNAM (which involved the addition of KEY pulses to PLAINTEXT message letters to produce the CIPHERTEXT). Binary digits are combined with a binary key stream produced by a key-generating COMPUTER. The result is the encryption, which offers strong protection for speech. Computers are also used to store key pulses on magnetic tape.

Purple, a U.S. CODENAME for a Japanese CIPHER MACHINE during World War II.

Purple was used to conceal Japanese diplomatic messages after February 1939. (It should be noted that many historians refer to the crucial 1941 Purple messages as the Purple CODE. Most CRYPTOLOGY experts refer to the mechanism itself as a cipher machine.) As tensions between Washington and Tokyo worsened, U.S. cryptanalysts increased their efforts to Herculean proportions in order to glean the secrets of this potential enemy.

The Purple Analog. (Courtesy of Gustavus Simmons.)

The Japanese called this cryptographic mechanism 97-*shiki O-bun Injiki*, or AL-PHABETIC TYPEWRITER 97. (Also written '97, the date was derived from 1937, the year of its invention and the 97th year of the 25th century in the ancient Japanese calendar.) It was an advanced version of a machine known as RED and has been referred to by several historians as the "B" machine, while Red is called "A."

PLAINTEXT was put into the 97 mechanism with an electrical typewriter keyboard. The touch of a given key sent a letter impulse on a journey through a plugboard, into an even more complex maze of telephone selector switches, and then to another plugboard that was the inverse of the input plugboard. The letter emerged as CIPHERTEXT on the output typewriter. A significant feature of this plugboard arrangement was that it was double ended—thus the output was the inverse of the input.

Late in 1938, decryptions of Red system messages announced the planned inception of a new machine cipher. A decipherment on February 18, 1939, announced that the new mechanism would be activated for Tokyo and its embassy transmissions two days later.

WILLIAM FRIEDMAN and the U.S. Army's Signal Intelligence Service (Army SIS) team included Robert Ferner, Samuel Snyder, and Genevieve Grotjan. Cryptology expert David Kahn credits Genevieve Grotjan with finding important patterns or intervals that revealed Purple secrets.

For a time, this group joined LAURENCE SAFFORD and the U.S. Navy's OP-20-G in a frantic attempt to decrypt the Purple messages. They were fortunate to have some comparative texts from both Red (to less important consulates) and Purple (to primary embassies).

More painstaking pencil-and-paper analysis revealed additional encryption arrangements. A very important break occured when a technician named Leo Rosen discovered that telephone selector switches would help in tests of solution ideas.

In autumn 1940, the SIS team, including Japanese-language specialist FRANK ROWLETT, had developed a blueprint for what they hoped was duplication of the Japanese system (by this time the OP-20-G members had been withdrawn to work on Japanese naval codes). By late fall, the first Purple analogs had been built by technician Rosen for $685.00 worth of hardware. Later versions were built with navy help.

A maze of wires and clattering relays housed inside a black wooden box, the analog was an astounding achievement of cryptanalysis and engineering, and it did indeed succeed in decrypting Japanese diplomatic exchanges.

The extent of SIS's success was realized at the end of the war, when it was discovered that the total of five Purple analogs were actually less likely to garble encryptions than were the Japanese originals. Furthermore, a captured Japanese 97/"B" machine was found to differ from the original U.S. analog by only two wire connections.

Q Code, a NONSECRET CODE developed to enhance worldwide radio communications. Like other international codes such as NAVAL SIGNALS, MORSE CODE, and the Z code, the Q Code was developed as a means to facilitate global commerce, travel, and emergency efforts. A series of meetings was called to regulate developments in radio, including the Berlin International Radiotelegraph Conference (1906), Washington Radiotelegraph Convention (1927), and the Madrid Conference (1932). The Q Code developed from these and others that convened until the outbreak of the World War II. With the end of hostilities, other conferences resumed and have maintained international standards into the age of satellite communications.

The Q Code covered such subjects as recognition between stations (exchange of names and positions), radio operation (order of telegrams, transit, and charges), control of aircraft (transmissions about height, speed, and visibility); airport locations, meterological conditions, and dangerous situations.

A series of abbreviations beginning with *Q* were used to convey such information. Some sample codeletters, along with their meanings, which could be in the form of either a question or an answer, depending on the context, is shown at left on the following page.

The Q Code has been revised over the years to reflect the technological advances affecting radio communications, such as use of geostationary satellites, and changes in maritime mobile services, radiotelegraphy, and radiotelephony. At right on the following page is a sample of recent equivalents.

Abbreviation	Question	Answer or advice
QAA	At what time do you expect to arrive at . . . ?	I expect to arrive at . . . at . . .
QTC	How many telegrams have you to send?	I have . . . telegrams for you.
QFS(b)	Please place the radiobeacon at . . . in operation.	The radiobeacon at . . . will be in operation in . . . minutes.
QFB	Are fresh meterological observations required?	Fresh meterological observations are required.
QTM(a)	Send radioelectric signals and submarine sound signals to enable me to fix my bearing and my distance.	I will send radioelectric signals and submarine sound signals.

Maritime Mobile Service—October 1986

Abbreviation	Question	Answer or Advice
QOA	Can you communicate by radiotelegraphy (500 kHz)?	I can communicate by radiotelegraphy (500 kHz).
QOB	Can you communicate by radiotelephony (2 182 kHz)?	I can communicate by radiotelephony (2 182 kHz)
QOH	Shall I send a phasing signal for . . . seconds?	Send a phasing signal for . . . seconds.
QOJ	Will you listen on . . . kHz (or MHz) for signals of emergency position-indicating radiobeacons?	I am listening on . . . kHz (or MHz) for signals of emergency position-indicating radiobeacons.

Quadratic Code, a CODE developed by Gen. Leslie Groves, who was in charge of the Manhattan Engineering District, the CODENAME for the top-secret effort to make the atomic bomb during World War II.

This widely based operation required Signal Corps cryptosystems to protect telegraphic messages. But telephone communications were also increasingly frequent as the project grew, and it was to protect these that Gen. Groves created what he called a quadratic code. He gave variations of it to important officials and was the only person who held all the methods.

The quadratic code was a 10 × 10 checkerboard, a typewritten square about 3½ × 4 inches in size. It could be carried in a wallet, and its loss was to be reported immediately. Such a code was used by Groves and Lt. Col. Peer da Silva, who was chief of security at Site Y (Los Angeles, New Mexico).

	1	2	3	4	5	6	7	8	9	0
1	I_8	P	I		O	U	O		P	N
2	W	E	U	T	E	K_6		L	O	
3	E	U	G	N	B_4	T	N		S	T
4	T	A	Z_2	M	D		I	O	E	
5	S_9	V	T	J		E		Y		H
6	N_7	A	O	L	N	S	U	G	O	E
7		C	B	A	F	R	S_5		I	R
8	I	C	W	Y_3	R	U	A	M		N_0
9	M	V	T		H_0	P	D	I	X	Q
0	L	S	R_1	E	T	D	E	A	H	E

Quadratic code. (Reprinted with permission from *The Codebreakers* by David Kahn, Macmillan, 1967.)

With this checkerboard, the general's last name could be encrypted as *33 76 48 92 22 39*, among other possibilities. This was done by locating each letter in the name and recording the numbers at the left of the letter's row and then at the top of its column. Decryption was accomplished using a copy of the same design.

In its time, the quadratic code had enough alphabet letters and numbers to counteract FREQUENCY counts of typical English letters by potential enemy spies. By all accounts, the Groves method was never compromised. However, the same cannot be said for the atomic research program as a whole, which was infiltrated by Soviet agents and undermined by traitors. (see IGOR GOUZENKO and KGB CABLES).

Radio Serials, radio adventure and mystery programs of the 1930s and '40s that mirrored their celluloid rivals by keeping their audiences breathless with a cliffhanger ending to each episode.

Scriptwriters and advertisers appealed to all ages with such characters as the Shadow, Dick Tracy, and Orphan Annie. Among other gimmicks devised to attract the younger audiences was the secret decoder, to be obtained by sending in boxtops or other proofs of purchase. The imaginative designs of these metal decoders and the colorful graphics of their accompanying manuals became a nationwide fad in the 1930s. They also allowed listeners to feel that they played an active role in the plot action. Soon other characters, ranging from Tom Mix to the Green Hornet, joined the CODE-sending trend.

The early decoders, often in rings or badges, contained a form of SYMBOL CRYPTOGRAPHY using daggers, stars, or other figures associated with a given hero or heroine. A message containing a CODEWORD was broadcast over the radio, with which the young listener would align the decoder's pointer. A matching line or arrow on the opposite side of the decoder indicated the secret word or name.

Jack Armstrong, the "all-American boy," had a "Secret Whistle Code" to communicate with his friends over the airwaves:

Signal	Message
One Whistle (short)	Attention
Two Whistles (short)	Be on guard for trouble

Signal	Message
Three Whistles (one long, two short)	In danger—come at once
Four Whistles (short)	We're being watched
Two Whistles (long)	Important news— meet me at once

2 A	4 B	6 C	8 D	10 E	12 F
14 G	16 H	18 I	20 J	22 K	24 L
26 M	28 N	30 O	32 P	34 Q	36 R
38 S	40 T	42 U	44 V	46 W	48 X
50 Y	52 Z	54 &			

A type of sign language developed from the Orphan Annie "secret salute" and "secret handshake" that identified club members. Accompanying a series of more elaborate decoders through the mid-1930s, the expanded sequence of gestures was known as the *Secret Wig-Wag Signs*. These signs included touching the ear with the first fingers of each hand to warn of eavesdroppers and holding the index finger and thumb together to form the letter *A*, the sign that Orphan Annie would soon be on the air.

By the late 1930s, in response to trouble overseas, the radio serials broadcast stories about spies, saboteurs, and traitors such as Ivan Shark. In opposing these subversive forces, Captain Midnight and his Secret Squadron used more complicated concealment methods that were actually CIPHERS similar to Orphan Annie's "Even-Number Code" (see above right). Their decryption mechanisms had radio-type dials containing numbers that were aligned with letters; while still called decoders, these mechanisms had evolved into types of CIPHER DISKS.

Rail Fence, a simple type of ROUTE or TRANSPOSITION cipher that has a prear-ranged order and is written in a predetermined though not rigid matrix.

The matrix of the rail fence is generally rectangular. The PLAINTEXT of the message is transcribed geometrically according to a planned direction and read in another prescribed direction to create the CIPHERTEXT. Reading up, down, and across apparently reminded someone of a rail fence, and this name became associated with the method.

A depth-two rail fence has two rows and an *n*-column array, with the number of columns determined by the length of the given message. The plaintext is written in columns along a cryptic route, that runs, in this example, from the top to the bottom of each column in succession. The ciphertext can be made by reading the letters left to right by groups of five, beginning with the top row:

Message: lamp signal her cottage at midnight

Rail fence: l m s g a h r o t g a m d i h
a p i n l e c t a e t i n g t

Ciphertext: lmsga hrotg amdih apinl ectae tingt

The intended receiver knows to interpret the ciphertext by dividing the letters into two equal groups with a vertical line, leaving 15 letters on each side:

lmsga hrotg amdih | apinl ectae tingt

Beginning at the left with *l*, the recipient reads each letter in the left half of the ciphertext followed immediately by the corresponding letter of the right, in this case *a*, continually alternating until the plaintext is recovered.

A three-level version of the rail fence yields a different combination of five-letter groups for the same plaintext:

```
l   s   a   r   t   a   d   h
 a p i n l e c t a e t i n g t
  m   g   h   o   g   m   i
```
Ciphertext: lsart adhap inlec taeti ngtmg hogmi

The rail fence was a popular method in the early decades of CRYPTOGRAPHY. It faded with the rise of more complex systems such as NOMENCLATORS in the Middle Ages and CODEBOOKS in the 1600s and 1700s, but it regained some of its popularity during the U.S. CIVIL WAR, when it was apparently used for concealments of military telegraph messages as well as the reports of agents for both the Union and the Confederacy.

Rebecca, a 1938 novel by Daphne du Maurier that was used as a CIPHER by German agents operating in Cairo during World War II. This cryptographic system was based on the prearranged use of particular pages of text on certain days. The concealed messages were broadcast to fellow agents who had copies of the novel for deciphering purposes.

A group of German agents involved in what was known as the Kondor mission sought to obtain information about the British forces opposing Gen. Irwin Rommel in the North African desert. The two key members of this mission were John Eppler and Peter Monkaster. The former was born of German parents in Egypt and had acted as an Abwehr *provocateur*, attempting to inflame long-smouldering Arab hatred of Great Britain. Peter Monkaster was a long-time German resident in East Africa working as an oil mechanic.

In May 1942 the two made their way through British and Egyptian checkpoints with the help of forged papers and their ability to speak English. Once in Cairo, they gathered a group of supporters, including staunch Arab nationalists, a pro-Nazi priest and an exotic dancer named Hekmeth Fahmy. A primary attraction at the Kit Kat Cabaret, Mademoiselle Fahmy was one of Egypt's most popular *danseuses du ventre* (belly dancers). She was also an agent for the Free Officers' Movement in the Egyptian army, and she was eager to undermine the British cause. Hekmeth was already actively involved in liaisons with a "Maj. Smith" of England's Government Headquarters in Cairo. During their trysts on her Nile River houseboat, Eppler was able to study the contents of the major's briefcase.

Monkaster and Eppler rented another houseboat nearby, in which they installed one of their transceivers. Taking advantage of the major's weakness for Mlle. Fahmy, they regularly studied his documents which contained facts about British troop dispositions and plans. The important details were enciphered with the *Rebecca* system and sent to one of two locations: Rommel's *Horch* (wireless intelligence) Company or the *Wehrmacht's* radio outpost in Athens.

Fortunately for the British Eighth Army, carelessness and a courageous counterespionage agent foiled the Germans' plans. While scouting for information, Eppler met a young woman named Yvette, paid her for her company, and asked to see her again soon. She agreed, but not because of his charm or his pound notes. She was a member of the Jewish Agency that was working with Britain's secret intelligence service, MI-6. Finding Eppler's behavior and plentiful money suspicious, she visited his houseboat again and made a very valuable discovery. While Eppler and Monkaster slept amid empty bottles and full ashtrays, Yvette found a copy of *Rebecca* and some notepaper covered with groups of letters and grids. But before she could reveal her discovery, she was arrested by local police, who were watching suspicious persons in the area.

Soon thereafter, Britain's field security in Cairo closed in on the Kondor pair, who refused to reveal their secrets despite thorough interrogation. Fortunately for England, Yvette finally got a chance to reveal her notes, which British cryptanalysts were able to use to solve the *Rebecca* cipher. Impersonators replaced the jailed Kondor team and began sending false information to Gen. Rommel. These faked reports were believed and had an important effect by confounding German actions in the region.

Red, color that was used to designate certain U.S. and Japanese encryption systems.

U.S. diplomatic CODEBOOKS were named for the colors of their bindings. Before World War I, the United States had had both Red and BLUE CODES using groups of five figures. The Red preceded the Blue, and both were thin masks at best. They were slightly improved by SUPERENCIPHERMENTS and then supplanted by the GREEN CIPHER (actually a codebook) in the period before World War I.

The Japanese Red Code was used during the 1920s. In the spring of 1920, the Office of Naval Intelligence and the FBI suspected that a Japanese vice-consul in New York City was actually a navy officer. Picking the locks on the consulate's door and safe, the ONI team discovered a Japanese naval codebook, which was duplicated in lengthy photography sessions and then translated. After further break-ins in 1926 and 1927, ONI analysts had produced two volumes, which they bound in red buckram and designated as the *Red Code* (also the *Red Book*). This material was given to LAURENCE SAFFORD, Joseph Rochefort, and their small Navy staff of cryptanalysts, including AGNES DRISCOLL. The team applied the Red Code to interceptions of Japanese radio traffic and managed to break some concealments.

In 1931, after HERBERT YARDLEY recounted the decryption of important Japanese telegrams in his book THE AMERICAN BLACK CHAMBER, Japanese military and intelligence officers determined never again to be so vulnerable. The result was a series of new Japanese military and diplomatic cryptosystems. One of these new machines that was used for diplomatic purposes was called Red by U.S. cryptanalysts.

This new CIPHER MACHINE depended

in part on the assumption that the Japanese language was a formidable obstacle to most Westerners. It consisted of a typewriter for message input, a telephone exchange plugboard, a ROTOR (or wired code wheel), a 47-pin wheel, and a typewriter for CIPHERTEXT output. (Some analysts believe that the Red, or at least one version of it, had two rotors.)

The one clearly identifiable wired code wheel was made in the half rotor design. Its exit points or contacts aligned with the standard fixed end plate for electric current transfer. The half rotor's input contacts were governed by slip rings, 26 of which were positioned on its shaft. The shaft, in turn, contained 26 input points that were contacted by the rings to transmit an electrical current. A step of the rotor and a turn of the shaft caused the rings to slip around the shaft as they maintained position with their input wires.

The stepping of the rotor was dependent on the 47-pin wheel, which also had 47 teeth, the arrangement of which determined the rotor's movement and thus the encryption. The current also entered the plugboard, first between the keyboard and the rotor input and a second time between the rotor exit and the output typewriter. Daily resettings of the plugs added to the polyalphabetic nature of the machine and further complicated decryption efforts.

Yet by 1936, cryptanalysts of the U.S. Signal Intelligence Service, particularly FRANK ROWLETT and SOLOMON KULLBACK, had broken the Red shield when they found that this machine encrypted Romaji, a Japanese type of Latin alphabet containing 26 letters. They were even able to predict what KEYS would be used to encrypt messages nine days before they were used. This first U.S. solution of an electromechanical device was an important accomplishment that paved the way for future decryptions of Japanese machine ciphers by U.S. analysts during World War II.

Retail Encryption Methods, cryptosystems historically used by retailers to conceal facts about financial matters.

From the bazaars of old to today's televised home shopping, retailers have always had various types of secret communications.

As commerce expanded during the Renaissance, secrets were kept from rivals and customers alike. Merchants developed JARGON CODES that maintained trade details and permitted conversations within earshot but beyond the understanding of outsiders. Altered word forms with NULLS, meaningless but purposely confusing syllables, constituted a type of secret language.

In modern times, businesses have developed other systems for the transfer of confidential information. In the 1890s, a Maryland-based theater chain used a CODE with its out-of-state locations in which specific words designated a given night's receipts at a particular theater. These encoded results were telegraphed to the headquarters in Baltimore, giving the owners a quick accounting and immediate feedback on the drawing power of *specific* performances.

Retail CRYPTANALYSIS was used in the 1950s by employees of Macy's in New York City. The store was obligated to comply with the minimum price levels set by manufacturers. However, Macy's suspected that its competitors were not honoring this practice, and its officials were able to uncover an illicit pricing plan being used by Masters, Inc., a New York City discounter.

The price-tag code was a tactic used by retailers to hide wholesale prices on price tags. The color of the ink used, the size of the tag, or a seemingly meaningless mark told merchants at a glance how much of a discount could be offered to customers who were unaware of the original cost. By breaking Masters' Code, Macy's was able to demonstrate that the store was selling merchandise below the prescribed price rules.

Some stores have used their own names as KEYWORDS to generate digits and thereby encrypt prices. An establishment with the name VALCO, for example, could choose the phrase "First VALCO" in order to encrypt the numbers 0 to 9.

F	I	R	S	T		V	A	L	C	O
1	2	3	4	5		6	7	8	9	0

Under this system, the three letters *FRO* would represent 130, $1.30, or $130. *FVLO* could be 1680, $16.80, or $1680. These letters could be placed in very small print on the fronts or backs of price tags for comparison with list prices so that a sales clerk could know, for instance, how deeply he or she could discount a product. Such letter groups could also serve as a way to identify stock.

Room 40, the name for Britain's premier CODE and CIPHER branch during the early 20th century.

The inadequacy of Great Britain's pre-World War I intelligence-gathering operations was revealed after the radio interception of the *Göben* message in August 1914. The message was deciphered, but too late to prevent the German battle cruiser from shelling Russian ports on the the Black Sea, prompting strategically located Turkey to ally itself with Germany and the Austro-Hungarian empire.

In the wake of this setback, Whitehall ordered a redoubling of the military's interception and solution efforts. Led by the director of naval education, Sir Alfred Ewing, an expanded CRYPTANALYSIS unit moved into new offices in room 40 of the Admiralty. Although the staff was known officially as section 25 of the Intelligence Division, the more popular "Room 40" became the common name for the group.

Lady Luck smiled on them with news from the *Kriegsmarine's* light cruiser, the MAGDEBURG. In September 1914 this ship ran aground in the Baltic Sea, and Russian sailors recovered a CODEBOOK (some accounts say two) from the partially wrecked vessel, which they turned over to the British Admiralty. Within three weeks the novice Room 40 analysts discovered that the codebook's CODEWORDS had been subjected to SUPERENCIPHERMENT, which enabled them to DECIPHER a series of earlier radio intercepts.

A second measure of good fortune was granted to the Admiralty in December when a British trawler recovered a chest that had been cast overboard by a *Kriegsmarine* warship during an October clash at Heliogoland Bight near Germany's northwestern coast. This yielded another codebook, which was added to the *Magdeburg* material. These discoveries, combined with an expanded radio direction-finding network and studies of the German vessels sending the wireless messages, all had a direct effect on countering the Kaiser's surface and U-boat fleets.

In January 1915, the resulting information was put to use when the British Admiralty learned that the German High Seas Fleet would be positioned in a shallow sector of the North Sea off the northern coast of England. Following a plan to intercept the enemy, the Royal Navy's Vice Adm. Sir David Beatty and his dreadnoughts steamed forward to stop the Germans from returning to their home base. In what came to be known as the BATTLE OF DOGGER BANK, the Royal Navy sank one German capital ship and badly damaged two others.

The next major naval engagement, the BATTLE OF JUTLAND (May 1916), also involved radio interception and encryption analysis. However, confusion about the location of the German flagship and a mistake in charting the Germans' course led to a missed opportunity for Britain's Grand Fleet.

During this period, the Room 40 staff were busy collecting codebooks from sources including a wrecked German zeppelin and sunken U-boats located by deep-sea divers. The leadership of Room 40 was passed from Sir Alfred Ewing to Capt. William R. Hall, director of naval intelligence, who was the man in charge when the most crucial interception of the war occurred.

This intercepted message came to be known as the ZIMMERMANN TELEGRAM. In January 1917, German Foreign Minister Arthur Zimmermann sent a cable message to the German embassy in Mexico. Although two transmission routes were used to ensure the arrival of the coded and superenciphered dispatch, both messages were intercepted and decrypted, revealing a plan that put a bayonet at the back of the United States.

Germany was about to engage in unrestricted submarine warfare against neutral shipping. Fearing that this would push an uncommitted United States clearly into England's camp, Zimmermann proposed an alliance with Mexico. In exchange for making war on the United States, Mexico was promised the region of Texas, Arizona, and New Mexico it had lost in the Mexican War (1846–48). The offer also involved "generous financial support" and indicated that Japan might join the scheme.

The telegram's decryption was made to look like a U.S. intelligence success so the Germans wouldn't suspect the contribution of the British cryptologists. After President Woodrow Wilson and his advisors agreed to inform the press, the March 1, 1917, banner headlines created a furor. The exposé shocked the United States and led to President Wilson's war address to Congress on April 1, 1917. A declaration of war passed decisively.

The Room 40 solution seekers were at their zenith of achievement as the United States entered World War I on the side of Britain and France.

Rosicrucians' Cipher, a cryptosystem applied by the Rosicrucians to conceal their secrets. The Rosicrucians were a secretive scholarly and religious group whose origins in the 15th century are still shrouded in mystery. Some historic sources refer to their founder as a far-sighted sage named Christian Rosenkreuz, whose early followers purportedly chose their symbol, a cross bearing a rose, from his name. Other texts describe the name as being derived from the Latin *rosa*, "rose," and *crux*, "cross."

A second point of debate concerns the secret writings at the core of the Rosicrucians' beliefs, called either the *Fama* or *Fama Fraternitatis.* Presenting ideas about mankind, nature, and the world that were considered heretical and enlightened, the documents were said to have been written by Rosenkreuz or Johann Valentin Andreä.

With members ranging throughout central Europe to the Mediterranean, the Rosicrucians were confronted with rival religious groups and were persecuted in some regions. To preserve their secrets, they used a form of CRYPTOGRAPHY similar to the FREEMASONS' CIPHER of the 1700s.

The Rosicrucians' systems baffled outsiders for a long time before disenchanted insiders revealed its secrets. The success of the CIPHER lay in its simplicity, since it did not require a hard-to-remember KEY or a CODEWORD that could be divulged to a third party. As shown in the example below, which uses the English alphabet, the cipher was arranged with a matrix of nine segments:

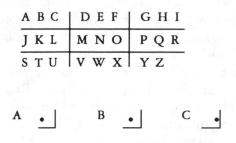

Each letter is represented by a dot marking its position in the segment of the matrix that institutes its cell. To an uninformed observer, the figures appear to be a type of SYMBOL CRYPTOGRAPHY, but they are actually a form of SUBSTITUTION. The Rosicrucians could spell their name this way:

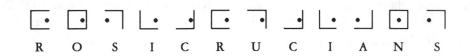

R O S I C R U C I A N S

Rossignol, Antoine (1600–1682), French cryptologist and political advisor. Rossignol's career began with a violent conflict between religious rivals in 1628. Catholic forces had surrounded the Hugenot town of Réalmont in southern France and captured a Huguenot carrying an encrypted message to his confederates. This missive was sent to young Rossignol, who decrypted its contents, revealing that the Protestants had a very low supply of ammunition. The Catholics showed the de-

cryption to the defenders of Réalmont, and, their weakness exposed, they abruptly surrendered.

Rossignol became the bane of the Protestants when he solved letters intercepted from their beseiged fortress of La Rochelle. On learning of the Huguenots' plan to be relieved by British naval forces, French Cardinal Richelieu ordered extra vessels into the area and strengthened the armaments of nearby forts to thwart the British navy. La Rochelle's beleaguered inhabitants were forced to give up the fight.

The French court rewarded Rossignal with money and favors and he began service to Louis XIII and Richelieu, as well as their successors Louis XIV and Cardinal Mazarin.

Rossignol also developed an improvement in the then-predominant NOMENCLATOR. He recognized that this cryptomethod, which combined CODEWORDS with a CIPHER alphabet, had a significant weakness. Both the plain terms and the code terms were listed in alphabetical or numerical order, regularity that had helped him to solve the concealments of others. Seeking a better way to protect French communications, he developed the two-part nomenclator. In the encoding part of this system the PLAINTEXT appeared in alphabetical order and the encrypting portions were randomly arranged, whereas in the decoding segment, the codetext, was alphabetized and the plaintext was randomly arranged.

Expertise with CODES and ciphers had given Antoine Rossignol a comfortable and respected life and he is said to have continued working with them into his retirement years. A noted poet immortal-

ized him, and he was the first career cryptologist to be included in the ranks of influential people.

Rote Kapelle, German for the "Red Orchestra," an organization of important contributors to SOVIET CRYPTOLOGY before and during World War II. Its name came from the Soviet radio transmitters, called "music boxes," that broadcast from inside the Third Reich and other countries of Europe, the operators of which were known as "pianists."

With its front operations, forged papers, false identities, and other tools of espionage, the multi-faceted network remained in a holding pattern until June 22, 1941, when *Wehrmacht* and *Luftwaffe* forces roared across the Soviet Union's borders, launching Operation Barbarossa. On cue, the orchestra quickly began to transmit a symphony of data about the Nazis, including battlefield plans and information on aircraft production, political decisions, and energy development and consumption.

The transfer of these secrets was protected by tested methods of CRYPTOGRAPHY. These included a checkerboard arrangement with a numeral KEY (see NIHILIST CIPHER, and STRADDLING CHECKERBOARD) used in conjunction with the text of designated books, including Honoré de Balzac's *La Femme de trente ans* and Guy de Téreamond's *Le Miracle du Professeur Wolmar*.

The application of such texts cannot provide perfect secrecy, since books are publicly available and the chosen text has a general order governed by the characteristics of the language in which it is written. For these reasons, keys based on books are less secure than truly random, nonrepeating keys. Still, this method proved useful up to a point.

Eventually, however, beginning about December 1941, HF DF on the part of the *Funkbbwehr* (radio counterespionage forces) succeeded in locating some of the *Rote Kapelle's* important broadcast sites. By December 1942 the orchestra had been effectively silenced, and some of the compromised sites and transmitters were used for a time by German intelligence in a FUNKSPIEL intended to create divisiveness between the Soviets and the Allies by indicating that the latter were conducting secret peace negotiations with the Nazis and even providing them with weapons and supplies.

However, surviving *Rote Kapelle* members managed to alert their superiors about this ruse. By a series of clever maneuvers, Soviet espionage officials forced the Nazis to disclose valuable information in order to maintain what they thought was a successful ruse. By the time the Berlin authorities realized that the tables had been turned, much damage had been done.

Along with the Soviet Lucy spies in Switzerland and the Sorge espionage ring in Japan, the *Rote Kapelle* members did much to counterbalance the Reich's early military success.

Rotor, invented around 1917, a means of combining the CIPHER-making skills of cryptographers with the increased speed and efficiency associated with machines. The rotor made more rapid and much more complex encryptions possible.

Rotors were generally of two principal types, pinwheel and wired. The former

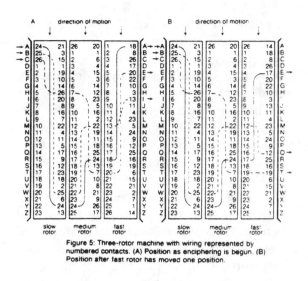

Figure 5: Three-rotor machine with wiring represented by numbered contacts. (A) Position as enciphering is begun. (B) Position after fast rotor has moved one position.

A schematic diagram of rotor positions and wiring. (Courtesy of Gustavus Simmons.)

Rotors. (Courtesy of the National Security Agency.)

consisted of a platelike disk with a series of projections on its circumference. The projections, or pins, were either fixed or moveable in either active or inactive modes.

The pinwheels were also seen in a version known as pin-and-lug machines, which had numbered or lettered positions on each rotor whereby the active/inactive pins were set. When set in motion, a group of rotors advanced one position with each step, thus extending the period before recycling began. The number of steps, equal to the product of the number of positions in each of the rotors, greatly increased CIPHERTEXT complexity and the difficulty of decipherment (see BORIS HAGELIN and M-209).

The other major type of rotor was the electrically wired wheel. Described in a patent of Swedish inventor Arvid G. Damm in 1919, the wired rotor was brought into practical use by American EDWARD HEBERN, who had rotors in mind as early as 1917 and received his U.S. patent in 1924. The modern rotor was developed from the Hebern "electric code machine."

The wired body of the rotor was made of an insulated, nonconducting material, such as rubber. Later, bakelite was used in the disks, which ranged in size from two to four inches in diameter, with a standard thickness of half an inch. On the disk's flat surface were 26 equally spaced electrical contacts. These studs were often made of brass and were randomly interconnected by a web of wires to the same number of contacts on the disk's opposite face. This formed a network by which an electric current could be conducted from one facing surface to the other, and the rotor thus became a commutator.

The contacts were equated with the letters of the alphabet. At the input stage they were PLAINTEXT and on the output step they were ciphertext. The different wire links formed a MONOALPHABETIC SUBSTITUTION alphabet subject to electromechanical variations.

The encipherment process was initiated by positioning the rotor between two insulated plates that also held 26 studs in a circle on each of their circumferences that corresponded to those on the disk. The contacts on the input plate were attached to a typewriter key (plaintext letter), and the linkage on the output plate was with an indicator such as an illuminated glass bulb containing a letter, or a device that printed characters on paper. By touching typewriter key l, the cipher maker caused an electric current to move from its power source (batteries or wall outlet) into the input plate's l contact. The electricity then passed to the rotor at the l stud, and through the wire maze to the rotor's output contact for a potential ciphertext letter, such as z. This contact connected to z on the output plate. Then the particular indicator mechanism was activated. A bulb lit under z to be transcribed by a clerk as ciphertext z, or it was printed by the CIPHER MACHINE on a paper tape.

Increasing the complexity introduced by the wire maze was the fact that the rotor moved forward and also backward in some machines. Thus the current begun at l, and reappearing at z, could emerge at q because a different contact–wire–contact sequence had occurred with a forward or backward step. This created a different POLYALPHABETIC SUBSTITUTION.

Next engineers expanded the number of rotors and grouped them in what was called a basket. The turning of one rotor caused the next to turn, with the multiple contact points and wires creating multiple encipherments. This provided yet greater secrecy by masking the FREQUENCY of letters used.

Wired rotor types and their uses multiplied through the 1920s. Dutch inventor Hugo Koch, German engineer Arthur Scherbius, and Willi Korn, of a company called *Chiffriermaschinen Aktiengesellschaft*, all contributed design advances to the ENIGMA machines that were later used by the armed forces of the Third Reich.

The Enigma (with improved variations) became the first commercially viable cryptographic machine and was thus purchased by different countries. Poland's General Staff used a version of it before World War II. The Japanese Enigma, labeled the Green machine by cryptosystem solvers in the United States, was anything but secure. The United States produced an advanced wired rotor machine, known as M-134-C/SIGABA by the U.S. Army and ECM by the U.S. Navy, which apparently were never broken by the Axis powers.

Rotor-based machines remained in prominent use by cryptologists until COMPUTERS come to dominate both encrypting and solving methods with their tremendous possibilities for both generating and analyzing data.

Route, a TRANSPOSITION cipher in which the direction is predetermined and the elements of the PLAINTEXT are entered in a geometric design (or matrix). While the design has usually been a rectangle, there have also been examples employing other GEOMETRIC PATTERNS, such as triangles, squares, and trapezoids.

Routes, such as the simple RAIL FENCE, came into prominence during the U.S. CIVIL WAR. During this conflict, the North developed expanded lists of routes that included a series of 12 ciphers, some of which consisted of dozens of pages for the routes and accompanying CODENAMES. Each of these routes was made up of a KEYWORD, codenames for important names, and nulls to complete lines and to confuse enemy interceptors. The keyword determined the size and the direction of the route. The alphabetical order of the keyword's letters preset the route, as shown here.

Keyword: watch
Codenames:

brass	(gunboats)
bronze	(Vicksburg)
copper	(bombardment)
gold	(General Grant)
iron	(Mississippi)
lead	(1:00 P.M.—message time)
metal	(New Orleans)
nickel	(wired)
ore	(telegram)
pewter	(five)
silver	(Admiral Farragut)
steel	(General Sherman)

Nulls: air, earth, fire, ice, water
Message (with codenames and nulls) to be sent:

gold	has	nickel	a	ore
to	metal	and	will	have
silver	send	pewter	brass	up
the	iron	to	bronze	for
copper	hold	your	sector	steel
lead	air	earth	ice	fire

The order of the alphabet letters in *watch* is *a*-1, *c*-2, *h*-3, *t*-4, and *w*-5, and its length is five letters, which becomes the width of the route. By prearrangement between the sender and the recipient, this route will go down column one, up two, down three, up four, and down five.

a	*c*	*h*	*t*	*w*
1	2	3	4	5
gold	has	nickel	a	ore
to	metal	and	will	have
silver	send	pewter	brass	up
the	iron	to	bronze	for
copper	hold	your	sector	steel
lead	air	earth	ice	fire

Completed route with keyword for directions:

> watch gold to silver the copper lead air hold iron send metal has nickel and pewter to your earth ice sector bronze brass will a ore have up for steel fire

Decrypted route:

> General Grant has wired a telegram to New Orleans and will have Admiral Farragut send five gunboats up the Mississippi to Vicksburg for bombardment hold your sector General Sherman 1:00 P.M. null null null null

For the clarity of this explanation, the codenames used here are all generally associated with metals and the nulls are variations of the basic elements. But in larger, actual routes, the words would have been far more varied for better secrecy since similar word discoveries gave analysts more angles.

Messages that were placed in rectangles allowed more variation than those set in columns. For example, the plaintext could be inscribed in alternate horizontals in the cells of a 5×5 matrix.

Plaintext: she hid that map inside her hat

Matrix:

s	h	e	h	i
t	a	h	t	d
m	a	p	i	n
h	e	d	i	s
e	r	h	a	t

The final CIPHERTEXT could then be transcribed beginning, for example, in the upper left-hand corner as (A) straight diagonal (*s*, down to *t*, up to *h*, and so forth), (B) alternate diagonal (*s* to *h*, down to *t*, down to *m*, up to *a*), or (C) clockwise spiral (*s* across to *i*, *d* down to *t* and over to *a* and back up the opposite side, *e*, *h*, *m*). Whatever the style, the letters were grouped in five-letter sets as a letter check and for convenience in transmission.

Ciphertext:

(A) sthma ehahh eepti rdidh inast

(B) shtma ehhah epeti didrh insat

(C) shehi dnsta hrehm tahti ideap

Other types of routes are simple horizontal, alternate vertical, and counterclockwise spirals begun from any corner of a rectangle or square and proceeding to the center of the matrix.

Rowlett, Frank (1908–   ), U.S. cryptologist.

After graduating from Emory and Henry College in 1929 with an honors degree in science, Virginian Frank Rowlett went to work for the Department of the

Army, where, in April 1930, he was hired by WILLIAM FRIEDMAN as the first junior cryptanalyst in the new Signal Intelligence Service (SIS). At a salary of $2,000 a year, Rowlett applied his mathematical skills and knowledge of German as a part of the small but eager Friedman team that included SOLOMON KULLBACK and ABRAHAM SINKOV. From the vantage point of modern message interception and analysis, it seems unbelievable that the SIS remained small with only seven employees and an average budget of $17,000 throughout most of the 1930s with which to develop cryptographic methods to protect U.S. Army messages as well as solving foreign encryptions.

Frank Rowlett and Solomon Kullback built on AGNES DRISCOLL's earlier work on the solving of Japanese CIPHER MACHINES. They in turn solved the Japanese machine designated as RED and helped reveal the secrets of a more involved encryption mechanism called PURPLE (see ALPHABETICAL TYPEWRITER '97). The enormously valuable data that was derived from these decrypted transmissions and other related solutions came to be called MAGIC and was of immense importance to the Allied war effort.

After the war, Rowlett achieved the rank of colonel in the U.S. Army while serving with the SIS and its successors, the Signal Security Agency and the Army Security Agency. From 1953 to 1958 he worked with the CIA, then became special assistant to the director of the NATIONAL SECURITY AGENCY.

At the NSA, Rowlett led the group that organized the National Cryptologic School, which was established in 1965. He served briefly as commandant of the school before his retirement in December of the same year. He was awarded the Distinguished Intelligence Medal and the National Security Medal, and holds patents for cryptographic equipment.

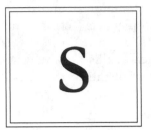

S

Sacred Three, The, nickname of Charles A. Tinker, Albert B. Chandler, and David H. Bates due to their efforts on behalf of the Union during the U.S. CIVIL WAR. The three telegraphers used CRYPTOGRAPHY to mask numerous messages from the War Department in Washington, D.C., as well as applying CRYPTANALYSIS to solve encrypted messages of the Confederacy.

Improved communications security was essential for the conduct of the war, which ranged from the Atlantic Ocean to the Mississippi River. The recently invented telegraph, in the hands of skilled cryptographers, became a formidable part of the North's arsenal.

Each of the Sacred Three had had experience with telegraphy before the war. David Bates began working as a telegrapher in Pittsburgh in March 1859 for the Pennsylvania Railroad and entered War Department service in April 1861. Albert Chandler had been a telegrapher in his native Vermont before he was hired by the Cleveland and Pittsburgh Railroad; he joined the Washington, D.C., telegraphers in June 1863. Charles Tinker was also born in Vermont and had railroad telegraphy experience; he served in the field with the Army of the Potomac before joining Chandler and Bates.

These men used a method developed by Anson Stager, a New York telegrapher. Stager's system was a word TRANSPOSITION on cards that had first been used by Maj. Gen. George McClellan in his early campaigns in western Virginia. The Sacred Three added to this system and devised others based on ROUTES. They worked as cryptanalysts as well, discovering that the South relied on the concealment system

Safford, Laurence / 185

named for BLAISE DE VIGENÈRE, a 16th-century French cryptologist, combining it with a brass CIPHER DISK. A KEYWORD was usually part of the Vigenère process, but the Confederates seemed to use only three during the war: *Manchester Bluff, Complete Victory*, and *Come Retribution.*

The trio also decrypted symbol ciphers. In December 1863, alert New York postmaster Abram Wakeman noticed a letter addressed to Alexander Keith, Jr., of Halifax, Nova Scotia, a known Southern sympathizer. The missive consisted of five varied types of symbols as well as letter substitutes. David Bates recalled similar figures from his boyhood employment in a store in Pittsburgh that had used such symbols on its price tags. The method was variously known as the pigpen, FREEMASONS' CIPHER, and ROSICRUCIANS' CIPHER (see FRATERNAL CRYPTOLOGY). When the letter was decrypted, the recovered PLAINTEXT told, among other things, of a large shipment of rifles to Halifax and a plan to seize a pair of steamers.

Two days later, a second postal intercept revealed an even more extensive plot. This cryptogram was from Christopher Memminger, the Southern secretary of the treasury. Decryption revealed that a counterfeiting operation had been set up in New York to print Confederate money. A man named Hilton was running a full-fledged operation in lower Manhattan. A subsequent raid led to the seizure of plates, machinery, and millions of dollars' worth of printed currency and bonds that were lost to the Confederate cause. As a reward for this achievement, the Sacred Three each received a $25-a-month raise. In the long conflict, their contributions proved invaluable to the Union's eventual victory.

Safford, Laurence (1893–1973), U.S. Navy officer and cryptologist.

A Massachusetts native, Safford graduated from the U.S. Naval Academy and was commissioned as an ensign in 1916. After serving in China, by 1924 he was Officer-in-Charge of the (Cryptologic) Research Desk of the Code and Signal Section of the Division of Naval Communications. With his tiny staff, Safford made his office in room 1621 of the old Navy Department building in Washington, D.C.

Under the guidance of AGNES DRIS-

Laurence Safford. (Courtesy of the National Security Agency.)

COLL, Safford put to use his own aptitude for mathematics and mechanical devices. In the 1920s, the Office of Naval Intelligence (ONI) surreptitiously photographed CODES kept in the Japanese consulate in New York. After decryption, this data was called the RED Code (also Red Book) because of the color of its binding. This material became a pillar upon which Safford and his lieutenant Joseph Rochefort built a full-fledged department staffed by well-trained personnel (nicknamed the ON THE ROOF GANG) as well as a network of listening posts in major naval operations areas.

With these improvements in the late 1920s came a new name for Safford's office and staff, OP-20-G. *OP* was from OPNAV, the Office of the Chief of Naval Operations: *20* referred to the 20th division of OPNAV; and *G* designated the Communications Security Section. OP-20-G was also known as Station Negat. However, with such expansion came division of responsibilities as well as personal rivalries for control of intelligence data.

Disputes over analysis and distribution of intelligence material erupted between ONI and OP-20-G in the early 1930s and in the late 1930s between OP-20-G and the Navy War Plans Division led by Rear Adm. Richmond K. Turner. The latter dispute continued while Stafford and OP-20-G worked with WILLIAM FRIEDMAN and his Army SIS staff that solved a Japanese diplomatic encryption given the name PURPLE. Amazingly, the Army group then developed a Purple analog and accomplished decryptions that became part of the United States' cryptanalytic MAGIC.

Tragically, the full range of Purple solutions and their implications about potential Japanese actions were not conveyed to U.S. commanders at Pearl Harbor and Safford became a central figure in the ongoing attempts to assign blame for the December 7, 1941, disaster. From the Congressional Hearings in 1946 he will always be remembered as the man who believed that a crucial warning sign of war called the WINDS CODE had been intercepted and should have been made known to the Hawaiian commanders.

Safford managed to survive the bitter debate about intelligence failures and coverups though his career was permanently damaged. After the war he served as Assistant Director of Naval Communications for Cryptographic Research until 1949. He later held the positions of Special Assistant to the Director of the Armed Forces Security Agency and Special Assistant to the Head of the Security Branch in the Division of Naval Communications. His active duties ended on March 2, 1953.

Despite his controversial link to the Pearl Harbor disaster, Laurence Safford is remembered for his pioneering work in naval intelligence when it was needed most.

Saint-Cyr Slide, a device named for the French military academy at which it was used for instruction in methods of CRYPTOGRAPHY. The man who named it was AUGUSTE KERCKHOFFS, a Dutch CODE and CIPHER scholar.

Its design was simple and consisted of a long strip of paper or cardboard called a *stator*, on which a standard alphabet was printed horizontally. Two openings, one on each side of the alphabet, enabled a

Saint-Cyr Slide. (From *The Science of Secret Writing* by Laurence D. Smith, Dover Publications, Inc., 1955.)

second, longer piece of paper or other material to slide under them. The slide, imprinted with two horizontal alphabets, was used to generate POLYALPHABETIC SUBSTITUTION.

Traditionally, the stator letters were the PLAINTEXT and the slide letters were the CIPHERTEXT. The first plaintext character on the stator was the index letter, and the keyletter of the slide was placed beneath it. The other plaintext letters were then located in the stator alphabet, and their encryption equivalents were found on the slide.

When the groups of letters are in standard *a*-to-*z* order, they resemble the table of letters associated with Frenchman BLAISE DE VIGENÈRE. The slide method is also considered a variation on the circular CIPHER DISK such as the one developed by GIOVANNI PORTA of Naples, a Renaissance CRYPTOLOGY expert.

Such devices permit numeral substitutions when digits, instead of letters, are printed on the slide. Because the enciphering possibilities are limited, slides did not provide superior security. Still, they proved to be an economical and easy-to-use instrument for both instructional purposes and field use in the years before electromechanical methods superseded manual systems.

Secret Adjunct Design, a CIPHER developed in 1805 by an Irish immigrant to the United States named Robert Patterson. Patterson, a native of northern Ireland, came to the American colonies in 1768. A store owner and academy director, he served during the colonial rebellion as a brigade major with a local militia group. He achieved his place in the history of CRYPTOGRAPHY by showing how the codes and ciphers used by U.S. ambassadors could be made more secure.

A member of the American Philosophical Society, Patterson's long-term interest in science and number theory influenced his studies with cipher designs. On Christmas Day in 1801, the Irishman presented his first cipher method in a letter to his friend and fellow scholar, THOMAS JEFFERSON.

The Patterson method involved a moderately complicated series of steps on ruled paper. It consisted of aligning letters in the "Chinese manner," one under the other and in lines written from left to right to complete a sequence of columns. No capitals, punctuation marks, or spaces were used between the PLAINTEXT terms. In a second step, sections of letters of no more than nine lines were numbered from

adj.	sig.	adj.	sig.
i	r	✝	d
i˙	n	✝	l
ı́	b	✝	r
ı̇˙	t	╪	n
˙ı	o	╪	u
˙ı	s	✝	v
ı	g	✝	and
ı̄	f	✝	e
ı̄	c	✝	of
ı̄	k	✝	k
¯ı	w	✝	t
¯ı	p	✝	s
ı̓	h	✝	h
ı̓˙	of	✝	x
ı̓˙	x	├	w
ı̓̓	y	✝	p
˙ı	v	⊦	the
˙ı	w	⊦	b
ı̓	th	⊢	m
ı̓	e	⌐	c
ı̓	j	⊦	j
ı	i	⊦	th
˙ı	z	⊢	f
̀ı	a	⊢	i
̀ı	l	⊦	o
ı̓	d	⊦	y
ı̓	q	├──	g
ı̄	the	├──	a
˙ı	and	⊢	q
̆ı	m	⊢	z
ı	space	⌡	space

Robert Patterson's Secret Adjunct Design. (Courtesy of Precedent Publishing.)

top to bottom and transcribed in random order. He used "insignificant letters" (see NULL) to fill out the lines. Deciphering involved knowedge of the number of lines per section, the pattern of how they were transcribed, and the number of nulls at the beginning of each line.

Though clever, the Patterson style proved too complicated for general usage among U.S. diplomats. It did, however, provide an example of the potential for variety and depth of concealment possible with quill, parchment, and imagination. Ever creative, Patterson developed a new "scheme of secret writing" and presented it to President Jefferson in December 1805.

Referring to his design of 1801, he stated that it was weak in that it was obviously a cipher to any third party who might intercept and see its rearranged letters. To remedy this he proposed a style that, according to today's cryptologic classifications, could be considered a form of STEGANOGRAPHY, an effort to conceal a message within an otherwise innocent text. Although Patterson presumed an overly polite attitude on the part of the "enemy" cryptanalyst, even in his day, his methodology was inventive.

Using but two letters, *i* and *t*, he developed a "dot and dash" style using their secondary marks or adjuncts, the *dot* of the *i* and the *dash* crossing the *t*. (The uppercase *Q* also had an adjunct, though *Q* was much less frequently used and its "dash" was at an odd angle for placement variety.)

He proposed that two sets of 26 adjunct varieties be equated with letters of the standard English alphabet, with three or four indicating double letters while other combinations would represent often-used words. In a detailed description of the adjuncts, Patterson mentioned the possibilities of the lowercase *j* being an adjunct of

As you always take a lively interest in the progress of the useful arts in your native country you will no doubt be gratifi   to hear that a certain M^r. Hawkins, I believe a native of The state of N.Y., has lately

A sample of text using the Patterson method. (Courtesy of Precedent Publishing.)

i. Some of the variations for *i* were: dots (strong and weak); obliques descending left (/) and right (\ ); and commas (regular and reversed). Different positions of these marks were near or slightly farther from the body of the letter, above the letter and to its left or right.

The adjuncts of the *t* consisted in variations of the horizontal line such as length, distance from the body of the *t*, crossing the stem, and so forth. Additionally, Patterson instructed that spaces between words, the conclusion of sentences, and the end of the message could be indicated by preplanned characteristics (for example, the omission of an adjunct might signify a space between words).

The letter from the Irish cryptographer to Jefferson on December 30, 1805, contained this line, exemplifying how the adjuncts appeared in a single sentence (see above).

Unusual as this style was, no current record exists of its ever having been used by President Jefferson or his diplomats. As historian Ralph E. Weber suggests, the varied clerical abilities and frequent writing miscues of State Department and embassy staffs alike may have worked against adopting a cipher that was dependent upon careful orthography.

Semagram, according to CRYPTOLOGY historian David Kahn, using the Greek *sema*, "sign," and *gramma*, "written" or "drawn," a form of linguistic concealment that is also a type of STEGANOGRAPHY.

The replacement elements of the CIPHERTEXT or CODETEXT are not letters or digits. Rather, they can be the dots on dominoes, objects in a photograph positioned so as to convey a prearranged meaning, or a painting in which two forms such as long and short tree branches represent the dashes and dots of MORSE CODE.

During World War I, German intelligence developed some clever semagraphic drawings and designs to try to elude Allied postal censors and to communicate with their distant agents and supporters. In one instance of this method, a well-to-do Englishwoman whose brother, an airman, was a prisoner of war in Holland, was approached by a woman purportedly representing a war relief charity. While the visitor was soliciting a donation on the terrace of the country house, she made a sketch on the blank page of a book, depicting birds in a nearby meadow. After discussing the captured airman, the Englishwoman gave the visitor some money for her charity. The fundraiser in turn suggested that the sketch be sent to the brother to give him a scene from his homeland. On this amicable note, the women parted.

Later, when the charity worker's papers

were found to be forgeries, the incident appeared to have been simply an elaborate ruse for a modest monetary theft. Nor did the donor realize the truth even after it was learned that her brother never received the sketch she sent. However, British authorities discovered that the charity worker had been drawing on paper pre-ruled from a reduced version of a particular survey. The sketch was far from innocent: the position of the birds actually showed the location of a mine field providing a defensive barrier for a strategic naval site. When the drawing was sent to Holland, it was intercepted by a Dutch agent cooperating with Germany. German agents also sent a semagram made with a knit sweater into Germany. Supposedly meant for a prisoner, it went instead to intelligence authorities. When the sweater was unraveled, its wool yarn was found to be full of knots. The yarn was straightened and the knots were compared to an alphabet printed vertically on a wall. Decipherment involved establishing a baseline such as the floor with the alphabet perpendicular to it. The end of the yarn was held to the floor beneath the alphabet, so that the first knot aligned with a letter. This knot was then placed on the floor and the second knot was checked for its letter matchup. In one instance, the knots revealed information about Allied naval vessels under construction and about to be launched.

Though semagrams succeeded during World War I, the need for rapid, multidirectional orders in warfare led to far greater dependence on cryptographic methods adaptable to telephone and radio. The Semagram eventually faded before the onslaught of electronic encryption.

Shakespeare Ciphers, CIPHERS purportedly in the works of Shakespeare attributing their authorship to someone else. The life and literary creations of William Shakespeare have generated a long series of books, critiques, articles, movies, and documentaries. Literary scholars and historians alike have searched his work for everything from information about actual events to the identities of real persons involved in his plot lines. Over the centuries, some people have also believed that someone other than Shakespeare actually penned several, if not all, of his works, proposing that cryptic clues within the plays and other writings held the secret of their real authorship.

The leading contender for the title was SIR FRANCIS BACON, a contemporary of the Bard of Avon. Bacon, a philosopher, essayist, and statesman, wrote about missive concealment and developed what he called a biliteral cipher, which represented all the letters of the alphabet in terms of *a* and *b* such as:

a	AAAAA
b	AAAAB
c	AAABA

This was used in a special way with different forms of printing type to create a method of STEGANOGRAPHY.

Bacon's interest in CRYPTOLOGY combined with past instances of hidden authorship (in which the first letter of each chapter combined to make an acrostic that spelled the actual writer's name, for example), gave credence to such speculations.

The first prominent person to claim a cryptic discovery among the Bard's works was a Minnesota politician named Ignatius

Donnelly. A lieutenant governor and representative of his state in the U.S. House of Representatives, Donnelly was also the successful author of *Atlantis: The Antedeluvian World* (1882). His book *The Great Cryptogram* (1888) caused a storm of protests by arguing that Bacon was the true author of works attributed to Shakespeare. Embroiled in controversy, his health failed, and he died a disillusioned man in 1901.

Others who took up Donnelly's cause came to be known as Baconians or enigmatologists. Among them was a Michigan high school principal, Elizabeth Gallup, who attempted a detailed study of the type fonts used in printing the Bard's works, in the hope of finding evidence there of Bacon's cipher. In 1899, she published *The Bi-literal Cypher of Sir Francis Bacon Discovered in his Works and Deciphered by Mrs. Elizabeth Wells Gallup.* Having gained a degree of notoriety, she continued her efforts into the new decade and accepted employment with a man who sought to carve his own niche in history by financing such causes—George Fabyan, a wealthy Illinois resident who founded the Riverbank Laboratories near the town of Geneva.

By a fortunate twist of fate, two of Gallup's assistants were WILLIAM FRIEDMAN and Elizebeth Smith (later Mrs. ELIZEBETH FRIEDMAN). The pair married and left Riverbank to become the most prominent couple in the history of cryptology. In their retirement years the Friedmans collaborated on a book that definitively debunked the cipher theorists, *The Shakespearean Ciphers Examined.* Letter counts, studies of acrostics, discoveries of multiple possible letter combinations, awkwardly contrived shifts of equivalents, and convenient deletions all validated the Friedmans' conclusion. There is no irrefutable evidence of a specific, unambiguous cipher or other cryptomethod in William Shakespeare's words to suggest that someone other than the Bard wrote the plays and poems and published under his name.

Shorthand, a system of speed writing whereby symbols can be made quickly to represent letters, words, and phrases. Shorthand systems have been used upon normal spelling (orthography), phonetics, or arbitrary symbols, and they may also be thought of as a type of SYMBOL CRYPTOGRAPHY.

The ancient Greeks used forms of rapid writing. Many historians link the beginning of rudimentary shorthand with the Greek Xenophon (434?–355? B.C.), who wrote the memoirs of Socrates. Later, in the Roman Empire, a shorthand form became more generally used, reputedly thanks to a freedman named Marcus Tullius Tiro. A learned member of the house of statesman and Stoic philosopher Cicero, Tiro invented his *notae Tironianae* (Tironean notes) in 63 B.C., and also wrote a form of shorthand dictionary. Taught in Roman schools and used by emperors such as Titus and Julius Caesar, the method survived for several centuries before meeting with disfavor in the Middle Ages because of its association with magic rituals and the occult. Nevertheless, when papal scribes began to take an interest in forms of abbreviated writing and discovered older shorthand texts, the method was granted acceptance once more because of inferred church approval.

In 1588, British physician Timothy

Bright published *Characterie: an Arte of Shorte, Swifte, and Secrete Writing by Character*, which described a system using combinations of lines, half-circles, and circles to represent the letters of the alphabet, an excerpt from which appears below:

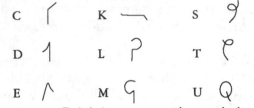

However, Bright's system demanded a great deal of study from its users and therefore did not prove to be rapid in practice.

Some 30 years later, Thomas Shelton invented a system called *tachygraphy* (from the Greek *tachys*, "swift," and *graphein*, "to write"). Described in his book entitled *Short Writing* (1620 or 1626), Shelton's method consisted of nearly a dozen forms that differed only slightly from the longhand. Greater concealment was accomplished by using dots for some vowels and having consonants replace other vowels in the middle of words. Also, digit-type characters were aligned with some 260 typical words (for example 2 for *to*, and **2** for *two*).

The most famous application of Shelton's system was in the diary of SAMUEL PEPYS, which was finally decrypted in the 19th century. Pepys heightened the cryptographic potential of this method by writing his more suggestive comments in French and Latin, among other languages, and applying his own personal NULLS.

In Colonial Virginia, William Byrd kept a similar journal on a part-time basis in the years between 1709 and 1741. The method used by Byrd was later identified as one created by William Mason, a London artist and stenographer. Mason's 1672 shorthand textbook, *A Pen pluck't from an Eagle's Wing*, was revised and appeared in 1707 as *La Plume Volante* (the flying pen).

Two of the most widely used shorthand methods were created by an Englishman and an Irishman, respectively. Sir Isaac Pitman's *Stenographic Sound-Hand*, published in 1837, incorporated special character forms to indicate omitted vowels. In 1852, Pitman's brother Benn brought this system to the United States where, with some modifications, it became the most widely used method on the East Coast by the 1890s.

Irishman John R. Gregg countered with his pamphlet *Light-Line Phonography* (1888), a system based on circles, hooks, and loops. In 1893 Gregg came to the United States and taught his method throughout the Midwest and South, where shorthand was virtually unknown. Gregg's efforts were rewarded when his style superseded that of Pitman. Both shorthand forms were designed to increase the speed of communications rather than conceal their contents.

During World War I, shorthand systems

Gabelsberger Shorthand.

were modified to add a further element of concealment to encrypted messages. Allied intelligence had special departments that studied German systems and postal censors scanned the mails for suspicious examples, which were then turned over to translators and encryption analysts. America's Military Intelligence Division (MI-8) had a section that made INVISIBLE INKS tests and could read several shorthand styles, including the German *Schrey*, *Stolze–Schrey*, and *Gabelsberger*.

In World War II, the written message was superseded by the much faster radio transmission. Even when the mails were used to pass intelligence, the MICRODOT, an advanced form of STEGANOGRAPHY, was much preferred over any type of conventional written communications, including shorthand.

SIGABA, or the U.S. Army's Converter M-134C. (Courtesy of the National Security Agency.)

SIGABA, the U.S. Army's short name for the Converter M-134C. It was developed from a series of predecessors that were based on the electric CIPHER MACHINE of EDWARD HEBERN, who had presented his device to the Navy in 1921.

In 1925, Navy officials began a search for a machine that incorporated the Hebern wired CODE wheel, or ROTOR, but that would be better suited for inclement weather, battle, and other conditions. Experimentation led to a new cryptograph in the period 1932–34.

The improved device had five rotors, each controlled by a pinwheel having 25 pins set in either an active or an inactive mode. An additional plugboard was attached to pass control from one rotor to another. Used with all five rotors and with

the pinwheels set carefully, the machine was reasonably secure. It was called the Electric Cipher Machine Mark I. Its successor, the ECM Mark II, became the premier U.S. cipher machine during World War II; it was this version that was designated SIGABA by the U.S. Army.

The ECM was active during the Japanese invasion of the Philippines and the siege of Corregidor, when the defenders transmitted encrypted messages in irrelevant data such as poems, sports scores, and old news articles to confound the Japanese analysts.

The U.S. Army also used the SIGABA/ECM in a version called the M-134A (or SIGMYK). This machine had a one-time tape using a form of the BAUDOT CODE and this arrangement regulated the SIG-MYK's rotors. The two-tape encryption method developed by GILBERT VERNAM was also applied.

To enhance Allied communications during the war, adapters were built to make the SIGABA/ECM compatable with British devices such as the TYPEX. One such adaptor, a U.S. Navy device called the CSP 1600, produced a hybrid device with five rotors designated the CSP 1700.

In the later stages of the conflict, an advanced SIGABA/ECM had 15 rotors, including 5 that gave multiple position changes to the other 10 which made the complex encryptions.

Sinkov, Abraham (1907–), U.S. cryptanalyst and intelligence officer. A Pennsylvania native, Abraham Sinkov graduated from the City College of New York in 1927. After teaching and gaining his master's degree in mathematics from Columbia in 1929, he was employed by WILLIAM FRIEDMAN of the U.S. Army's Signal Intelligence Service. As a junior cryptanalyst in 1930, he served as the SIS French specialist (see CRYPTANALYSIS).

At the SIS, Sinkov worked with SOLOMON KULLBACK, Genevieve Grotjan, FRANK ROWLETT, and cryptographic clerk Harry L. Clark to expand the early hard-won advances of the U.S. "pencil-and-paper" analysts who were true pioneers of their craft. The new generation took on the challenges of electromechanical CIPHER MACHINES (see EDWARD HEBERN and ENIGMA), and their efforts were especially fruitful against the enciphered messages of the expanding Japanese empire in the late 1930s.

By this time, Abraham had left the Washington, D.C., area to head a signals intercept station in Panama, a locale of special importance due both to its ideal position for snaring cross-continental messages and to the strategic Panama Canal.

In January 1942, with the United States directly involved in World War II, Sinkov received a crucial assignment. Now a major, he was chosen to replace the exhausted William Friedman on a secret mission to England. Accompanied by another Army Signal Corps officer and two members of the U.S. Navy's OP-20-G CIPHER-solving team, Sinkov was responsible for conveying a pair of PURPLE analog machines, along with other encryption material, to embattled Great Britain. He returned with some advanced British cryptographic equipment. After a promotion to colonel, Sinkov became assistant director, then director, of the Central Bureau, a joint U.S.–Australia communications intelligence operation. With the war's conclusion, he served with SIS successor organizations, including the Armed Forces Security Agency and the NATIONAL SECURITY AGENCY. For a time he was the latter's deputy director of the Office of Production. After his retirement in 1962, he returned to university life as a professor of mathematics at Arizona State University.

Skytale, the first known cryptographic device. Developed by the Spartans in the 5th century B.C., it was one of the very few developments for the TRANSPOSITION of letters.

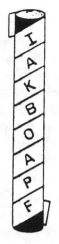

Skytale. (Courtesy of Crown Publishers, Inc.)

The skytale was made of a cylinder of wood or, in some cases, an officer's baton around which a strip of leather or papyrus was tightly wrapped. The PLAINTEXT was written on this strip and down the length of the staff. When the papyrus or leather was unwound, the loosened strip of letters appeared a jumble to a third party. A courier then took the dispatch to another Spartan camp, where the communication was wrapped around another staff of the same length and thickness, realigning the proper letter order and revealing the message.

Soldiers' Messages, cryptosystems used by soldiers attempting to evade military censors and communicate with distant family and friends.

Attempts to sneak past the censors have been made with cables and telegrams using a type of OPEN CODE called a NULL CIPHER. In this method, only a few specific letters or terms are important; all the remaining words are nulls that serve as concealments.

One amusing instance from World War II involved a GI attempting to inform his parents that he was stationed in Tunis, the capital of Tunisia. On the envelopes of the letters he sent, he used his father's middle initial, beginning with a *T*, then a *U*, and so forth. However, he failed to date the letters, and when they arrived out of order, his parents searched their atlas in nervous frustration looking for "Nutsi."

A much more serious example involved a U.S. prisoner of war in Japan who succeeded in getting a postcard with a null CODE past the camp censor:

Front:

FRANK G. JONELIS, 1st Lt. U.S.A.
ZENTSUJI WAR PRISONERS CAMP
NIPPON

       MR. F. B. IERS
       c/o FEDERAL BLDG. COMPANY ROOM 1619. 100 MAIN ST.
       LOS ANGELES CALIFORNIA U. S. A.

Back:

DEAR IERS:
AFTER SURRENDER, HEALTH IMPROVED
FIFTY PERCENT. BETTER FOOD ETC.
AMERICANS LOST CONFIDENCE
IN PHILIPPINES. AM COMFORTABLE
IN NIPPON. MOTHER: INVEST
30%, SALARY, IN BUSINESS. LOVE
       FRANK G. JONELIS

An FBI agent discovered that only the first two words of each line were the message: *After surrender, 50 percent Americans lost in Philippines; in Nippon, 30 percent.*

Soviet Cryptology, encryption systems developed in czarist Russia and in the Soviet Union.

The early concealment systems of Russia under the czars were on a par with those of European nations in the period from the 1100s to the 1700s. The Russian examples follow a typical pattern ranging from few letter SUBSTITUTIONS in the 12th century to a more involved two-part NOMENCLATOR in the 1750s. Peter the Great, along with his modernization programs in other areas, was responsible for improving the cryptographic efforts of his government. By the late 1700s, INVISIBLE INKS were being used and BLACK CHAMBERS were operating at postal centers to open, study, and reseal intercepted mail.

The Okhrana, the secret police of the czars, used the black chambers to intercept and analyze the mail and then the telegrams of their enemies. The Okhrana sought to uncover anarchist plots concealed by the NIHILIST CIPHER and other encryption systems.

It took major military setbacks during World War I to send the tottering Russian monarchy over the brink. Such a disaster occurred at the August 1914 BATTLE OF TANNENBERG, in which two large Russian armies suffered a huge defeat near this East Prussian town. A dependence on radio dispatches carelessly sent in CLEARTEXT (plain language) was a factor in this defeat. Other setbacks followed, due in part to poor encryptions by the Russians and to superior CIPHER solving by the Central Powers. These defeats inexorably undermined the average Russian soldier's faith in the Czar.

After their victory over the White Russians, Lenin and the Bolsheviks consolidated their power. With the *Cheka* and then the G.P.U. controlling internal security, ciphers were used to convey messages to espionage operatives and local Party members. The Amtorg Trading Corporation in New York City was discovered to be a front for a well-organized Soviet espionage operation. Though a number of the group's cables were obtained for a Congressional investigation in 1930, their encryption shield could not be broken.

During the Spanish Civil War (1936–39), the Soviets supported the anti-Fascist Loyalists, providing them with encryption methods such as the STRADDLING CHECKERBOARD as well as other aid. However, such assistance was not enough to save the Loyalists from defeat.

After the Soviets signed a nonaggression pact with the Third Reich in 1939, they maintained in Germany full-fledged espionage networks, such as the ROTE KAPELLE, to watch the Nazis. Nevertheless, Stalin failed to heed numerous enciphered warnings about the Germans' impending attack in June 1941.

While the sieges of Leningrad and Stalingrad grabbed the headlines, poor CODES and good CRYPTANALYSIS played more subtle yet important roles on the Eastern Front. When a period of stalemate occurred during 1943, the *Wehrmacht* made some gains through radio intercepts in which the Red Army continued to show some carelessness with its enciphered codes (see ENCICODE).

However, in general, Soviet cryptosystems at this time were superior to those of Germany. While Hitler's Foreign Office was compromised by spies and traitors, Soviet ambassadors protected their vital diplomatic transmissions with ONE-TIME PADS. When properly used and provided with fresh random KEY material, these pads were, and are, truly UNBREAKABLE CIPHERS.

During the war, Communist espionage groups like the "Lucy" organization in Switzerland and the Sorge ring in Japan used a particularly strong encryption that combined the straddling checkerboard with a KEYWORD and a one-time key of numbers listed in books of trade statistics. Because the digits were taken from published texts that may have had some repeated numbers and that could have been discovered by enemy analysts, the method could not be classified as truly unbreakable. Nevertheless, it sufficed to stymie the Nazis.

After World War II, Soviet agents were linked in a radio network, using one-time pads to exchange information. Occasionally a costly mistake was made, such as that involving the KGB CABLES. During the Cold War, the USSR gained access to U.S. and other Western cryptographic data from sources in military and intelligence agencies. The infamous John Walker family of spies, for example, divulged U.S. Navy encryption methods among other secrets from the late 1960s into the 1980s. Weaknesses in NATO security have also allowed the transfer of several top-security code and cipher secrets. Such penetrations remained a Soviet intelligence goal during the warming of the USSR's relations with the West. Now with the breakup of the Soviet Union, many factors, including cryptologic practices, remain uncertain.

Sports Signs and Signals, hand and body gestures, as well as sounds, used in team sports to communicate with one's own teamates. CODES and CIPHERS are very much a part of our favorite pastimes, from the football quarterback's line-of-scrimmage signals to the third-base coach's baseball batting signs.

Baseball managers instruct batters and baserunners to swing away, bunt, or steal a base through a series of gestures that include touching the brim of their cap, their nose, or elbow flashed from the manager to the third-base coach and thence to the players. These transfers of information are NONSECRET CODES in that they are visible to the competing team. In the sense that such gestures are used by people in a particular line of employment, they convey the meanings of words in the realm of ARGOT and JARGON CODES.

Square Table, invented by the German scholar and abbot JOHANNES TRITHEMIUS (1462–1516), it was the first alphabet table (tableau) for POLYALPHABETIC SUBSTITUTION in cryptology.

This table was one of the early GEOMETRIC PATTERNS used to arrange alphabets, numbers, and symbols to make an encryption. It was square because it contained as many rows as there were letters in the alphabet. Generally the same series of letters was repeated, with shifting positions creating the necessary variation. This provided a different group of cipher alternatives for the PLAINTEXT words. I and j were considered equivalent, as were u and *v.* A partial table illustration is shown below:

```
a b c d e f g h i k l m n o p q r s t u x y z w
b c d e f g h i k l m n o p q r s t u x y z w a
c d e f g h i k l m n o p q r s t u x y z w a b
d e f g h i k l m n o p q r s t u x y z w a b c
e f g h i k l m n o p q r s t u x y z w a b c d
f g h i k l m n o p q r s t u x y z w a b c d e
g h i k l m n o p q r s t u x y z w a b c d e f
h i k l m n o p q r s t u x y z w a b c d e f g
i k l m n o p q r s t u x y z w a b c d e f g h
. . . . . . . . . . . . . . . . . . . . . . . .
w a b c d e f g h i k l m n o p q r s t u x y z
```

Trithemius called this the *tabula recta.* He enciphered a plaintext message by taking its first letter and masking it with one from the first alphabet row of the tableau, masking the second plaintext letter with the one beneath it in the second alphabet row, and so forth. Thus the Latin *Pax Romana* would become *pbz usrgui. P* is enciphered by *p* in the top row, since the first plaintext letter gets its substitute from the first cipher alphabet. Then *a*, the second original letter, is concealed by *b*, the second cipher alphabet row letter beneath it. In this manner, *m*, the sixth plaintext letter, is replaced by the letter *r.*

A new alphabet row was used for each letter. After the total of 24 was reached, the alphabets were repeated in groups of 24 until the entire plaintext was hidden. Such polyalphabetic encryption avoids the weakness of repeating cipher letters being used to conceal repeating plaintext ones, such as in the message: she wi*ll* arr*i*ve at n*oo*n.

Trithemius's creation was the first progressive KEY with which all possible cipher alphabets were used before one was repeated. This practical system was described in Book V of his classic 6-part *Polygraphiae libri sex* (Six Books of Polygraphy). Both polyalphabetics and a progressive key contributed to the widespread acceptance of this method by the Neapolitan GIOVANNI PORTA, the Frenchman BLAISE DE VIGENÈRE, and other cryptologists.

Steganography, from the Greek meaning "covered writing," a primary form of communications security involving the concealment of the presence of a secret message, which may or may not be additionally protected by a CODE or CIPHER.

Steganography often appears in popular literature as secret compartments, hidden pockets, and hollowed-out books and umbrella handles, among other examples. The practice has a long and fascinating history.

The *Histories* of Herodotus, a Greek historian of the 5th century B.C., contains an account of a revolt against Persian rule that directly benefited from steganography. Two regional strongmen communicated secretly by shaving a slave's head and tattooing it with a secret message. After his hair grew back, the slave was sent to coconspirators, who shaved his head again and read the message. The communication was successful, and the revolt became a reality.

A major form of steganographic concealment involved the use of INVISIBLE INKS. Described in early Arabic writings as well as by scholars of the Middle Ages, these substances included onion juice and ammonium chloride and were used to write be-

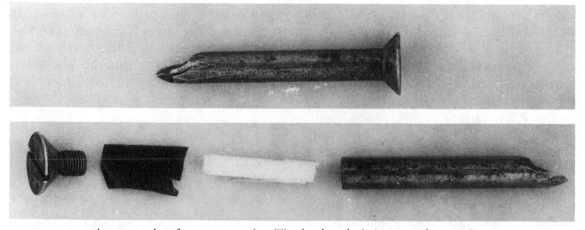

An example of steganography. The broken bolt is opened, revealing tissue-wrapped microfilm. (Courtesy of the Federal Bureau of Investigation.)

tween the lines of an innocuous letter or on blank parchment in a stack of seemingly empty pages. They were made visible again by applications of heat or other chemicals among varied methods.

These inks, or "stains" as they were called during the American Revolutionary War (1775–1783), helped convey important information in missives between Gen. George Washington and agents such as BENJAMIN TALLMADGE.

In the 20th century, chemistry provided additional concealment tools. During both world wars, postal censors searched for secrets in letters with test-tube marvels such as the iodine–vapor test. The World War I spy Maria de Victoria was arrested in 1918 at a Long Island, New York, hotel due largely to the work of British intelligence and the U.S. Military Intelligence Division's Codes and Ciphers Unit, which discovered invisible inks in her correspondence from Berlin that exposed her plans

for sabotage. Indicted but never brought to trial, she reportedly met her demise through drug addition in 1920.

The Nazis contributed to the advancement of steganography with the MICRODOT, which concealed full-size typewritten letters on tiny squares or dots the size of the period at the end of this sentence.

Miniaturizing techniques continued into the Cold War era. Soviet master spy Rudolph Abel, for example, hid strips of microdots in segments of the binding of U.S. magazines that were sent to a predetermined address in Paris.

Present day forms of electronic steganography include quick burst/spurt broadcasts, frequency hopping, and spread spectrum techniques of diminished signals covered with specially produced "noise" (see TRANSMISSIONS SECURITY).

Straddling Checkerboard, a checkerboard-based CIPHER used by communist forces during the Spanish Civil War (1936–1939) and later conflicts.

The opponents of fascism controlled most of Spain's major cities in the beginning of the struggle and protected their communications, including radio transmission, with a variety of encryption methods, such as the straddling checkerboard.

The communists' version was called straddling because of its unique use of ciphers of one and two numbers. The cipher builder would use the difference in the digits to add extra puzzlements for a would-be solver. Since the analyst could not be sure of the location of single numbers contrasted with paired digits, he or she might match a single with a member of a numeral pair while analyzing the CIPHERTEXT. This "straddles" a correct pair of equivalents or combines numbers that should be separate and thereby forms an incorrect pair, ending up with scratch pads full of nonsense.

The straddling checkerboard generated a particular one-number encipherment of the letters of PLAINTEXT in contrast to the paired digits of previous checkerboard styles such as that of the NIHILISTS. The method creates one-number versions by deleting a side coordinate from one of the rows. A letter in such a row has only one coordinate (above it) as an equivalent rather than one from the top and one from the side.

With the arrangement complete, the coordinates are read from the side and then the top. A KEYWORD initiates the alphabet sequence in the cells of the checkerboard. The cells of the second and third rows are filled with the remaining letters. None of the chosen single numbers (0 to 3) to begin a digit pair, in order to avoid confusion. The matrix has a period (.) and shift sign (/) to fill out the bottom row. An example follows, using the keyword *guernica* (all lower case).

```
    0  9  8  7  6  5  4  3  2  1
    g  u  e  r  n  i  c  a
 1  b  d  f  h  j  k  l  m  o  p
 2  q  s  t  v  w  x  y  z  .  /
```

In order to encipher the message *save madrid*, the cipher maker would begin by locating the coordinates for *s*, or 29, then *a*, or 3, and so on through the plaintext, and then place the letters alongside each other to form the digit-covered cipher 293278133197519. The addressee knows that whenever a 1 or 2 appears, it will pair with another digit but will not appear as a single number. Therefore, 29 is obviously a pair while 32 is not, because in this matrix there is no side coordinate 3. A successful interception of such a message by a third party would reveal a series of numbers, but the enemy solution seeker could not be sure which numbers represented singles and which pairs.

Substitution, a method of CRYPTOGRAPHY in which the PLAINTEXT is replaced by letters, numbers, or other symbols while its original word or letter order remains unchanged.

For example, the word *security* could be replaced by *rdbtqhsx*, which is comprised simply of the letters directly preceding each letter of the plaintext in the English alphabet. It could also be replaced by the digits 19, 5, 3, 21, 18, 9, 20, and 25, which reflect the numerical position of each letter in the alphabet, or SYMBOL CRYPTOGRAPHY could be applied, as follows: #&*$-/= +. Each of these examples is a substitution CIPHER since individual letters are replaced.

Substitutions are sometimes combined with a process called TRANSPOSITION, in which the positions of letters are changed but their identities remain the same.

Besides ciphers, substitution is also used to form CODES, in which whole words are replaced at once, as opposed to the letter-for-letter substitution used to create ciphers (see CODEWORDS and CODENUMBERS).

It is generally accepted that the earliest forms of substitutions were hieroglyphics written by scribes in ancient Egypt to record their leaders' lives and times. Centuries later, papal and royal court scribes developed lists of letter and word replacements and the process of substitution became a standard part of concealment systems.

By the early 1400s in Europe, MONOAL-PHABETIC SUBSTITUTION, in which one cipher alphabet is used, became a basic form. In addition to letter-for-letter equivalents, many such substitutions used two- and three-element equivalents, such as 220 for *f*, 221 for *g*, and 222 for *h*. The example below shows a mixed cipher alphabet beneath a plaintext one:

Plain: a b c d e f g h i j k l m
Cipher: I X E Q Y O H F V Z A U D

Plain: n o p q r s t u v w x y z
Cipher: B L S G K M P W C R J T N

Encipherment is accomplished by replacing the letters of the plaintext message with the cipher equivalents beneath them.

Message:

o u t p o s t o f d e m o c r a c y i n d a n g e r
L W P S L M P L O Q Y D L E K I E T V B Q I B H Y K

Concealments using only one alphabet are relatively easy to solve. Therefore, by the latter 1400s, cryptographers began to turn to POLYALPHABETIC SUBSTITUTION, which involves more than one alphabet. This type of substitution is achieved by aligning the original letters with various alphabet groups by such means as tableaus (tables), CIPHER DISKS, and letter-generating grids that create pairings of letters.

A multi-alphabet table is arranged with a plaintext alphabet, KEYLETTERS and/or KEYNUMBERS to identify the chosen alphabet, and a series of cipher alphabets.

Plaintext

KEYS	a	b	c	d	e	f	g	h	i	j	k	l	m
1 I	I	X	E	Q	Y	O	H	F	V	Z	A	U	D
2 X	X	E	Q	Y	O	H	F	V	Z	A	U	D	B
3 E	E	Q	Y	O	H	F	V	Z	A	U	D	B	L
.		.											.
.		.											.
.			.										.
26 N	N	I	X	E	Q	Y	O	H	F	V	Z	A	U

KEYS	n	o	p	q	r	s	t	u	v	w	x	y	z
1 I	B	L	S	G	K	M	P	W	C	R	J	T	N
2 X	L	S	G	K	M	P	W	C	R	J	T	N	I
3 E	S	G	K	M	P	W	C	R	J	T	N	I	X
.	.												.
.	.												.
.	.												.
26 N	D	B	L	S	G	K	M	P	W	C	R	J	T

Encipherment is accomplished by locating a keynumber or keyletter on the left and the plaintext across the top of the table. Then the cipher letter is found at the row and column coordinates. With key letter *x*, for example, plaintext *n* equals cipher *L*. With keynumber 3, plaintext *v* becomes cipher *J*. Even from this brief example, the advantage of polyalphabetic substitution can be seen: It renders messages more difficult to decrypt by decreasing the level of letter repetition from one communication to the next.

Superencipherment,

a method of CRYPTOGRAPHY in which a CODE or CIPHER is itself enciphered by TRANSPOSITION (especially for numbers) or SUBSTITUTION (for words and numbers) in order to provide an extra layer of cryptographic protection. The result is called an ENCICODE, also known as an enciphered code.

In the chart, both a PLAINTEXT word and an original number are shown being concealed by an encicode. The CODEWORD *signatory* is not transposed because the sense of the letters could be changed too much by mixing them. When *signatory* is replaced by substituted letters, the original word *blueprint* has been encicoded.

In terms of the digits *4916*, their CODENUMBER is *2370*. The numerals' positions can be transposed, then substituted (replaced) with other numbers, resulting in the encicode *5068*.

Plaintext	blueprint
Codeword	signatory
Transposition	———
Substitution	dxqkmjvfz

Encicode	dxqkmjvfz
Original number	4916
Codenumber	2370
Transposition	7203
Substitution	5068
Encicode	5068

When decrypted, the original recovered word or number is the *placode* (condensed from plain code).

Swaim's Signals,

a system of visual signals devised by James Swaim during the U.S. CIVIL WAR.

James Swaim was a U.S. Navy man whose service prior to the U.S. Civil War had exposed him to various methods of visual communication. Hoping to be awarded a war contract, he arrived in the nation's capital in November 1862, bringing with him a signal system and gained the attention of two telegraphers of the War Department, David Bates and Charles Tinker (see THE SACRED THREE).

Swaim presented Bates and Tinker with a CODEBOOK of several thousand phrases, words, and numerals that were represented by combinations of as many as four digits, which in turn were conveyed by six visual signals using a flag or a torch. In this system, which was similar to the one devised by ALBERT MYER, the flag or torch was moved through different positions to form a visibly NONSECRET CODE. It was secure as long as the true meanings of the movements were kept secret.

The signalman held the flag or torch up and to the right to indicate the number 1, straight out to the right for 2, and to the right and down for 3. The numbers 4, 5, and 6 were indicated by the same movements performed to the left side of the signalman. These positions were equated with number pairs that indicated alphabet letters and digits:

A	G	M	S	Y	5
11	21	31	41	51	61
B	H	N	T	Z	6
12	22	32	42	52	62
C	I	O	U	1	7
13	23	33	43	53	63
D	J	P	V	2	8
14	24	34	44	54	64
E	K	Q	W	3	9
15	25	35	45	55	65
F	L	R	X	4	0
16	26	36	46	56	66

Swaim proposed a mnemonic device to help signalmen remember the KEY to the alphabet. His formula asked, "Who is the inventor?" The answer was found by repeating the first four horizontal letters of the chart rapidly, so that *AGMS* sounded like "a Jeems" (or "James," Swaim's first name). The next question was "Why?" (*Y*). Thus, *A, G, M, W, Y* recalled the first letter of each column.

Although Bates and Tinker found the method relatively easy to learn and Abraham Lincoln was encouraging, unfortunately for Swaim, his proposal never gained favor with the War Department hierarchy or the field commanders.

After the war, Swaim entered a series of business ventures, including a widely publicized remedy named Swaim's Panacea, which he sold at medicine shows.

Symbol Cryptography,

a form of CRYPTOGRAPHY in which the PLAINTEXT is replaced by a symbol, such as a design or a written or printed mark.

Writing has been both defined and concealed by symbols since ancient times. Egyptian hieroglyphics were picture-type symbols that represented a word, syllable, or sound. Similar symbols were found in different civilizations, from the cuneiform inscriptions of Assyria and Babylonia, to the stone carvings of the Mayans in Central America, and the runic inscriptions of the Celts in northern Europe. At different times, high priests and scribes introduced new forms to impress either their rulers or the masses. Insofar as this created a secret meaning, the practice can be seen as a very early stage of cryptography.

From about 1400 to 1850, the NOMENCLATOR was the primary means of masking communications. This system, consisting of CIPHERS and CODEWORDS, often used symbols, including NULLS, or meaningless characters intended to confused prying third parties. During the same period, practitioners of occult rituals concealed their secret records with symbols.

Beginning in the 17th century, formalized methods of speed writing called SHORTHAND also provided standardized symbols to represent words. Britain's SAMUEL PEPYS used shorthand and nulls in his personal journal. His system was similar to that of William Byrd in colonial Virginia, who kept a private journal intermittently between 1709 and 1741, concealed with a speed-writing style called *La Plume Volante* (the flying pen). During the American Revolution, symbol cryptography masked secret correspondence with de-

A   B

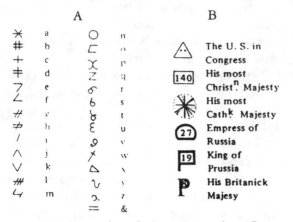

Two examples of symbol cryptography. (Courtesy of Precedent Publishing.)

signs replacing alphabet letters and words as shown above.

The types shown in part *B* are representative of those used by diplomats of the United States after freedom from Great Britain had been achieved. At this time, nomenclators were still predominant.

The U.S. CIVIL WAR saw a brief resurgence of a variety of covering methods from detailed TRANSPOSITIONS (Union) and CIPHER DISKS (Confederacy) to "home-made" drawings that resembled pictographs or rebuses conveyed by friends on both sides of the struggle.

HOBOES have a shared pattern of drawings that represent such factors as "safe town," "danger," "generous person," and so forth. Placed on tree trunks or lamp posts in chalk, these depictions were more numerous when many Americans were tragically uprooted during the Depression. FRATERNAL CRYPTOLOGY such as that practiced by the Masons and the Rosicrucians continues to use symbols in rituals and on documents exchanged between members.

Tallmadge, Benjamin (1754–1835), Colonial army officer and congressman.

During the American Revolution, Maj. Benjamin Tallmadge, of Connecticut's second regiment, light dragoons, led the Culper Ring of spies, which maintained espionage activities with skill, daring, and CRYPTOGRAPHY.

Tallmadge was a Yale graduate and a Connecticut school superintendent before being commissioned a lieutenant in the Continental Army in June 1776. After seeing combat at White Plains, Brandywine, and Germantown, Gen. George Washington asked him to form a secret intelligence network in New York City and Long Island.

Given the CODENAME John Bolton, Tallmadge began his organization in 1778. Among his most important recruits was Abraham Woodhull, a Long Island farmer. Tallmadge and Woodhull are credited with recruiting a dry goods merchant named Robert Townsend to serve as the primary agent in New York City. Woodhull came to be known as Samuel Culper, Senior, and Townsend as Samuel Culper, Junior. Robert Townsend worked in the city as a journalist for the *Royal Gazette*, owned by secret rebel supporter James Rivington. Through this contact point and in conversations at a Wall Street coffee house, Townsend garnered details about fortifications, troop dispositions, and royalist vessels, among other information.

The ring members sent some of their early intelligence in plain language. Fortunately, they soon began to practice better communications security, using an INVISI-

Benjamin Tallmadge. (Courtesy of the Library of Congress.)

BLE INK, or "stain," sent to them by Gen. Washington.

The passing of communications was conducted with elaborate precautions. Woodhull and other messengers, such as Austin Roe, took Townsend's messages to a drop site, a box hidden in a Long Island pasture owned by Woodhull, who in turn picked up the missives and looked for a petticoat hanging on a clothesline along Strong's Neck creek. This was a sign that Caleb Brewster was nearby with his whaleboat. Brewster's exact location, from among six

possibilities, was indicated by the number of handkerchiefs on the line. Brewster continued the transfer by rowing across Long Island Sound to Tallmadge or to another selected agent along the Connecticut coast. Dragoons then completed the relay to Gen. Washington's headquarters.

For additional protection, Tallmadge developed a one-part NOMENCLATOR of around 760 components. Patterned after the nomenclators used during the Renaissance, and based on *Entick's Spelling Dictionary* and its most often-used words, he had the system ready by July 1779. The nomenclator was arranged in alphanumerical order and also included a mixed alphabet to encrypt terms and digits not listed. The system was somewhat vulnerable because its components were listed in sequence. Still, it provided a reasonable level of security.

Below are sample words with their numerical equivalents, followed by the mixed alphabet:

37	attone	143	defense
38	attack	144	deceive
39	alarm	145	delay
40	action	146	difficult
306	industry	550	ruler
307	infamous	551	rapid
308	influence	552	reader
309	infantry	553	rebel
711	G. Washington	726	James Rivington
723	R. Townsend	727	New York
724	Austin Roe	728	Long Island

a	b	c	d	e	f	g	h	i	j	k	l	m	n	o	p	q	r	s	t	u	v	w	x	y	z
E	F	G	H	I	J	A	B	C	D	O	M	N	P	Q	R	K	L	U	V	W	X	Y	Z	S	T

With this method, the message *rapid infantry attack* was indicated by 551.309.38. Periods signaled the completion of a full number so that digits would not be misconstrued. To form the past tense, a flourish (˜) was placed over the number; 1444̃, for example, meant *deceived*.

The Tallmadge-led Culper Ring had a direct effect on military actions in 1780. Robert Townsend learned that Sir Henry Clinton, commanding British officer in New York, was planning to attack French troops and ships in Newport, Rhode Island. Townsend passed important details on troop strength and vessel movements along a circuitous 150-mile chain to Gen. Washington, who warned the French.

When Clinton's forces were poised on Long Island to begin the attack on July 30, he received a double shock. First, reports from the Newport area showed it to be heavily fortified. Second, news came that Gen. Washington had moved a large body of men to the eastern bank of the Hudson River, close to New York City. The strong defenses ahead and the potential threat to the city behind him forced Clinton to cancel his plans.

Benjamin Tallmadge also played an important role in thwarting the spy activities of Maj. John André in September 1780. By now a major himself, Tallmadge suspected that André was conspiring with Benedict Arnold and thus would not permit the two to reunite after André's capture. Arnold fled to New York, while André was hanged for his involvement in Arnold's plot against West Point.

Tallmadge continued to direct the Culper Ring until the conclusion of the war for independence. When peace was restored, he became an entrepreneur in Litchfield, Connecticut. After becoming a bank president and postmaster, he served from 1801 to 1817 as a Connecticut representative in the Congress that his highly dangerous espionage efforts helped to make a reality.

Tannenberg, Battle of (August 17–31, 1914),

a pivotal confrontation of World War I that is a classic battlefield example of the necessity of communications security (COMSEC).

When World War I began in August 1914, Czar Nicholas of Russia and his generals initiated their plan for two huge armies to attack strategically important East Prussia, which was defended by only one major German army. But the Russians didn't have the necessary communications equipment or encryption methods to protect the many dispatches needed to complete their sweeping plan.

Without enough CIPHERS to conceal messages, Russian wireless operators began sending dispatches in unprotected CLEARTEXT. Alert German eavesdroppers heard these exchanges and reported them to their German commanders, who planned a brilliant counteroffensive. In a series of engagements through the last days of August, the Kaiser's generals won a crushing victory. Poor cryptomethods and carelessness had helped inflict Russian losses of some 30,000 men killed, nearly

100,000 troops captured and the loss of vast quantities of materiel.

Teapot Dome, a U.S. political scandal that exposed corruption in the Republican administration of Warren G. Harding.

Teapot Dome was the name of a U.S. Navy oil reserve located in Wyoming. Rumors had circulated for years that officials of the Harding administration, including Veterans Bureau and Justice Department employees, had profited from illegal tampering with government oil bases. In 1924, the Senate launched an official inquiry through the Public Lands Committee. Committee staff persons discovered CODED messages, including one sent to Edward Doheny of the Pan American Petroleum Company. Unable to DECODE them, the Senate sent them to the U.S. Army Signal Corps and its code section, headed by WILLIAM FRIEDMAN.

Friedman testified that the message to Doheny was sent in a private code belonging to the Pan American Petroleum Company and that messages exchanged with *Washington Post* president Edward McClean were encoded with either a method belonging to the Bureau of Investigation of the Department of Justice or *Bentley's Complete Phrase Code*, a five-letter code that was widely used for business concealments.

Newspaper readers had their curiosity piqued by such communications such as that dated January 9, 1924, which included CODEWORDS like *opaque, hosier, bedaggled,* and *chinchilla.* Anything but bland, the code itself was rife with mysterious and scintillating terms.

Friedman DECODED these communica-tions and others, by studying the Bureau of Investigation's CODEBOOK, which McClean had obtained after being accepted as a special agent of the Justice Department. The Friedman decryptions showed that McClean's interest in the oil lease scheme was all too clear.

The Friedman findings and further Senate inquiries eventually exposed widespread fraud and bribery. Secretary of the Interior Albert Fall had secretly leased the Elk Hills, California, oil reserve to Edward Doheny and Teapot Dome to the oil company of Harry F. Sinclair. Doheny, in return, had "loaned" $100,000 to Fall. Sinclair had added to the bribery with a herd of cattle for Fall's ranch, $85,000 in cash, and $223,000 worth of bonds.

In 1927 the government won a suit to have the leases canceled. Though a jury acquitted Sinclair, Doheny, and Fall of conspiracy to defraud the government, Sinclair was convicted of jury tampering. Albert Fall was convicted of bribery, fined $100,000, and sentenced to a year in prison.

TELINT, telemetry intelligence. Telemetry (from the Greek *tele*, "far off," plus *metron*, "a measure") is the self-diagnosis sent by a missile to tracking stations on the ground. This information, which includes the rocket's on-board instrumentation and in-flight status, is a primary target for enemy electronics intelligence (ELINT) with special sensors such as those mounted on satellites.

In the past, such interceptor equipment has included special antennas and tape recorders. more recent space eavesdroppers have the technology to pick up microwave signals that carry telemetry. When signaled from their own command center, the observer satellites return their captured encryptions in very rapid spurts that make them more difficult to intercept too. The ground-based analysts then try to break these encryptions to learn more about a particular missile's own records of the launch, guidance systems, speed, the interaction of the technology on board, and so forth. Of course, even with the help of super-high-speed COMPUTERS, decryptions don't always succeed. A good example of Soviet telemetry protection and signals security occurred with the U.S. Rhyolite satellites.

The first Rhyolite satellite was put into space in March 1973 specifically as a signals intelligence orbiter eavesdropping on Soviet microwave signals and telemetry data. The usually secrecy-conscious Soviets had not believed that either transmission method could be intercepted. Thus, for about four years, the United States had a very valuable advantage. However, by the middle of 1977, a spy named Christopher Boyce at TRW, a California defense contractor, had informed the Soviets about their vulnerability. Soon the USSR was concealing its telemetry with ONE-TIME PADS and/or a "tape bucket" system. With the former, special single-use number groups covered the telemetry data, making decipherment virtually impossible since there is no FREQUENCY pattern that might make the transmission decryptable even by computer before the data becomes obsolete. In the "tape bucket" system, telemetry data are tape-recorded on board the missile, then parachuted back to earth in a capsule, thereby avoiding any transmission at all.

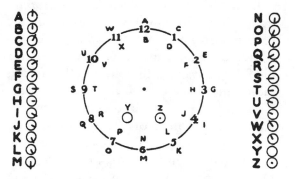

A time code. (From *Secret Writing* by Henry Lysing, Dover Publication, Inc., 1974.)

Time Code, a CODE using a clock face.

The numbers of a clock face can designate 24 alphabet characters (1 through 24 in the A.M. and the same in the P.M.). With this system, relative rarities such as *q* and *z* or letters such as *i* and *j* or *u* and *v* can be combined to reduce the alphabet to 24 characters. A.M. and P.M. can then be differentiated by using a 24-hour military-style clock, on which 1 P.M. is 13, 2 P.M. is 14, and so forth.

A clock or watch face can also be adapted for a version of SYMBOL CRYPTOGRAPHY, in which the numbers used alone are represented schematically by drawings of a clock face on which a single hand points to the number's position. For example, "A" is indicated by the hand pointing to 12 o'clock with the hand extending just outside the circle. "B" is also found at 12 o'clock, but the hand remains inside the circle.

Tokumu Han ("Special Section"), a decryption unit introduced into the communications department of the Japanese naval general staff in 1925.

In 1929, a fully organized *tsushintai* (radio intercept unit) was set up in the navy ministry and in 1932, when Japan occupied Shanghai, an "X Facility" accompanied the naval landing force. It was this radio unit that provided the analysts of the *Tokumu Han* with intercepts from the Kuomintang forces of Chiang Kai-shek.

During this time, the *Tokumu Han* was also actively trying to break the U.S. State Department's GRAY CODE, a ONE-PART CODE used by diplomats in the Far East. First, the Japanese cryptanalysts discovered a series of vowels and KEYWORDS with the assistance of the Tokyo *kempeitai* (military police), who clandestinely obtained telegram scraps from U.S. embassy wastebaskets. The solvers finally removed the mask by identifying *nadad* as *stop/period*, opening the door to further discoveries that ultimately compromised the U.S. State Department's cryptosystem.

The solving of the Gray Code led to a military reversal for China. In 1932, "X Facility" analysts in occupied Shanghai were able to break a Chinese CODE similar to a digit code used to send business telegrams. When its message was compared to a *Tokumu Han* decryption of a Gray transmission, the combined solutions exposed a planned Chinese airstrike on Japanese troops. Reacting quickly, Japanese carrier-based planes struck the Nationalists' aircraft on the ground at Ch'ang-sha, dealing them severe losses.

In the autumn of 1932, the Japanese tanker *Erimo*, shadowing U.S. maneuvers in the Pacific, learned that the U.S. Navy was using an encrypting machine built by EDWARD HEBERN. The Japanese had already been studying similar rotary systems, and they soon penetrated this

version. U.S. technicians had also noted the machine's weaknesses, however, and opted instead for a strip cipher method with sliding card strips imprinted with different alphabets. Gradually, as U.S. cryptosystems multiplied in number and complexity, the successes of the *Tokumu Han* shrank in number. After the start of World War II, the balance of intelligence-gathering and encrypting capabilities shifted in favor of the United States.

Transmissions Security, an electronic form of concealment in the area of communications security that is similar to STEGANOGRAPHY. Like this method of covering written text, transmissions security tries to hide the existence of secret messages in electrical exchanges, whether or not they are encrypted.

Burst or spurt radio transmissions are high-speed broadcasts of often prerecorded data in supercompressed form, sent at exact prearranged intervals and at speeds so high that they are difficult to detect by signals intelligence monitors. This technique has military and espionage applications, such as the conveyance of dispatches to submarines and undercover agents.

Other examples include spread spectrum, in which a signal is diluted to a millionth of its original intensity and mixed with background "noise" before being sent, and frequency hops, which move messages from frequency to frequency, at speeds greater than a thousand times a second.

Transposition, a system of CRYPTOGRAPHY whereby the letters of a message are rearranged.

For example, the word *sentinel*, when

transposed, could become *netsilen*. In its basic form this method does not conceal messages as well as does its partner SUB-STITUTION, wherein letters or words are replaced by other letters, words, symbols, or numerals.

Letter transposition existed in some of the earliest attempts to conceal the contents of writing. The Neapolitan scholar GIOVANNI PORTA discussed transposition as a primary concealment method in his classic *De Furtivis Literarum Notis*, published in 1563. By then, however, the NO-MENCLATOR was achieving ascendancy as the principal masking system, a position it would occupy until the middle of the 19th century, when the invention of the telegraph began to cause important changes in such methods.

During the U.S. CIVIL WAR, a transposition form called ROUTE was used by northern forces to conceal telegraph messages from Confederate wiretappers and CRYPTANALYSTS. To form the route, PLAINTEXT was written in horizontal lines that formed columns. The words were transcribed by moving down some columns and up others in a prearranged direction (the route). A KEYWORD defined the size and direction of the route for the addressee. CODE terms for certain persons and places, meaningless NULLS, and also diagonal term alignments further helped to conceal the messages.

An example of a modern transposition style is the columnar transposition. It can be arranged with a keyword such as *LA-SERS*. The numerical order of the keyword's letters in the alphabet sets the order in which the columns are transcribed from the transposition table and placed in the enciphered message. Re-peating letters in the keyword are given sequential digits from left to right.

The plaintext message *he is a high tech thief for their side* is written horizontally in a block below the keyword. The repeated *S* in the keyword is assigned a 5 and a 6.

L	A	S	E	R	S
3	1	5	2	4	6
h	e	i	s	a	h
i	g	h	t	e	c
h	t	h	i	e	f
f	o	r	t	h	e
i	r	s	i	d	e

Reading down the columns according to their numerical order and placing the letters in groups of five yields the CI-PHERTEXT *egtor stiti hihfi aeehd ihhrs hcfee*.

An additional encryption step is used in double columnar transposition. The letters derived from the original transposition are placed horizontally in another block with a new keyword. Then they are transcribed in groups of five, again by reading down the columns in numerical order. (If the bottom row should happen to be incomplete, nulls can be added to complete the line before the columns are transcribed.)

B	E	A	M	S
2	3	1	4	5
e	g	t	o	r
s	t	i	t	i
h	i	h	f	i
a	e	e	h	d
i	h	h	r	s
h	c	f	e	e

Ciphertext: *tiheh fesha ihgti ehcot fhrer iidse*

One structural variation of this method is interrupted columnar transposition, wherein blank cells are placed at preset points in the columns. The location of the blanks is part of the KEY sent to the addressee. The empty cells introduce variety to the lengths of the segments, making decryption more difficult.

The message is inscribed horizontally around the spaces, then transcribed from the columns according to their numerical order, and placed in five-letter groups for transmission.

L	A	S	E	R	S
3	1	5	2	4	6
h	e	_	i	_	s
a	_	h	_	i	_
g	h	t	e	c	h
_	t	h	i	_	e
f	_	f	o	r	_
t	h	_	e	i	r
_	s	i	_	d	e

Ciphertext: *ehths ieioe hagft icrid hthfi shere*

Pairs of transposition tables also help to complicate concealments. Such is the case with the VIC CIPHER used by Soviet spy and defector REINO HAYHANEN. The VIC is considered by several experts to be a virtually UNBREAKABLE CIPHER in practice, because of its combination of mnemonic keys, a version of the STRADDLING CHECKERBOARD, and sequences of numeric encryptions. These are developed through a standard columnar transposition, plus a second table with a series of planned interruptions.

Transposition in combination with other methods is also exemplified by versions of FRACTIONATING CIPHERS. Some of these processes involve substitutions for plaintext characters. Then they are split into two elements (the "fractionating" aspect), that are then transposed for additional encipherment (see ADFGVX and BIFID CIPHER).

Trithemius, Johannes (1462–1516),

German abbot, author, and cryptographer. Ridiculed by a stepfather for his interest in learning, the young Trithemius nevertheless persevered, studying at the University of Heidelberg and becoming an abbot of a Benedictine order in Germany at a very young age. His energetic mind generated collections of sermons, histories, and biographies, earning him the title "Father of Bibliography." He also become deeply involved in studies of the occult and the practices of alchemy. From this realm of mysticism and pseudoscience, his interest in CRYPTOLOGY developed.

In 1499 Trithemius began a series of volumes entitled *Steganographia* (Greek for "covered writing"). In its early sections, he wrote about methods of vowel–consonant SUBSTITUTION, how nonsense words can be meaningful, and how letters can be used as NULLS, having no significance other than to confuse prying eyes. The text remained in manuscript form for more than a century because of its heretical contents about magic, other-worldly beings, and secret powers. After it was finally printed in 1606, it was placed on the Catholic Index of Prohibited Books.

Trithemius's direct contribution to CRYPTOLOGY was in his *Polygraphia*, published by a friend in 1518, a year and a half after his death. A collection of six books, the *Polygraphia* contained columns of Latin terms, words equated with PLAINTEXT letters, and the first SQUARE TABLE in cryptographic writings, the foundation of POLYALPHABETIC SUBSTITUTION. Its CIPHER alphabets were arranged in rows, with each shifted one position to the left of the one above it. He used his *tabula recta* to encipher the first letter with the first alphabet, the second letter with the second alphabet, continuing in this way through the end of the message. According to David Kahn's history of cryptology, *The Codebreakers*, Trithemius had developed the original progressive KEY whereby all the cipher alphabets were used before repeating any one of them.

Trithemius's influence as a scholar and author did much to promote an understanding of secret-writing techniques. His work laid the foundations for many who came after him, including LEON ALBERTI of Florence and GIOVANNI PORTA of Naples.

Two-key Cryptography, also known as the PUBLIC KEY method, a relatively recent advance over the long-used single-KEY style of concealment. Even the advanced commercial security process known as the Data Encryption Standard (DES), developed in the 1970s, was a single-key algorithm. The two-key breakthrough occurred in 1976 at Stanford University in California. There, Professor Martin Hellman and research student Whitfield Diffie developed what they called a public key cryptosystem.

Hellman, Diffie, and another student named Ralph Merkle collaborated on the public key as a solution to the problems inherent in the distribution of keys. Their system has two keys, one publicly available (in a directory) and the other private. In most cases the public key is used for encrypting and the private one for decrypting.

The Stanford researchers built their concept on a series of mathematical "secret-entrance" problems known as trap doors, which are planned openings in COMPUTER systems that permit authorized users to bypass existing security to test operating systems and software. However, they have also been used by hackers and computer criminals. In mathematical terms, trap doors are easier to solve in one direction; trying to work back from the solution to the beginning problem can be very difficult.

Merkle and Hellman proposed a trap door called a knapsack as the model for their cipher algorithm. Solving the knapsack is frequently described as trying to determine the number of cylinders, of the same width but varying length, that are held end to end in a cylindrical knapsack of the same diameter. The power of the algorithm was in the difficulty for the analysts who tried to discover the exact sequence of the components as they were arranged to make the sum.

Hellman and Merkle developed complementary key pairs. A message encrypted with one member of the pair was decrypted by the other member. Encryption involved assigning a digit to each message letter and then adding these digits together. The decryption key separated the original numerals from their sum, and the PLAINTEXT was recovered. For the third-party analyst, unable to discern the secret decrypting key, the only alternative was believed to be a "brute-force," trial-and-error computer attempt to find every possible key, necessitating costly and time-consuming electronic guesswork.

The Hellman/Diffie/Merkle system was lauded as one of the very few UNBREAKABLE CIPHERS. This seemed to be the case until 1982, when Adi Shamir of the Massachusetts Institute of Technology solved the trap-door knapsack. Not long thereafter, Shamir's former MIT associate Leonard Adleman used Adi's formula to solve the knapsack on a home computer.

Shamir, Adleman, and associate Ronald Rivist of MIT had a competitive two-key process that became known as the RSA cryptoalgorithm. Its public and private keys were also based on a trap door, but had combinations of prime numbers (numbers that can be evenly divided only by themselves and the numeral *1*, such as 3, 5, or 7).

When a prime integer is multiplied by another, the product is one that cannot be produced by any other pair of prime numbers. The inventors of the RSA system recommended very large integers to make the private and public keys. Thus an RSA-based computer program would randomly select a pair of prime numbers around 100 digits long, then multiply them together, with the product becoming the basis of the two keys. As with the complementary pair system of Hellman and Merkle, an analyst trying to remove such a concealment was faced with the immense difficulty of factoring these large integers in a "brute force" attempt.

Throughout most of the 1980s, the

RSA cryptoalgorithm was described as being computationally cryptosecure; potential advances in both factoring theory and computer-enhanced decryptions for practical time frames make the term *unbreakable* more difficult to apply.

Two-part Code, a CODE having elements that are out of sequence in relation to the PLAINTEXT words, which are in alphabetical order. More complicated than a ONE-PART CODE, it requires a second list or a book of code groups that are compiled in numerical or alphabetical order for DECODING. Friendly communicators have both versions. The following is an example of a segment of a two-part code with CODENUMBERS used for army communications.

Encoding		Decoding	
advance	2400	3812	attack
attack	3812	3815	refuel
battalion	3826	3820	front line
battle	3647	3826	battalion
begin	3849	3830	east
besiege	1390	3837	weather
binoculars	2629	3842	company
bivouac	7812	3849	begin
bridge	9151	3853	supply route
brigade	4170	3857	river

The general of an army in battle may give hundreds of orders that in turn initiate thousands of radio messages and replies along the chain of command such as this:

4925	3577	6193	8610	5728
6232	5341	8072	1546	3642
3826	7823	5695	3285	9370
5843	1418	3849	4491	8252
1706	3739	6430	5325	6047
3423	8656	2829	7727	3812

According to the decoding section above, these numbers contain the command:

battalion	begin	attack
(3826)	(3849)	(3812)

For added security, the senders could practice SUPERENCIPHERMENT by means of a book code (not to be confused with a CODEBOOK containing lists of CODE-WORDs and their replacements by terms or numerals), that has prearranged KEY-NUMBERS each derived from a page, line, and word of a book. For example, 1041 could be page 10, line 4, word 1. This number is then added to 3826 (battalion) to make 4867. Other digits derived from the book and known to both parties could be added to the other codenumbers in turn. The sequence of their sums would constitute the complete cryptogram.

Typex (AKA "Type X"), British adaptation of the German CIPHER MACHINE ENIGMA. British authorities had bought and analyzed commercial Enigmas in the 1920s. After about a decade of tests and improvements, they considered their own machine ready for service.

The Typex had five typical ROTORS (wired disks) and a sixth, specialized one that resembled the half rotor, or reflecting rotor, of the Enigma. The sixth disk reversed the electric current it received, sending it back through the other rotors along a different pathway through their wire mazes.

This reflector enabled the machines to turn out CIPHER alphabets that were reciprocal. For example, if *c* was enciphered by *n*, then *n* was enciphered by *c*. No letter represented itself, because the direct rotor pattern never crossed the reflected one. By arranging the rotors in the same order and original position for encipherment, one could simply type the cipher letters to recover the PLAINTEXT.

The Typex also had ratchet wheels that resembled those on advanced models of the Enigma. The ratchets had notches that affected the movement of the rotors. At the point where the notch on the most rapid rotor came to a certain place in its revolution, a pawl pushed the medium-speed rotor a step forward. The same operation repeated for the next-fastest rotor. This enhanced the number of rotor letters available for multiple-alphabet encipherments.

On one version of the Typex, the first two rotors were stators. Once preset, these did not move again during the encryption process. In practice, the function of these was similar to that of plugboards on German machines, adding another level of complexity to the cipher. The three other moving wired disks had ratchets with several notches (from five to nine per wheel). At the other end of the sequence was the reflector.

Some Enigma versions had so-called alphabet rings, imprinted with either the standard alphabet or the digits 1 through 26, to assist in setting the rotors. The Typex, however, did not have an alphabet circle similar to that of the Enigma. On the Typex, the primary encryption cylinder body was generally a slug that could be removed from the rotor housing to enable different notched rims to be used (5, 7, 9, and even-notched). Some slugs were arranged with 52 contacts on each side, or two rings of 26, or one set of a pair that only performed a back-up function.

Some Typex versions had rotors at the entry point of the electric current that moved automatically, thus creating still greater diversity in polyalphabetic encryptions. Some of their rims had standard alphabets, but others had varied alphabet sequences. Cipher machine experts Cipher Deavours and Louis Kruh propose

that the starting positions of the rotors were probably encrypted and were used as a key for beginning the process.

The keyboards of the Typex machines often had both numbers and letters. The infrequently used letters x, z, and v served for word divisions, figure shifts, and letter shifts respectively. The complete CIPHERTEXT was printed on paper tape.

The eventual results of the war showed that the Typex held up against German code and cipher breakers far better than the Enigma machines did, guarding their communications against Britain's ULTRA operation of interception and analysis.

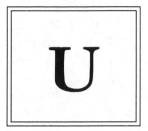

U

Übchi, a double columnar TRANSPOSITION CIPHER used by the Germans during World War I. It was broken by French CIPHER solvers, thanks in part to a radio message sent in unprotected CLEARTEXT early in the conflict.

The Übchi had a KEYWORD or KEYPHRASE that was represented by numerals according to the position of its letters in the alphabet (A = 1, B = 2, and so forth). Two identical letters were numbered consecutively if they appeared in the same keyword or keyphrase. The German word *Herrschaft* (domination) demonstrates this method below:

Keyword: h e r r s c h a f t
                5 3 7 8 9 2 6 1 4 10

Original communication:

> First army X Plan five activated
> X Cross Marne at set hour

The encipherment involved six stages. First, the original message was placed in rows below the number series:

5	3	7	8	9	2	6	1	4	10
f	i	r	s	t	a	r	m	y	x
p	l	a	n	f	i	v	e	a	c
t	i	v	a	t	e	d	x	c	r
o	s	s	m	a	r	n	e	a	t
s	e	t	h	o	u	r			

The cryptographer then wrote the letters by columns according to the order of the KEYNUMBERS: *mexe aieru ilise yaca fptos rvdnr ravst snamh tftao xcrt.*

These groups were then transcribed horizontally into another block beneath the same number sequence:

217

5	3	7	8	9	2	6	1	4	10
m	e	x	e	a	i	e	r	u	i
l	i	s	e	y	a	c	a	f	p
t	o	s	r	v	d	n	r	r	a
v	s	t	s	n	a	m	h	t	f
t	a	o	x	c	r	t			

The next step was to add as many NULL letters as there were words in the original phrase, or in this case, keyword. Thus *one* null (*z*) was added after the last letter in the last row (in this example, *t*).

The encipherer once more took these letters from the block by columns in the numerical sequence: *rarh(z) iadar eiosa ufrt mltvt ecnmt xssto eersx ayvnc ipaf.*

The new series of letters was written in horizontal rows and divided into the standard five-letter groups. If there were less than five in a group, the first letter or letters of the next column in the order was added to make five, until the message was completed. Thus, the final encryption was *rarhz iadar eiosa ufrtm ltvte cnmtx sstoe ersxa yvnci paf.*

To DECIPHER the message, the recipient first had to discern the size of the transposition rectangle in order to learn how long the columns were.

This was accomplished by dividing the total number of key numbers into the total number of letters in the communiqué, including the null (48 ÷ 10). The quotient (4) was the number of complete lines. The remainder (8) was the number of letters in the incomplete lines.

The succeeding steps simply reversed the corresponding steps in the enciphering process.

UKUSA, the United Kingdom–United States Security Agreement, a top-secret pact among, originally, the United States, Great Britain, Canada, Australia, and New Zealand, to share signals intelligence information. The pact was signed in 1947 and gave each member nation a sphere of influence where it was best able to gather intelligence. The United States took precedence in covering certain Chinese frequencies from its listening posts in Japan, Taiwan, and Korea. England had priority over other Chinese channels from its position in Hong Kong. Australian eavesdroppers covered regions across to the South Pacific islands as well as sections of the Indian Ocean. Canada and the U.S. shared monitoring stations in North American and the vital northern polar region.

The UKUSA arrangement had its unofficial beginnings with information and technical exchanges in the early months of World War II. This included such important technology as two PURPLE decrypting machines from the United States and radar and sonar data provided by Britain.

In May 1943, with both nations fully involved in the war, the United Kingdom and the United States signed the BRUSA Agreement, which included careful plans for data exchanges, security procedures, and a new lexicon of CODENAMES and CODEWORDS, among other arrangements. Previously, U.S. COMINT (communications intelligence) had the codenames *Dexter* (for the enemy's top CODE method), *Corral* (for the enemy's moderately important systems), and *Rabid* (for traffic analysis). The English counterparts were *Ultra, Pearl,* and *Thumb.* The specific highest-level ULTRA intelligence obtained from decipherents of the German ENIGMA cryptosystems was not made known to U.S. representatives until April 1943.

Meanwhile, the United States cooperated by placing the more general Ultra secrecy designation before its own codenames. Eventually the Pearl and Thumb identifications were replaced by the codename *Pinup*.

In Europe, at circulation levels below that of commanding general, Ultra data was referred to as *Pearl*, *Thumb*, and sometimes *Zeal*. These terms came to be closely associated with low-level wireless intercepts. By these and other means, the very top-security Ultra-labeled data from the decryptions of the German Enigma machines and other machine CIPHERs was kept secret throughout the war, even from English intelligence staffs in other departments. The same protection was afforded Ultra by U.S. authorities. At lower distribution levels, the codename MAGIC was used as a type of general cover. Thus Magic concealed both the U.S. decryptions of Japanese messages and the material from British decryptions of Nazi transmissions. (Only in 1974, with the publication of Frederick Winterbotham's *The Ultra Secret*, did the facts about Ultra become known to the general public.)

The mutually agreeable results of BRUSA led to meetings with Australia and Canada. Two years after the Axis was defeated, UKUSA became a reality. Later, NATO countries as well as South Korea and Japan joined as signatories designated as third parties with restricted access. Though now broader in scope, the specific intent of the pact continues to be the maintenance of a highly secret signals intelligence network.

Ultra, the CODENAME for the successful British operation, during World War II, to read the CIPHERs generated by the German ENIGMA and other encryption machines. One of the best kept secrets in all of military and espionage history, Ultra was not revealed to the general public until 1974 with the publication of Frederick Winterbotham's *The Ultra Secret*. Ultra had been the name of the English Admirals' Code from the days of the Battle of Trafalgar. In World War II it was applied to both the project to decrypt the Enigma cipher and other Nazi cryptosystems, and to the data derived from this process.

British intelligence had early knowledge of the Enigma device from French and Polish sources.

Polish analysts had had access to an early Enigma version sold commercially in the 1920s, and their intelligence agents had photographed and drawn diagrams of an Enigma machine mistakenly shipped to Warsaw in 1929. Scholars at the University of Poznan also solved important mathematical problems regarding Enigma decipherments. In late 1931 or early 1932, a German Ministry of Defense clerk, codenamed *Asche* (or Source D) and reportedly named Hans-Thilo Schmidt, began selling secret cryptographic documents to the French. Over an eight-year period, deliveries reputedly included an instruction manual for a military Enigma, a CODEBOOK of KEYS, sample encipherments with PLAINTEXT equivalents; and machine modifications.

Later, in the mid-1930s, Poles at the AVA radio factory near Warsaw and French technicians both built versions of the Enigma that enhanced Allied research, and in 1938 Polish efforts with multiple motor-driven rotors led to a machine dubbed the *bombe* that helped decrypt improved Enigma machine variations.

In 1939 secret meetings in Paris and Warsaw led to a necessary division of effort among the Poles, the French, and the British. Bowing to Great Britain's broader scientific and technical base, Poland and France agreed to entrust contributions to teams of British analysts such as those at BLETCHLEY PARK, a Victorian estate about 45 miles northwest of London. There, members of Britain's Government Code and Cipher School, chief British cryptanalyst Alfred D. Knox, and Cambridge mathematicians Gordon Welchman and Alan Turing, along with other scholars, began work on new attacks against the Enigma system.

Months of labor led to the development of the British *bombe* (AKA "the bomb"). Beginning in 1939, construction of this machine began and by late April 1940, the result was a copper-hued cabinet around eight feet high and eight feet wide at its base. Its inner works were a maze of wires arranged in electrical circuits that tried to imitate the Enigma's rotors. The machine was set up in Hut 3, a large structure built on Bletchley's grounds.

With the help of England's intercept stations, recordings were made of messages sent by enemy military, diplomatic, and intelligence organizations. When Enigma transmissions were identified, they were placed on tape and fed into the *bombe*. With a noise like a series of rapidly working knitting needles, the apparatus often was able to find the keys enciphering the communications. Then the analysts endeavored to unravel their concealments (working in Hut 6 for army and air force transmissions and Hut 8 for those of the navy). The *bombe* became the precursor of

a series of devices that counteracted Nazi cryptographs throughout World War II, as described below.

German naval ciphers (such as Hydra and Triton) were solved through *bombe*/ Ultra intelligence with the aid of a naval Enigma and documents retrieved from captured U-boat 110 in May 1941. These successes were crucial to winning the BATTLE OF THE ATLANTIC.

A Bletchley-based machine called "Heath Robinson" was an electronic *match* for Germany's early *Geheimschreiber* (secret writing machine). A 1943 solution of this device, which had advanced teleprinter aspects of the BAUDOT CODE and the MURRAY CODE, gave the Allies some knowledge of Hitler's directives and German Foreign Office exchanges, among other high-level traffic.

A COMPUTER predecessor named CO- LOSSUS was used to break an improved *Geheimschreiber* that had 10 rotors. Colossus was established at Bletchley in December 1943. Its photoelectric cells, radio tubes, high-speed drive system, and extra tape-reading mechanisms helped the cryptanalysts to check thousands of cipher characters a second. In 1944–45, Colossus and a Mark II successor provided data about the most secret radio transmissions within the hierarchy of the Third Reich.

This Ultra data, including information on enemy plans, defensive measures, troop movements, industrial production, and air and naval strategies, contributed greatly to the defeat of the Axis powers.

Unbreakable Ciphers, include one- time methods and computationally secure cryptosystems. An unsolvable cryptosys-

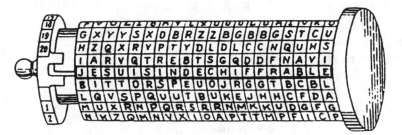

"I am indecipherable." The ideal cryptosystem. (Courtesy of Headquarters CECOM, Fort Manmouth, New Jersey.)

tem was and is the dream of amateur and professional cryptographers alike.

A Frenchman with cryptographic talents named BLAISE DE VIGENÈRE (1523–1596) was credited for years with having created *le chiffre indéchiffrable* (the indecipherable cipher). Yet this system, involving an alphabet table, fell short of the goal. Nor was his original polyalphabetic tableau a perfect form of message protection.

It was not until the 20th century that truly impenetrable cryptomethods were devised. The foundation was laid by GILBERT VERNAM, an AT&T engineer who was studying security problems with the teletypewriter in 1917. He developed a process with paper tapes and sequences of marks (holes) and spaces (no marks). Encipherment of standard teletype characters was accomplished with a KEY of holes and spaces that was added to the marks and spaces of the PLAINTEXT message. The sum of this electromechanical process was the CIPHERTEXT.

Vernam's base was built upon by U.S. Army Maj. JOSEPH MAUBORGNE, who applied his experience in military security and CRYPTOGRAPHY to the AT&T system. In 1918, Mauborgne proposed a non-repeating, unintelligible key used to encrypt the plaintext. This advance came to be known as the "one-time system." With the Vernam/AT&T equipment, this procedure became the one-time tape. The random key characters added to the original message pulses made for a lack of predictability that confounded the standard procedures of outside analysts.

During the same period, other concealment experts apparently experimented independently with single-use techniques. Between 1918 and the early 1920s, one such system, the ONE-TIME PAD, was formalized. Used by Germany's Foreign Office, its name derived from the two sheets of paper that were typed with a sequence of random numbers that became the key. A series of these pages were placed in two identical groups, or pads, one for the sender and one for the receiver. The numbers on the pads' pages were intended to be used just once, then discarded.

In this system, the encipherer first converts the plaintext letters into digits using a KEYWORD and a type of matrix called a monome–dinome table. The keyword (*consul*, in this example) is written horizontally, with the remaining alphabet characters placed beneath it in rows. Each of the numbers 0 through 7 is aligned with one of the often-used letters *a, e, o, n, i, r, s,* and *t* according to its location in the columns, reading left to right. Number pairs are assigned to the other characters in combinations starting with 8 or 9 and ranging in order down the columns from 80 to 99. They are written vertically and placed in the table that also has a diagonal for digit–character shifts in the plaintext and a period for stops.

c	o	n	s	u	l
80	1	4	6	92	96
a	b	d	e	f	g
0	84	86	7	93	97
h	i	j	k	m	p
81	2	87	89	94	98
q	r	t	v	w	x
82	3	5	90	95	99
y	z	.	/		
83	85	88	91		

The next stage is to begin SUBSTITUTION of the message letters with the numbers from this table. For transmission clarity, all numerals in the plaintext are repeated in triplicate.

Plaintext:

c o u r i e r / 1 0 / h a s i t
80 1 92 3 2 7 3 91 111 000 91 81 0 6 2 5

These numbers are then added to the digits of the key, which is a series of nonrepeating numerals. Noncarrying addition is applied (for example, $4 + 8 = 2$, with the 1 deleted). This prevents carryover errors and permits addition from left to right.

Plaintext: 80192327391111100091810625
Key: + 17034853954260239146085l7
Ciphertext: 97126170245371239054181332

Such an encryption is considered unbreakable, since the odds against solving it are astronomically high and the time required for decipherment, even if successful, would be so long that any information gained would be obsolete. The absence of any predicable aspect in the key undermines such standard analytical tools as same key encryption matchups, FREQUENCY counts of letters, or searches for familiar words and typical opening and closing phrases.

Universal Product Code (UPC), is a generally NONSECRET CODE intended to assist in the sale and distribution of consumer items.

Product coding in the United States began as early as the 1930s. However, the process did not become widespread until the 1970s, with the grocery industry taking the lead, motivated primarily by the need for improvement in checkout speed and the processing of sales data, stock counts, and inventory records.

After much study, an 11-digit CODE (plus a check digit) was chosen in April 1971 by an oversight committee representing grocery manufacturing, wholesaling, and retailing. Still more study was necessary to choose the standard machine-readable symbol to accompany these numerals. After extensive tests, the UPC symbol design was revealed on April 3, 1973.

During the code and symbol development phases, plans were made for an organization to oversee and manage the application and supervision of the Universal Product Code. In early 1972, the Uniform Code Council (UCC) was set up to regulate overall activity. Since then, the UPC system, popularly known as the "bar code," has been used in virtually every type of retail business.

The first digit of the code, the number system character, has a function similar to a cryptographic KEY, in that it determines the meaning and category of each of the other numbers. There are seven categories of the number system character (*A* in the illustration below):

0—assigned to all nationally branded products *except* the following:

2—random weight items such as meat, cheese, and poultry

3—drug and certain health-linked products

4—products marked by the retailer for sale only in his store or stores

5—coupons

6, 7—valid for assignment to retail products since the first quarter of 1990.

The number system character is included within a six-part numeral series (B) that identifies the manufacturer. This number is assigned by the Uniform Code Council, Inc.

The next five-digit sequence (C) is a product code number. Controlled by the manufacturing company, this numeral is unique for each of the manufacturer's products and includes color, size, flavor, and other qualities.

The final number (D) is the check digit, which helps to reveal error in the other numbers.

0   12345   67890   5
(A)   (D)
          (B)   (C)

At the supermarket, the checker passes the UPC-labeled item over an optical scanner, which "reads" the UPC symbol, decodes it into the UPC code digits, and transmits these digits to a small COMPUTER. The computer records the product's sales data and transmits the item's description and price to the checkout stand for visual display and printing on a receipt tape. The UPC has also been adapted for use on shipping containers and business forms.

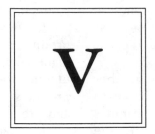

Vernam, Gilbert (1890–1960), U.S. inventor and amateur cryptographer. When the United States entered World War I, Vernam was working for the American Telephone and Telegraph Company in New York City. He and his fellow engineers had been given the task of trying to protect the messages of the printing telegraph, or teletypewriter.

This mechanism was rather new at the time, but that was no guarantee of security. Changing the internal connections enabled the sender to encrypt one letter with another, in a form of MONOALPHABETIC SUBSTITUTION. Yet this was known as a very basic concealment that could be easily discerned by experts. Then Gilbert had an idea that was based on the traditional BAUDOT CODE.

French telegrapher Emile Baudot's method replaced the letters of the alphabet with electrical pulses, called *units.* Every character was given five units that signified either a pulse of electric current (marks) or its absence (spaces) during a given period. This made 32 combinations of spaces and marks, 26 of them being for the standard alphabet and 6 for operational processes such as number and letter shifts and carriage return.

By 1917 the teletypewriter had evolved into a second mode called *indirect.* In this version the initiation of typing and activating the electrical processes caused the signals to be changed into marks (holes) that were punched in a paper tape. The absence of pulses left spaces in the tape strip, thereby creating a pattern of spaces and marks that put the Baudot Code on paper. The tape was "read" by a device that had metallic fingers. These slipped through the strips at the openings, made contact with another part of the mechanism, and thus sent a pulse. The spaces (unperforated segments) kept the contact points apart, so that no pulse was sent.

Well aware of this process, Gilbert devised a CIPHER using the very same items. He took a tape of KEY characters and added its pulses to the pulses of the PLAINTEXT letters. The total of the two became the CIPHERTEXT that concealed the teletyped communication. He developed a convenient plan for reversing this addition so that the intended addressee could subtract to recover the original plaintext. With the mark-and-space process as the foundation, he had four variations:

Plaintext		Key		Ciphertext
space	+	space	=	space
space	+	mark	=	mark
mark	+	space	=	mark
mark	+	mark	=	space

When the plaintext and key pulses were both the same (two marks or two spaces), the ciphertext was always a space. The two different combinations always meant a mark as the cipher. The Baudot letter *I* was designated as *space mark mark space space* (in digital terms, 01100). The key letter *O* was *space space space mark mark*, or 00011. The cipher sum became 01111, or *V* in the Baudot alphabet.

Plaintext	0 1 1 0 0 (I)
Key	0 0 0 1 1 (O)
Ciphertext	0 1 1 1 1 (V)

At the recipient site, the ciphertext pulses

were added with the prearranged key pulses for the particular message sequence in order to find the plaintext. The previously mentioned rule of space and mark equivalents applied here (*mark + mark = space*):

Ciphertext	0 1 1 1 1 (V)
Key	0 0 0 1 1 (O)
Plaintext	0 1 1 0 0 (I)

The electrical adding of the pulses was accomplished with a device that included magnets and relays. Keytape and plaintext tape-reading mechanisms generated pulses to go into Vernam's enciphering device. Incoming pulses that were different closed a circuit and made a mark; like pulses resulted in a space. The encrypted spaces and marks were then sent as a regular teletype transmission. The Vernam mechanism at the transmission's destination was arranged so as to restore the plaintext pulses, which were then put into a teletype receiver that in turn printed the plaintext.

By introducing "on-line encipherment," Gilbert Vernam brought automation to a process formerly dependent on clerks with varying degrees of skills.

Nevertheless, the method was vulnerable. The Baudot Code was publicly known, and its alphabet variations, though polyalphabetic, were limited. A cryptanalytic genius named JOSEPH MAUBORGNE recognized these weaknesses and, building on Vernam's work, developed a truly secure one-time system.

Very Light, developed by Edward Very in the 1870s, a method of signaling using pyrotechnics (from the Greek *pyros*, "fire," + *techne*, "art").

A native of Maine, Very served in the U.S. Navy during the U.S. CIVIL WAR before he began ordnance experiments at the Washington Navy Yard. His Very signal, as it was also known, had a pistol designed to take a 10-gauge, center-fire, brass-headed paper shotgun shell. The original pistol was single-loading and had a steel barrel around nine inches long that was tapered at the muzzle. To operate it, one pressed the barrel catch and broke open the barrel by pushing it down. The cartridge then was inserted and the barrel closed and locked.

The cartridge was very similar to a standard shotgun shell, with a primer and a firing charge of about 25 grains of musket powder. The cartridge propelled a "star" skyward. These stars, of red, green, or white, were cylinders packed with pyrotechnic material. Each was reinforced with wire and wrapped with a quick match, and one end was primed with a small portion of black powder to ensure its ignition at full illumination just before it reached its maximum height of 200 to 400 feet.

Each star color had a distinctively shaped top for easier handling at night. In comparison with earlier pyrotechnic methods such as the Rogers or the Coston systems, which had 18 to 20 different accessories, the Very Light was a much less awkward and thus more practical NON-SECRET CODE.

Its code was quite similar to telegraphic systems. In a form resembling the alternating dots and dashes of MORSE CODE, the Very system signaled numbers with different four-part sequences of red (*R*) and green (*G*) bursts. The digits 0 through 9 were indicated by such a pattern:

1	R	R	R	R	6	G	G	R	R
2	G	G	G	G	7	R	G	G	G
3	R	R	R	G	8	G	R	R	R
4	G	G	G	R	9	R	G	G	R
5	R	R	G	G	0	G	R	R	G

The CODE was nonsecret in that it was intended as a highly visible signal to improve communications. The method did have encryption potential, however; extra star bursts could be inserted into the numeral or letter sequences to render their patterns unintelligible to third-party observers.

The Very Light was also discussed by the U.S. Navy as a means to transmit flag code signals in its *General Signal Book.* The U.S. Army soon adapted the Very method as well, adding it to its Ordnance Board manual.

Although by the time of World War I the Very Light was considered ill-suited for the transmission of Morse code, a system did exist for translating its colored flashes into dots and dashes:

Night	*Day* (colors not distinguishable)
red = dot	one shot = dot
white or green = dash	two shots (fired simultaneously) = dash

Many Very signal codes were impromptu arrangements in the midst of conflict. These included quick messages such as "mission succeeded" or "begin supporting advance" rather than long sequences of star bursts amid bomb hits and artillery fire.

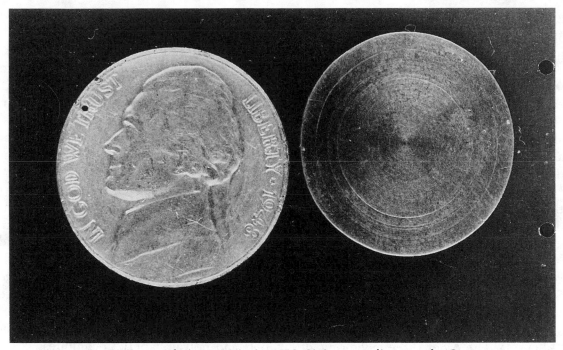

The hollow nickel in which the VIC Cipher was discovered. (Courtesy of the Federal Bureau of Investigation.)

VIC Cipher, an encryption method deriving its name from the Soviet CODE-NAME of spy and defector REINO HAYHANEN. Alienation from his espionage superior Rudolph Ivanovitch Abel (codenamed *Mark*) and chronic alcohol abuse led to Hayhanen's being recalled to Moscow for a "rest." Instead, he stopped at the U.S. Embassy in Paris in May 1957, where his confession resulted in the FBI capture of Abel in New York City the following month.

Hayhanen's cooperation also led to the solution of a puzzling encryption that had been in the possession of the FBI for almost four years. The mystery had begun in 1953, when a Brooklyn newspaper boy found an unusual nickel among his change. It had fallen, split in two, and revealed a piece of microfilm 5/16ths of an inch square, covered in tissue paper. Turned over to the New York police and then the Bureau, the microfilm was enlarged, revealing 21 rows of numbers in a series of five-numeral groups, with a total of 1,035 digits.

The VIC cryptosystem had been given to Hayhanen by his Moscow bosses for communications concealment. Its KEY terms and numbers are not purely random, as are those of a properly used ONE-TIME PAD; nevertheless, several experts consider it to be a virtually UNBREAKABLE CIPHER. It proved so in actual use.

According to historian David Kahn, in technical terms, a CIPHER like the VIC is a straddling bipartite MONOALPHABETIC SUBSTITUTION superenciphered with modified double TRANSPOSITION. As Hayhanen divulged it, the method was built upon four mnemonic keys that varied for each Soviet agent. Hayhanen's keys consisted of the first seven letters of the Russian word for snowfall (*snegopad*); part of a folk song ("The Lone Accordion"); the date of victory over Japan in World War II (3/9/1945—Continental date style), and the number 13 (Hayhanen's personal digit, changed to 20 in 1956).

These four keys controlled the development of the alphabet for a substitution process as well as two transposition tables. Specifically, the KEYWORD for *snowfall* affected the arrangement of the letters and symbols in a type of STRADDLING CHECKERBOARD. The other three mnemonic devices helped develop a series of numbers that then governed the numerical keys for the checkerboard and both transposition tables.

Because of the mnemonic keys with no need for any key lists (a weakness of one-time pads) and because of its complex encryption procedures, a cipher like the VIC remains a very formidible challenge to analysts. In fact, it has been suggested that the Soviets planted the nickel with the microfilm so that it would be found, as a test of U.S. solution capabilities.

Vigenère, Blaise de (1523–1596),

French diplomat, cryptographer, and author. Born in the small French town of Saint-Pourçain between Paris and Marseilles, Vigenère managed to secure a position as a junior secretary to French diplomats. Thus initiated in the realm of embassies and affairs of state, he remained involved with such work all his life. For 30 years he worked in ambassadorial circles, interrupted only by studies and service to his mentor, the French Duke of Nevers.

After retiring from court life, he began to write about cryptographic practices; however, he did not have a total grasp of the entire field of CRYPTOLOGY. He considered CRYPTANALYSIS to be a time wasting brain exercise. Still, his *Traicté des Chiffres* (*Treatise on Ciphers*) (1586) is considered an important work in the field. Similar to JOHANNES TRITHEMIUS and GIROLAMO CARDANO, among other scholars of his time, Vigenère mixed a large dose of occult lore and pseudoscience with practical text. He described a number of systems of his day that had varied alphabets and polyalphabetic techniques.

Vigenère also studied others' methods and improved on them. He developed a SQUARE TABLE like the *tabula recta* of Trithemius, but added different alphabets along the top and at the side. He also enhanced the AUTOKEY system of Cardano in two ways, by introducing a priming KEY and by making the key running (not repetitive).

Cardano:

Key:	the	theth	the	thet	theth
Plaintext:	the	first	was	from	Milan

Vigenère (priming key *Q*):

Key:	(Q)H	EWA	S	AFRENCHMA
Plaintext:	h e	wa s	a	F r e n c h m a n

Vigenère's priming key indicated the particular alphabet of the alphabet tableau used to encipher the first PLAINTEXT letter. With the primer, the recipient had a known starting point and could use the first plain letter to decrypt the second CIPHER character. The second plain character was used to DECIPHER the third encrypted letter, and so on.

Vigenère developed a second autokey, with a priming key and a CIPHERTEXT as the key to encrypt the body of the message. This differed from Cardano's style, in which the plaintext was the key.

The *Traicté* and these keys were Vigenère's primary contributions to cryptology. However, despite their cleverness, the primer and the two autokeys were not applied in cryptography for many years; they were forgotten until the late 1800s, when others discovered the practicality of such concealments, apparently independently.

In the meantime, Vigenère's name had become most closely associated with a much less secure system not of his making. This version had typical alphabet characters and a short KEYWORD that was repeated (*sign* in the example below).

Key:	S I G N S I G N S I G N
Plaintext:	r e c e i v e t h e e m
Ciphertext:	J M I R A D K G Z M K Z

Key:	S I G N S I G N S I G
Plaintext:	i s s a r y t o d a y
Ciphertext:	A A Y N J G Z B V I E

This ciphertext is found by using the table below. Each of the 26 cipher alphabet rows is positioned one letter to the left of the one above it. The plaintext characters are at the top, and the key alphabet is at the side. From the starting position of each, the cryptographer moves down

and across to a coordinating point. For key *S* and plaintext *r* the cipher letter is *J*, found at the intersection of their row and column, respectively. This procedure continues in the same manner until all the plain letters are hidden.

```
  a b c d e f g h i j k l m n o p q r s t u v w x y z
A ABCDEFGHI J KLMNOPQR S TUVWXYZ
B BCDEFGHI J KLMNOPQR S TUVWXYZA
C CDEFGHI J KLMNOPQR S TUVWXYZAB
D DEFGHI J KLMNOPQR S TUVWXYZABC
E EFGHI J KLMNOPQR S TUVWXYZABCD
F FGHI J KLMNOPQR S TUVWXYZABCDE
G GHI J KLMNOPQR S TUVWXYZABCDE F
H HI J KLMNOPQR S TUVWXYZABCDE FG
I I J KLMNOPQR S TUVWXYZABCDE FGH
J J KLMNOPQR S TUVWXYZABCDE FGHI
K KLMNOPQR S TUVWXYZABCDE FGHI J
L LMNOPQR S TUVWXYZABCDE FGHI J K
M MNOPQR S TUVWXYZABCDE FGHI J KL
N NOPQR S TUVWXYZABCDE FGHI J KLM
O OPQR S TUVWXYZABCDE FGHI J KLMN
P PQR S TUVWXYZABCDE FGHI J KLMNO
Q QR S TUVWXYZABCDE FGHI J KLMNOP
R R S TUVWXYZABCDE FGHI J KLMNOPQ
S S TUVWXYZABCDE FGHI J KLMNOPQR
T TUVWXYZABCDE FGHI J KLMNOPQR S
U UVWXYZABCDE FGHI J KLMNOPQR S T
V VWXYZABCDE FGHI J KLMNOPQR S TU
W WXYZABCDE FGHI J KLMNOPQR S TUV
X XYZABCDE FGHI J KLMNOPQR S TUVW
Y YZABCDE FGHI J KLMNOPQR S TUVWX
Z ZABCDE FGHI J KLMNOPQR S TUVWXY
```

The intended recipient knows to use the same alphabet table. Beginning with the first keyletter, he or she moves along the horizontal row beside it until arriving at the first enciphered letter. Next, the column of characters above it is traced up to the plaintext letter atop the column (*S* across to *J*, then up to *r*).

This method was, surprisingly, considered *le chiffre indéchiffrable* (the indecipherable cipher) for generations. A version of it was found in the BEAUFORT CIPHER developed by Royal Navy Adm. Sir Francis Beaufort in 1857. The Beaufort form had a key of words from a poem or the name of a well-known location and a tableau with standard alphabet characters on all four sides, making 27 characters across and down, with an *A* in each corner. Placed on a 4×5-inch card, it was pro-

moted as a security measure for telegrams and postcards.

Four years later, during the U.S. CIVIL WAR, the Confederates had a "Vigenère" square to protect their dispatches and telegrams. They believed it inviolate, but it was in fact broken by the Union analysts known as THE SACRED THREE.

Yet such a strange concoction of myths and false assumptions had wrapped themselves around this method that versions of it were still extant as late as the 20th century. In 1914, the United States Army's Larrabee cipher was based on the Vigenère tableau. It offered very low protection and was replaced by other methods as the United States entered World War I.

Wallis, John (1616–1703), mathematician known as the "Father of English Cryptology." An ordained clergyman, Wallis amused himself with problems of numerical complexity. As with others skilled in arithmetic or music, his talents seemed to lead to a special understanding of cryptic messages.

Wallis's first experience with an enciphered letter came during the English Civil War (1642–1652), when a letter belonging to the supporters of Charles I was found after the battle for Chichester. Asked to solve it, Wallis lifted the veil of this rather easy CIPHER (presumably a Cavalier dispatch). He later solved more difficult numerically encrypted missives and his career in CRYPTANALYSIS was established. Soon he was helping the Puritan cause by reading intercepted letters and orders written by King Charles. Historians

have credited Wallis's solutions with providing the evidence that Parliament used against the king before he was beheaded in 1649.

Wallis's services were valued so highly that he was retained by Charles II after the end of Puritan rule. His mathematical achievements during the Restoration years included his classic *Arithmetica Infinitorum*, which provided Sir Isaac Newton with the foundations for his own discoveries.

Wallis later became a secret-writing analyst for William and Mary. In this capacity, he solved some detailed NOMENCLATORS and even influenced international affairs with his findings. In 1689 he was able to read the missives exchanged between Louis XIV and the French embassy in Poland. Wallis revealed plots by the Bourbon king that included a war against Prussia and an arranged marriage between a member of Polish royalty and a Hanoverian princess. These exposures caused a deep rift between France and Poland, to the delight of Wallis's royal employers.

Upon his passing in 1703, Wallis's grandson and protégé William Blencowe assumed his cryptanalytical responsibilities.

Wheatstone Cryptograph, cryptosystem designed by Sir Charles Wheatstone (1802–1875). A scientist and inventor, Wheatstone pursued a host of interests, ranging from acoustics to dynamos and phonetics. He built an electric telegraph before Samuel Morse (see MORSE CODE) and designed the Wheatstone Bridge, a means for measuring electrical resistance. In the field of CRYPTOGRAPHY, Sir Charles was equally creative.

In 1854 he devised a manual, polygraphic cryptomethod that was the first literal digraphic CIPHER, with two alphabet characters being encrypted so that the final product was dependent on both letters (see GIOVANNI PORTA). Yet because Wheatstone's friend Baron Lyon Playfair promoted the concealment among British officials, it came to be known as the PLAYFAIR CIPHER (this system served British forces in the Boer War and in Australia during World War II).

Twelve years later, the imaginative member of the Royal Society developed his cryptograph, a mechanism with alphabets in circular form and "hands" similar to those of a clock that moved by gears. It was officially presented to the public in 1867.

This instrument was an advance over the similar CIPHER DISK, whereby letters, symbols, and digits were arranged in circles on their respective disk faces and aligned in various patterns to produce SUB-STITUTION ciphers. Wheatstone's cryptograph also had two alphabets on its face. The outer, fixed ring held the PLAINTEXT. It had 27 places (26 letters and a blank), arranged in alphabetical order. Aligned beneath the letters A through J and N through W were two sets of the numbers 1 through 0. The inner circle had 26 nonsequential alphabet letters. There were no numerals, and this ring's movable section was considered the CIPHERTEXT.

The cryptograph had clock-type hands connected by gears in a ratio of 27 : 26. This meant that for every space the long hand moved clockwise around the outer alphabet, the short hand was shifted one position clockwise around the inner mixed letter sequence. Both hands were moved with the help of small knobs, and the larger was arranged to move over the smaller.

Encipherment was initiated by moving the longer hand and its pear-shaped opening to the blank while a beginning cipher character was aligned with the shorter pointer. Then the aperture was moved to the first plaintext letter or number. This activated the gears and realigned the short pointer with another letter, which was written as the ciphertext. Double letters were either varied with an infrequently used Q or Z or were transmitted as single characters rather than a pair. Decipherment moved in reverse from the encrypted letters found with the smaller hand, to the larger hand that aligned with the plaintext on the outer ring.

While the instrument boasted one of the smoothest operations in manual cryptography (it even had a compact case for easy transport), it never saw any practical use. One reason may have been that its alphabet differential was just one letter. This was by no means a great barrier to a skilled solution seeker knowledgeable about letter pairs and FREQUENCY.

Willes, Edward (1684–1773), British clergyman and cryptanalyst.

Like his predecessor, JOHN WALLIS, Edward Willes was a minister with a flair for solving secret messages. Also like Wallis, Willes influenced English history with his talents.

Early in his career, he found the solution for several hundred pages of a Swedish CIPHER, revealing a plan by some influential Swedes to start an uprising in Great Britain. The scheme was foiled, and Willes's stature (including his position in the Church of England) rose accordingly.

His most direct effect upon his nation occurred in 1723, when he gave expert testimony before the House of Lords, where the Bishop of Rochester, Francis Atterbury, stood accused in a conspiracy to put a false claimant on the English throne. Willes and a fellow member of the Decyphering Branch testified as to what they had found among intercepted letters, which did indeed link Atterbury to the plot involving James Francis Edward Stuart, the pretender James III. Primarily because of this testimony, Atterbury was declared guilty and exiled.

Thereafter, Willes achieved the position of Canon of Westminster and continued to gain important ecclesiastical employment. The Willes family made encryption solutions a family affair when his sons Edward, Jr., and then Francis Willes also became official decipherers.

Winds Code, a World War II OPEN CODE designed by the Japanese to an-

nounce a state of diplomatic emergency. On November 19, 1941, a U.S. Navy interception outpost, Station S at Bainbridge Island (in the Puget Sound near Seattle), intercepted from the airwaves a message sent from the Japanese foreign office in Tokyo to its embassy in Washington, D.C. The staff at Bainbridge sent the encrypted contents by teletype to the Navy's top-secret analysts at OP-20-G in the nation's capital. The cryptosystem solvers determined that the Japanese CODE was one called J-19, and they were able to break it soon thereafter. Circular 2353 from Japan's foreign office was a special plan for an alert in case of a sudden change in the then extremely tense Pacific region. It was an open code arrangement with phrases linking winds to compass points and countries according to their respective directions from Japan:

Regarding the broadcast of a special message in an emergency:

In case of emergency (danger of cutting off our diplomatic relations) and the cutting off of international communications, the following warning will be added in the middle of the daily Japanese language short-wave news broadcast:

1. In case of Japan–U.S. relations in danger: *Higashi No Kaze Ame* [east wind rain]
2. Japan–USSR relations: *Kita No Kaze Kumori* [north wind cloudy]
3. Japan–British relations: *Nishi No Kaze Hare* [west wind clear]

This signal will be given in the middle

and at the end as a weather forecast, and each sentence will be repeated twice. When this is heard, please destroy all code papers, etc. This is as yet to be a completely secret arrangement.

Forward as urgent intelligence.

Some U.S. naval officers and intelligence staff persons believed that the broadcast of *Higashi No Kaze Ame* (east wind rain) would signal an imminent attack on the United States by Japan. ON THE ROOF GANG radio monitors were instructed to listen to every Japanese weather broadcast. But in the swirl of other intercepts relating to several possible points of conflict in the Pacific, it still is not clear whether the radio alert was ever broadcast. When Japanese naval forces attacked Pearl Harbor on the morning of December 7, 1941, the assault came as a total surprise.

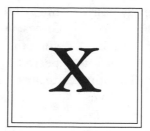

X

XYZ Affair, a 1797 scandal affecting U.S.–French relations. The former allies that had defeated Britain in the American Revolution (1776–1783) were dangerously at odds during the following decade. By 1797, the United States and France had seen their military and diplomatic ties decline to a point of mutual recrimination and threats. The anarchy of the French Revolution had disgusted even the most embittered anti-royalists in the United States. Added to this background of social upheaval was U.S. distrust of the French diplomatic ministers, Edmond Genêt and Pierre Adet. When Genêt assumed powers far beyond those of a foreign envoy, George Washington demanded that France recall him. Adet, the succeeding French envoy to the United States, later added fuel to the fire when he announced that France would consider U.S. seamen serv-

ing on British vessels to be buccaneers. As the new president, John Adams, assumed office, a clamor arose demanding that he take action.

Adams reacted by sending a special commission to France that included Charles C. Pinckney, John Marshall, and Elbridge Gerry. The first two of these men represented the conservative Federalist point of view on foreign relations, while Gerry was partial toward the liberal Jeffersonian view.

The U.S. trio arrived in late September 1797 and became involved in dangerous political and financial intrigue. A Swiss banker, Jean Hottinguer ("X"), requested a $250,000 *douceur* (gift) for French officials. Soon a Hamburg merchant, Mr. Bellamy ("Y"), offered a secret treaty in exchange for a sizable loan. Not long thereafter, Lucien Hauteval ("Z"), a messenger for Talleyrand, French minister of foreign affairs, also sought monetary commitments from the commissioners.

Marshall, Pinckney, and Gerry used a NOMENCLATOR to send the account of these affairs to Secretary of State Timothy Pickering. These details included summaries of their discussions, encoded with number–letter combinations such as the following:

449 no	456 N. Carolina	1191 sort
450 nob	457 not	1192 south
451 nom	458 noth	1193 A
452 non	459 notify	1194 ab
1176 sy	26 ped	493 ce
1177 sive	27 pen	494 ced
1178 six	28 people	495 ceive
1179 sixteen	29 per	496 cent

From this list came a famous reply in the diplomatic history of the United States. When told by Monsieur Hottinguer that monetary payments were an expected part of such negotiations, the answer of the commissioners was:

449.449.457.1193.1178.27.493.

As can be seen in the nomenclator examples, this decoded as:

no	no	not	a	six	pen	ce
449.	449.	457.	1193.	1178.	27.	493.

The representatives of a young but proud nation had answered. The outrage of many U.S. citizens also served to cause a moderation in the French position over time. Though additional problems with France continued, the United States was making its claim to a place of respect in the world community (see MURRAY CODE).

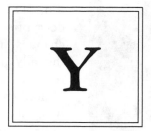

Yardley, Herbert (1889–1958), U.S.
cryptologist and author. Herbert Osborn
Yardley may very well be the number-one
"character" of CRYPTOLOGY. While not as
brilliant as his contemporaries WILLIAM
FRIEDMAN of the United States and
GEORGES PAINVIN of France, Yardley's
life was quite colorful, as well as important to some of the modern developments of U.S. CODES, CIPHERS, and
CRYPTANALYSIS.

Born in Worthington, Indiana, Yardley
became first a railroad telegrapher and
then a code clerk with the U.S. State Department, where he saw the expansion of
communication in business and in worldwide diplomacy.

Yet as the United States flexed its industrial muscles and looked for new markets
and alliances, its supposedly private embassy exchanges were not well protected.

Yardley amused himself by solving some
State Department codes and thereby enhanced his reputation as an expert.

As the United States entered World
War I, Yardley persuaded his superiors to
give him a captain's commission and the
direction of MI-8, the new cryptologic section of U.S. military intelligence. His energy and creativity helped to build MI-8
into a very credible organization that
developed new Army codes, broke international encryptions, and produced IN-
VISIBLE INKS, as well as the chemicals to
reveal them. He continued with MI-8
until the November 1918 armistice and
remained in France to direct the cryptology section of the U.S. delegation to the
Peace Conference.

In 1919, back at the State Department
code room, Yardley became concerned
about maintaining a full-time cryptologic

Herbert Yardley. (Courtesy of the National Archives.)

department amid peacetime financial cutbacks. He directed his efforts toward this cause and achieved it in 1919 with a new organization jointly funded by the State and War departments. Due to government spending technicalities, it was decided to shift the staff and the tools of its trade to New York City, where the new group came to be known as the AMERICAN BLACK CHAMBER.

The group had some of its greatest difficulties and most brilliant successes with decryptions of intercepted Japanese telegrams. Once language problems were surmounted and it was ascertained that the Japanese codes used KATA KANA, Yardley and his team made important discoveries. Some of the most crucial involved a disar-

mament conference that began in Washington, D.C., in November 1921. The decryption of Japan's diplomatic exchanges helped U.S. negotiators to gain the advantage during the meetings. The resulting Five-Power Treaty gave the United States superior ship-tonnage ratios, especially in relation to Japan, a growing rival in the Pacific.

Yet in spite of this success and others (reputedly around 45,000 international telegrams were decrypted), funding cuts and isolationistic political sentiment combined in the decisions that led to the closing of the chamber in October 1929.

Embittered by this and financially drained by the Depression, Yardley published his memoir, THE AMERICAN BLACK CHAMBER. Published in 1931 by the Bobbs–Merrill Company of Indianapolis and serialized in *The Saturday Evening Post*, the book was a commercial success and created a furor at home and abroad. Its revelations alarmed Tokyo's cryptographers, who quickly adopted improved secrecy procedures. WILLIAM FRIEDMAN of the U.S. Army Signal Corps and other U.S. government officials were aghast.

Yardley struck back at his critics in magazine articles indicating that his book was intended as a warning to the United States to strengthen its own encryptions. While his reputation suffered in some circles, Yardley's literary efforts produced two novels, *The Red Sun of Nippon* and *The Blonde Countess*. While neither book had widespread success, the latter reached the silver screen with the title *Rendezvous* in 1935 (see MOVIE CIPHERS AND CODES).

With money from his books and the movie, Yardley made some New York

City–area real estate deals. When these faltered, he signed on as a cryptanalyst for Chiang Kai-shek, whose China was already under assault by Japan. From 1938 to 1940, he mixed CRYPTOGRAPHY with his long-time interest in poker, as well as with a series of female companions and a *joie de vivre* that historians say masked a growing cynicism.

After leaving China in 1940, he was variously involved in a failed restaurant deal, the Canadian Department of External Affairs (cryptanalysis work), and the Office of Price Administration in Washington, D.C. Nonfiction rewarded him a second time in 1957 with his successful book *The Education of a Poker Player.* He died in 1958.

Despite his highly questionable revelations, Herbert Yardley is credited with stimulating public interest in cryptology to a degree not seen since the days of author and amateur cryptologist EDGAR ALLAN POE.

Z

Zimmermann Telegram, a German World War I document proposing a military alliance with Mexico against the United States.

On January 16, 1917, German Foreign Minister Arthur Zimmermann sent a telegram of about a thousand numbered CODE groups from Berlin. It was wrapped in a strong TWO-PART CODE called 0075 that was used by German diplomats. Most chroniclers agree that the communication was sent by two routes. One was on a Swedish cable line to South America by a point of British access. The second route was from Berlin on U.S. diplomatic cables that passed through Copenhagen and then London before crossing the Atlantic. By both routes, the dispatch went to Washington, D.C., and Count Johann von Bernstorff, the German ambassador in the United States. It was then sent to the Kai-

ser's ambassador in Mexico City, Heinrich von Eckardt.

The telegram was intercepted by British intelligence, whose ROOM 40 staff discerned that Germany was planning unrestricted submarine warfare, a direct threat to neutral nations, including the United States.

Moreover, Zimmermann also proposed a German military alliance with Mexico, offering financial rewards, the return of New Mexico, Arizona, and Texas to Mexico, and the possibility that Japan might also join the scheme to threaten the U.S. in the Pacific.

The Room 40 staff had deduced these facts from further intercepted exchanges commenting on the telegram as well as from other German transmissions using Code 0075. Capt. William Hall, naval intelligence director, and his associates had

The Encrypted Zimmermann Telegram. (Courtesy of the National Archives.)

also devised a plan to fill in the blanks of the dispatch. They knew that the exchange between Bernstorff in Washington and Eckardt in Mexico City was probably not in Code 0075 because the latter embassy had not used that cryptosystem in its previous communications. Thus Hall tried to obtain the telegram that arrived in Mexico in order to study a hopefully weaker encryption.

Reputedly, a British agent CODENAMED *T* is said to have obtained a copy of the Bernstorff-to-Eckardt message from the Western Union office in Mexico City. It was masked by Code 13040, with which

the Room 40 analysts were familiar. Code 13040 had 75,000 CODENUMBERS and approximately 25,000 PLAINTEXT items in a form that was a hybrid of a ONE-PART CODE and a two-part code.

The encoding segment had hundreds of codenumbers arranged alongside sequential words, but the numbers were in segments that were purposely disarranged. The decoding section had words in mixed arrangements similar to these and a standard numerical order:

Encoding	Decoding
3827 ambassador	1289 signatory
3910 ambassadorship	1301 treaty
4156 consul	1320 treaty port
5161 consular	1361 ceremony
5304 consular agent	1423 courier
6177 consulate	1440 document
10728 consul general	1517 emissary
10949 consulship	1556 legation
8293 diplomacy	1602 minister
8605 diplomat	1644 mission
7012 diplomatic corps	1680 negotiation
7134 embassy	1715 plenipotentiary

The mixed blocks of numbers made analysis of this code more difficult than that of a simpler one-part code. Still, the position of some of the words in the list helped reveal others that were bracketed by the known terms in 0075.

The solution of typical words and proper names in 13040 gave Capt. Hall and his staff more information to verify their work on 0075. Extended effort enabled them to fully decrypt the Germans' Washington-to-Mexico transmission. They then gave this data to the U.S. authorities who could plausibly present it as their own intelligence coup, thereby hiding the involvement of, and even the existence of, Room 40.

On February 22, 1917, Capt. Hall showed the recovered PLAINTEXT of the telegram to a U.S. embassy official in England. A top-level decision was made to release the telegram and some limited supporting details to the Associated Press. A March 1, 1917, publication resulted in a furor of anti-German sentiment and a call to arms. When Zimmermann admitted his involvement in the scheme, it swept away all suspicion of a conspiracy to dupe the United States into entering the conflict. President Wilson asked for a declaration of war and Congress agreed on April 2, 1917.

Zip Code, originally, a five-digit NONSECRET CODE designed to facilitate the processing of U.S. mail. On November 28, 1962, Postmaster General J. Edward Day revealed the Post Office Department's new mail-sorting and distribution system called the *Zone Improvement Plan,* or zip code. The new process was formally initiated on July 1, 1963.

At first, zip codes were intended to be used mainly by large-volume mailers to help speed mail delivery. Yet the response of the general public was so positive that the system was expanded to include other business and personal usage as well.

In the beginning, the numbers had a slightly different meaning for rural and for urban areas. In less populated regions, the first three numerals of the CODE identified the central focal points of air, highway, and railroad transportation. The last two digits identified the post office or delivery station. In cities that had local postal zones, the first three numbers identified the city and the last two designated the local zone number.

Sample zip code 54321 provides a sequence of information for the mail-delivery system. The first digit, 5, designates one of a series of national service areas. The second number, 4, identifies the service area subdivision. The third numeral, 3, signifies the city post office. The fourth and fifth digits, 2 and 1, are the station from which the mail is delivered.

The recently activated "zip + 4" system is an elaboration of the location designator digit. The four additional numerals classify the sector of the route and then the segment of the route.

Codes remain directly linked to the future of postal service. By 1995 plans call for a very rapid sorting and distribution system using scanner mechanisms and barcode type addresses.

Bibliography

Abernethy, Thomas Perkins. *The Burr Conspiracy.* New York: Oxford University Press, 1954.

Allen, Thomas B. *War Games.* New York: McGraw-Hill, 1987.

Bakeless, John. *Turncoats, Traitors and Heroes.* Philadelphia: J.B. Lippincott, 1959.

Bamford, James, *The Puzzle Palace.* Boston: Houghton Mifflin, 1982.

Barker, Wayne, ed. *The History of Codes and Ciphers in the United States during the Period Between the World Wars. Part II, 1930–1939.* Laguna Hills, CA: Aegean Park Press, 1989.

Bates, David Homer. *Lincoln in the Telegraph Office.* New York: Century, 1907.

Bazeries, Étienne. *Les chiffres secrets dévoilés.* Paris: Librairie Charpentier et Fasquelle, 1901.

Beker, Henry, and Fred Piper. *Cipher Systems.* New York: John Wiley, 1982.

Bennett, Ralph. *Ultra in the West: The Normandy Campaign, 1944–45.* London: Hutchinson, 1979.

Bernikow, Louise. *Abel.* New York: Trident Press, 1970.

Bond, Raymond T. *Famous Stories of Code and Cipher.* New York: Rinehart, 1947.

Bowers, William M. *The Bifid Cipher, Practical Cryptanalysis, 2.* American Cryptogram Association, 1960.

——. *The Trifid Cipher, Practical Cryptanalysis, 3.* American Cryptogram Association, 1961.

Cave Brown, Anthony. *Bodyguard of Lies.* New York: Harper & Row, 1975.

Chant, Christopher. *The Encyclopedia of Codenames of World War II.* New York: Methuen, 1988.

Cookridge, E. H. (pseud.). *Spy Trade.* New York: Walker, 1971.

Costello, John. *Mask of Treachery.* New York: William Morrow, 1988.

——. *The Pacific War.* New York: Rawson, Wade, 1981.

Dallin, David. *Soviet Espionage.* New Haven, CT: Yale University Press, 1955.

Davies, D. W., and W. L. Price. *Security for Computer Networks.* New York: John Wiley, 1984.

Deacon, Richard. *The Chinese Secret Service.* New York: Taplinger Publishing, 1974.

Deavours, Cipher A., and Louis Kruh. *Machine Cryptography and Modern Cryptanalysis.* Dedham, MA: Artech House, 1985.

de Toledano, Ralph. *The Greatest Plot in History.* New York: Duell, Sloan and Pearce, 1963.

Donovan, James B. *Strangers on a Bridge: The Case of Colonel Abel.* New York: Atheneum, 1964.

Dorwart, Jeffery M. *Conflict of Duty: The U.S. Navy's Intelligence Dilemma, 1919–1945.* Annapolis: Naval Institute Press, 1983.

——. *The Office of Naval Intelligence: The Birth of America's First Intelligence Agency, 1865–1918.* Annapolis, MD: Naval Institute Press, 1979.

Erickson, John. *The Soviet High Command: A Military-Political History, 1918–1941.* London: Macmillan, 1962.

Farago, Ladislas. *The Broken Seal: "Operation Magic" and the Secret Road to Pearl Harbor.* New York: Random House, 1967.

——. *The Game of the Foxes: The Untold Story of German Espionage in the United States and Great Britain During World War II.* New York: David McKay, 1971.

Foote, Alexander. *Handbook for Spies.* Garden City, New York: Doubleday, 1949.

Frank, Thomas, and Edward Weisband, eds. *Secrecy and Foreign Policy.* New York: Oxford University Press, 1974.

Friedman, William F. *American Army Field Codes in the American Expeditionary Forces During the First World War.* War Department. Washington, DC: GPO, 1942.

——. *Cryptography and Cryptanalysis Articles* Vol. 1 and Vol. 2. Laguna Hills, CA: Aegean Park Press, 1976. (Reprinted from "The Use of Codes and Ciphers in the World War and Lessons to be Learned Therefrom." *Articles on Cryptography and Cryptanalysis.* Signal Corps Bulletin. Washington, DC: GPO, 1942.)

——. *Elementary Military Cryptography.* Laguna Hills, CA: Aegean Park Press, 1976.

——. *History of the Use of Codes.* Laguna Hills, CA: Aegean Park Press, 1977. (A reprint from *Report on the History of the Use of Codes and Code Language, the International Telegraph Regulations Pertaining Thereto, and the Bearing of This History on the Cortina Report.* International Radiotelegraph Conference of Washington, 1927, Delegation of the United States of America. Washington, DC: GPO, 1928.)

——. *Military Cryptanalysis II.* Laguna Hills, CA: Aegean Park Press, 1984.

——. *Solving German Codes in World War I.* Laguna Hills, CA: Aegean Park Press, 1977.

Friedman, William, and Charles J. Mendelsohn. *The Zimmermann Telegram of January 16, 1917 and Its Cryptographic Background.* Laguna Hills, CA: Aegean Park Press, 1976.

Friedman, William F., and Elizeth Friedman. *The Shakespearean Ciphers Examined: An Analysis of Cryptographic Systems Used as Evidence That Some Author Other Than William Shakespeare Wrote the Plays Commonly Attributed to Him.* Cambridge, England: Cambridge University Press, 1957.

Gaines, Helen F. *Cryptanalysis: A Study of Ciphers and Their Solution.* New York: Dover Publications, 1956.

Givierge, Marcel. *Cours de cryptographie.* Paris: Berger-Levrault, 1925. Translated as *Course in Cryptography* by John B. Hurt, Washington, DC: GPO, 1934. Reprinted by Aegean Park Press, Laguna Hills, CA, 1978.

Glover, Beaird. *Secret Ciphers of the 1876 Presidential Election.* Laguna Hills, CA: Aegean Park Press, 1991.

Gyldén, Yves. *The Contribution of the Cryptographic Bureaus in the World War.* Laguna Hills, CA: Aegean Park Press, 1978. Translated from the original *Chifferbyraernas Insatser I Världskriget Till Lands* (Stockholm, Sweden, 1931).

Hamming, Richard W. *Coding and Information Theory.* 2d ed. New York: Prentice Hall, 1986.

Hitt, Parker. *Manual for the Solution of Military Ciphers.* Laguna Hills, CA: Aegean Park Press, 1976.

Holmes, W. J. *Double-Edged Secrets: U.S. Naval Intelligence Operations in the Pacific during World War II.* Annapolis, MD: Naval Institute Press, 1979.

Howe, Russell W. *Mata Hari.* New York: Dodd, Mead, 1986.

Hoy, Hugh C. *40 O.B., or How the War Was Won.* London: Hutchinson, 1935.

James, William. *The Codebreakers of Room 40.* New York: St. Martin's, 1956.

Johnson, Brian. *The Secret War.* London: British Broadcasting Corporation, 1978.

Kahn, David. *The Codebreakers: The Story of Secret Writing.* New York: Macmillan, 1967.

——. *Hitler's Spies: German Military Intelligence in World War II.* New York: Macmillan, 1978.

——. *Kahn on Codes.* New York: Macmillan, 1984.

Keiser, Bernhard E., and Eugene Strange. *Digital Telephony and Network Integration.* New York: Van Nostrand Reinhold, 1985.

Kennan, George F. *Memoirs, 1923–1950.* Boston: Little, Brown, 1967.

Kessler, Ronald. *Moscow Station: How the KGB Penetrated the American Embassy.* New York: Charles Scribner's Sons, 1989.

Koch, Edward. *Cryptography or Cipher Writing.* 2d ed. Belleville, IL: Buechler Publishing, 1942.

Konheim, Alan G. *Cryptography: A Primer.* New York: John Wiley, 1981.

Krivitsky, Walter J. *In Stalin's Secret Service.* Frederick, MD: University Publications of America, 1985.

Ladd, James, and Keith Melton, and Captain Peter Mason. *Clandestine Warfare.* London: Blandford Press, 1988.

Laffin, John. *Codes and Ciphers.* New York: Abelard-Schuman, 1964.

Lamphere, Robert J., and Tom Shachtman. *The FBI–KGB War: A Special Agent's Story.* New York: Random House, 1986.

Lange, André, and E. A. Soudart. *Treatise on Cryptography.* Laguna Hills, CA: Aegean Park Press, 1981.

Layton, Edwin T., with Roger Pineau and John Costello. *"And I Was There": Pearl Harbor and Midway—Breaking the Secrets.* New York: William Morrow, Inc., 1985.

Lewin, Ronald. *Ultra Goes to War: The First Account of World War II's Great-*

est Secret Based on Official Documents. New York: McGraw-Hill, 1978.

Lindsey, Robert. *The Falcon and the Snowman.* New York: Simon & Schuster, 1979.

Locard, Edmond. *Traité de criminalistique,* 6. "Les Correspondances secrètes," 831–931 at "Cryptographie à l'aide des objets," 901–903. Lyon, France: Joannès Desvignes, 1937.

Macalister, R. A. Stewart. *The Secret Languages of Ireland.* Cambridge, England: Cambridge University Press, 1937.

Macintyre, Donald. *The Battle of the Atlantic.* New York: Macmillan, 1961.

Mead, Peter. *The Eye in the Air.* London: Her Majesty's Stationery Office, 1983.

Meister, Dr. Aloys. *Die Anfänge der Modernen Diplomatischen Geheimschrift.* Paderborn: Ferdinand Schoningh, 1902.

——. *Die Geheimschrift im Dienste der Päpstlichen Kurie.* Paderborn: Ferdinand Schoningh, 1906.

Meyer, Carl H., and Stephen M. Matyas. *Cryptography: A New Dimension in Computer Data Security.* New York: John Wiley, 1982.

Moore, Dan Tyler, and Martha Waller. *Cloak & Cipher.* Indianapolis: Bobbs-Merrill, 1962.

Myer, Albert J. *A Manual of Signals.* New York: D. Van Nostrand, 1868.

Nanovic, John (Henry Lysing, pseud.). *Secret Writing: An Introduction to Cryptograms, Ciphers and Codes.* New York: Dover Publications, 1974. Republication of original by David Kemp & Company, 1936.

Newbold, William R. *The Cipher of Roger Bacon.* Philadelphia: University of Pennsylvania Press, 1928.

Noggle, Burl. *Teapot Dome: Oil and Politics in the 1920s.* Baton Rouge, LA: Louisiana State University Press, 1962.

Norman, Bruce. *Secret Warfare.* Washington, DC: Acropolis Books, 1973.

Ore, Oystein. *Cardano—The Gambling Scholar.* With a translation from the Latin of Cardano's *Book on Games of Chance* by Sidney Henry Gould. Princeton, NJ: Princeton University Press, 1953.

O'Toole, G.J.A. *The Encyclopedia of American Intelligence and Espionage: From the Revolutionary War to the Present.* New York: Facts on File, 1988.

Parker, Donn B. *Fighting Computer Crime.* New York: Charles Scribner's Sons, 1983.

Pennypacker, Morton. *General Washington's Spies on Long Island & in New York.* Brooklyn: Long Island Historical Society, 1939.

Perrault, Gilles. *The Red Orchestra. (L'orchestre rouge,* 1967.) Translated by Peter Wiles. New York: Simon & Schuster, 1969.

Persico, Joseph E. *Piercing the Reich: The Penetration of Nazi Germany by American Secret Agents During World War II.* New York: Viking Press, 1979.

Pitt, Barrie, and the editors of Time-Life Books. *World War II: The Battle of the Atlantic.* Alexandria, VA: Time-Life Books, 1980.

Plum, William R. *The Military Telegraph During the Civil War in the United States.* Vols. I and II. Chicago: Jansen, McClurg, 1882.

Prange, Gordon W., with Donald M. Goldstein and Katherine V. Dillon. *At Dawn We Slept: The Untold Story of Pearl Harbor.* New York: McGraw-Hill, 1981.

Preston, Keith, trans. *De Furtivis Literarum Notis* by Giovanni Porta (1563). Fabyan Collection, Library of Congress.

Price, Derek J. *John Baptista Porta's Natural Magick.* New York: Basic Books, 1957.

Princess de Lamballa. *Secret Memoirs of the Royal Family of France during the Revolution.* Vol. 2. London: H.S. Nichols, 1895.

Rachlis, Eugene. *They Came to Kill: The Story of Eight Nazi Saboteurs in America.* New York: Random House, 1961.

Richelson, Jeffrey T. *The U.S. Intelligence Community.* Cambridge, MA: Ballinger, 1985.

Roskill, S.W. *The War at Sea: 1939–1945.* London: Her Majesty's Stationery Office, 1954.

Rowan, Richard W., and Robert Derndorfer. *The Story of Secret Service.* New York: Elsevier-Dutton, 1956.

Russell, Francis, and the editors of Time-Life Books. *World War II: The Secret War.* Alexandria, VA: Time-Life Books, 1981.

Ryan, Cornelius. *The Longest Day: June 6, 1944.* New York: Simon & Schuster, 1959.

Sacco, Luigi. *Manual of Cryptography.* Reprinted from a translation of *Manuale di Crittographia* (Rome, 1936). Laguna Hills, CA: Aegean Park Press, 1977.

Sarton, George. *Six Wings: Men of Science in the Renaissance.* Bloomington, Indiana: Indiana University Press, 1957.

Simkins, Peter. *Air Fighting 1914–1918.*
London: The Imperial War Museum, 1978.

Smith, Laurence Dwight. *Cryptography: The Science of Secret Writing.* New York: Dover Publications, 1955.

Spector, Ronald H. *Eagle Against the Sun: The American War with Japan.* New York: Free Press, 1985.

——. *Listening to the Enemy.* Wilmington, Delaware: Scholarly Resources, 1988.

Stallings, William. *Data and Computer Communications.* New York: Macmillan, 1985.

Stern, Philip Van Doren. *Secret Missions of the Civil War.* New York: Crown, 1959.

Stevenson, William. *A Man Called Intrepid.* New York: Harcourt Brace Jovanovich, 1976.

Thayer, Charles W. *Diplomat.* New York: Harper & Brothers, 1959.

Thompson, James W., and Saul K. Padover. *Secret Diplomacy: Espionage and Cryptography.* New York: F. Ungar, 1963.

Thompson, George Raynor, and Dixie R. Harris. *The Signal Corps: The Outcome (Mid-1943 through 1945) (United States Army in World War II: The Technical Series)* Department of the Army, Office of the Chief of Military History. Washington, DC: U.S. Government Printing Office, 1966.

Thompson, George Raynor; Dixie R. Harris; Pauline Oakes; and Dulany Terrett. *The Signal Corps: The Test (December 1941 to July 1943) (United States Army in World War II: The Technical Series)* Department of the Army, Office of the Chief of Military History. Washington, DC: U.S. Government Printing Office, 1957.

Thorndike, Lynn. *A History of Magic and Experimental Science.* New York: Columbia University Press, 1926–1958.

Time-Life Books. *Understanding Computers: Computer Basics.* Alexandria, VA: Time-Life Books, 1985.

——. *Understanding Computers: Computer Security.* Alexandria, VA: Time-Life Books, 1990.

——. *Understanding Computers: Military Frontier.* Alexandria, VA: Time-Life Books, 1988.

Tuchman, Barbara W. *The Guns of August.* New York: Macmillan, 1962.

——. *The Zimmermann Telegram.* New York: Viking Press, 1958.

Van Doren, Carl. *Secret History of the American Revolution.* New York: Viking Press, 1941.

Voorhis, Harold V. B. "Masonic Alphabets." *A History of Royal Arch Masonry.* Vol. 3. Lexington, KY: Royal Arch Masons, 1956.

Way, Peter. *Undercover Codes and Ciphers.* London: Aldus Books, 1977.

Weber, Ralph E. *United States Diplomatic Codes and Ciphers, 1775–1938.* Chicago: Precedent Publishing, 1979.

Welchman, Gordon. *The Hut Six Story: Breaking the Enigma Codes.* New York: McGraw-Hill, 1982.

Whitehead, Don. *The FBI Story: A Report to the People.* New York: Random House, 1956.

Willoughby, Malcolm F. *Rum War at Sea.* Washington, DC: GPO, 1964.

Wolfe, Jack M. *A First Course in Cryptanalysis.* Revised. 3 vols. Brooklyn: Brooklyn College Press, 1943.

Woods, David L., ed. *A History of Tactical Communication Techniques.* Orlando, FL: Martin-Marietta Corporation, 1965.

——. *Signalling and Communicating at Sea.* Vols. 1 and 2. New York: Arno Press, 1985.

Wright, Louis B., and Marion Tinling, eds. *The Secret Diary of William Byrd of Westover 1709–1712.* Richmond, VA: Dietz Press, 1941.

Wright, Peter, with Paul Greengrass. *Spycatcher: The Candid Autobiography of a Senior Intelligence Officer.* Harrisonburg, VA: Donnelley & Sons, 1987.

Yardley, Herbert. *The American Black Chamber.* Indianapolis: Bobbs-Merrill, 1931.

Yates, Frances A. *Giordano Bruno and the Hermetic Tradition.* Chicago: The University of Chicago Press, 1964.

Periodicals

Attansio, C. R., and R. J. Phillips. "Penetrating an Operating System: A Study of VM/370 Integrity." *IBM Systems Journal* 15, no. 1 (1976): 46.

August, David. "Cryptography and Exploitation of Chinese Manual Cryptosystems, Part I: The Encoding Problem." *Cryptologia* 13, no. 4 (October 1989): 289–302.

——. "Cryptography and Exploitation of Chinese Manual Cryptosystems, Part II: The Encrypting Problem." *Cryptologia* 14, no. 1 (January 1990): 61–78.

Beard, William W. "YIYKAEJR GZQSYWX." *U.S. Naval Institute Proceedings* 44, no. 8 (1918).

Bowers, William M. "F. Delastelle—Cryptologist," *The Cryptogram* 30 (March–April, 1963): 79–82, 85.

——. "F. Delastelle–Cryptologist," *The Cryptogram* 30 (May–June, 1963): 101, 106–109.

——. "Major F. W. Kasiski—Cryptologist." *The Cryptogram* 31 (January–February 1964): 53–54, 58–60.

Broadhurst, George. "Some Others and Myself." *The Saturday Evening Post* 199 (October 23, 1926): 42.

Chase, Pliny Earle. "Mathematical Holocryptic Cyphers." *The Mathematical Monthly* I (March 1859): 194–96.

"Cryptophotography." *International Criminal Police Review* 102 (November 1956): 284–90. N.A. Culenaere (Criminalistics Laboratory), University of Ghent, Belgium.

Davies, Donald W. "Charles Wheatstone's Cryptograph and Pletts' Cipher Machine." *Cryptologia* 9, no. 2 (April 1985): 155–61.

——. "The Early Models of the Siemens and Halske T52 Cipher Machine." *Cryptologia* 7, no. 3 (July 1983): 235–53.

Friedman, William F. "Edgar Allan Poe, Cryptographer." *American Literature* 8 (November 1936): 266–80.

Friedman, William F., and Charles Mendelsohn. "Notes on Code Words." *The American Mathematical Monthly*. (August–September 1932): 394–409.

Givierge, Marcel. "Questions de Chiffre." *Revue Militaire Français* (June 1, 1924): 398–417, (July 1, 1924): 59–78. Translated as "Problems of Code" in *Articles on Cryptography and Crypt-*

analysis Reprinted from the *Signal Corps Bulletin.* Washington, DC: GPO, 1942.

Hardie, Bradford. "The Potus–Prime Connection." *Cryptologia* 11, no. 1 (January 1987): 40–46.

Helmick, Leah Stock. "Key Woman of the T-Men." *The Reader's Digest* (September 1937): 51–55.

Hill, Lester. "Concerning Certain Linear Transformation Apparatus of Cryptography." *The American Mathematical Monthly* 38 (March 1931): 135–54.

——. "Cryptography in an Algebraic Alphabet." *The American Mathematical Monthly* 36 (June–July 1929): 306–12.

Hoover, J. Edgar. "The Enemy's Masterpiece of Espionage." *The Reader's Digest* 48 (April 1946): 1–6.

Kapany, Narinder S. "Fiber Optics." *Scientific American* (November 1960): 72–81.

——. "Picture Tube." *Time* (December 3, 1956): 69–70.

Kahn, David. "Pearl Harbor and the Inadequacy of Cryptanalysis." *Cryptologia* 15, no. 4 (1991): 273–94.

——. "The Wreck of the Magdeburg." *MHQ: The Quarterly Journal of Military History* 2, no. 2 (Winter 1990): 97–103.

Keegan, John. "Jutland." *MHQ: The Quarterly Journal of Military History* 1, no. 2 (Winter 1989): 110–12.

Knight, Mary. "The Secret War of Censors vs. Spies." *The Reader's Digest* 48 (March 1946): 79–83.

Kruh, Louis. "The Genesis of the Jefferson/Bazeries Cipher Device." *Cryptologia* 5, no. 4 (1981): 193–208.

Kruh, Louis, and Cipher Deavours. "The Typex cryptograph." *Cryptologia* 7, no. 2 (April 1983): 145–165.

Levine, Jack. "Some Elementary Cryptanalysis of Algebraic Cryptography." *The American Mathematical Monthly* 68 (May 1961): 411–18.

Matthews, W. "Samuel Pepys, Tachygraphist." *Modern Language Review* 29 (October 1934): 397–404.

McKay, Herbert C. "Notes from a Laboratory." *American Photography* 60 (November 1946): 38–40, 50.

——. "Stereo Photography." *U.S. Camera* 13 (October 1950): 16.

Mendelsohn, Charles J. "Blaise de Vigenère and the 'Chiffre Carré.'" *Proceedings of the American Philosophical Society* 82 (March 22, 1940): 103–29.

——. "Cardano on Cryptography." *Scripta Mathematica* 6 (October 1939): 157–68.

Morris, C. Brent. "Fraternal Cryptography: Cryptographic Practices of American Fraternal Organizations." *Cryptologia* 7, no. 1 (January 1983): 27–36.

Morris, Robert. "The Hagelin Cipher Machine (M-209)." *Cryptologia* 2, no. 3 (July 1978): 267–89.

Niblack, Albert. "Proposed Day, Night and Fog Signals for the Navy with Brief Description of the Ardois Night System." *Proceedings of the United States Naval Institute.* Annapolis: U.S. Naval Institute, 1891.

Paltsits, Victor Hugo. "The Use of Invisible Ink for Secret Writing During the American Revolution." Bulletin 39 (May 1935): 361–64. The New York Public Library.

Post, Melville D. "German War Ciphers."

Everybody's Magazine 38 (June 1918): 28–34.

Simmons, Gustavus J. "Cryptology: The Mathematics of Secure Communication." *The Mathematical Intelligencer* 1, no. 4 (1979): 233–46.

——. "Scanning the Issue on Cryptology." *Proceedings of the IEEE* 76, no. 5 (May 1988).

Smith, David E. "John Wallis as a Cryptographer." *Bulletin of the American Mathematical Society* 24 (1917): 83–96.

Smith, Richard A. "Business Espionage." *Fortune* 53 (May 1956): 118–26.

Vogel, Donald S. "Inside a KGB Cipher." *Cryptologia* 14, no. 1 (1990): 37–51.

Documents

Data Encryption Standard. Federal Information Processing Standards. Publication 46-1. U.S. Department of Commerce. National Bureau of Standards. January 1988.

Eberhart and Taschner. "Criminal Codes and Ciphers," FBI Bulletin. January 1985.

Friedman, Elizebeth. "History of Work in Cryptanalysis, April 1927–June 1930." Washington, DC, National Archives, Record Group 26.

The General Signal Book of the United States Navy. Washington, DC: GPO, 1898.

The History of Army Strip Cipher Devices. U.S. War Department. Army Security Agency, 1948.

Influence of U.S. Cryptologic Organizations on the Digital Computer Industry. May 1977. National Security Agency.

Instructions for Using the Cipher Device M-94. U.S. War Department. Washington, DC: GPO, 1922.

"Interservice Instructions for Ground/Air Recognition and Identification 1943." The War Office, England. November 1943.

National Intelligence Reorganization and Reform Act of 1978. Senate Bill (s. 2525). U.S. Congress, Washington, DC.

O'Neill, E. F., ed. *A History of Engineering and Science in the Bell System—Transmission Technology, 1925–1975.* AT&T Bell Laboratories, 1985.

"Pioneers in U.S. Cryptology." Part 1 (1987): 9–11, and Part 2 (1987): 12–14. History and Publications Division. National Security Agency, Ft. George Meade, MD.

Record Group 59. Department of State Decimal File 411/421/424. Record Group 457. SRH Histories: SRH 20, SRH 044, SRH 355. National Archives, Washington, DC.

Index